# THE WATCHMEN

## Being Prepared and Preparing the Way for Messiah

## by
## Tom Hess

Published by:
**MorningStar Publications**
**16000 Lancaster Highway**
**Charlotte, NC  28277 • USA**

**For a free catalog of other MorningStar Books and Resources call 1-800-542-0278.**
Unless otherwise noted, Scripture quotations in this book are from the New International Version, Copyright © 1983 by B.B. Kirkbride Bible Co., Inc. and the Zondervan Corporation.

# TABLE OF CONTENTS

# Dedication and Acknowledgment

First and foremost, this book is dedicated to our awesome God, the Watchman who has infinite vision. He is watching all things in all the galaxies of the universe at the same time, as He is omnipresent everywhere simultaneously and omniscient. He knows everything and is watching even all the hairs on your head which He has numbered. He has total vision—He is both farsighted and nearsighted. An eagle can see eighty times better than man- -but that is nothing compared to God!

This book is dedicated to the Watch Leaders, Pastors and Congregational Leaders in Jerusalem, Israel, the Arab nations, the *10/40 Window* nations, and all nations with whom together we have the high honor of serving King Messiah, the Chief Watchman, and all believers who are called to be watchmen. We pray that the Lord will help us all to be exemplary watchmen, watching the Lord, watching the enemy, and faithfully watching over ourselves, our families and flocks by day and by night. May we be watchmen in all the ways He has called us to watch, as we watch and long for Messiah's appearing.

This book is also dedicated to two special women of God, Susan and Kathy, watchmen who have each spent hundreds of hours sacrificially editing this book. Susan, who is Jewish, made *Aliyah*[1] from the USA to Israel after reading my first book, *Let My People Go*, and has since been a great blessing as my assistant— watching, working and praying with *Jerusalem Watch of the Lord- Jerusalem House of Prayer for All Nations*. She also did a yeoman's service of helping coordinate both the 1994 and 1996 *All Nations Convocations Jerusalem*

---

1.  lit. "going up"—a return to the Land of Israel, specifically, Jerusalem.

with 140 and 188 nations represented respectively. Kathy came to Israel to work with us in 1991 as our first Watch Coordinator. While she was with us, God placed a desire in her heart to return to Kansas City, Missouri, USA to start a watch there, which was birthed in 1992. She returned to be with us in 1996 and worked literally day and night to help finish this book. May God bless Susan and Kathy for their labors of love in helping with editing.

*May we bless the Chief Watchman for continually watching over all of us. I bless God for the strength, inspiration and grace that He gave me to write* The Watchmen. *May His Word in this book bring forth one hundredfold fruit for God's kingdom, and be anointed by the Holy Spirit like a fire and a hammer to consume all who read it by giving vision, calling forth birthing, anointing and blessing upon thousands of watchmen and watches in all nations as we work, watch and wait for Messiah's appearing.*

# Chapter 1

# The Watchmen

## Being Prepared and Preparing the Way for Messiah

Though a vision tarry, wait—for it shall surely come to pass (Habakkuk 2:3). The vision, revelation and developments that make this book complete have come progressively over the last seven years. Many times I tried to finish it, but it was not the appointed time. There is a time and a season for everything under heaven (Ecclesiastes 3:1). This is the appointed time! I believe the Lord gave *The Watchmen* to His people as a gift to help accomplish multifaceted purposes in being prepared ourselves and preparing the way for His coming. As you read, I pray the Lord will impart His revelation to you concerning these seven purposes:

1. To help us know God as a Watchman. We can only understand ourselves as watchmen as we know God—Father, Son and Holy Spirit—as the Chief Watchman, for we are created in His image and likeness.

2. To help us learn, know and practice all the twenty different aspects of watching (incorporated in faithfully keeping a daily watch time), and to learn from the different models of Biblical, Historical and Contemporary watches.

3. To help strengthen the 24-hour watches established in approximately one hundred nations, to encourage the birthing and development of 24-hour watches in all of the two hundred nations of the world to pray for the peace of Jerusalem, their nation and all nations, and to encourage the development of millions of watch groups worldwide.

4. To watch the "Fig Tree" of Israel and the Arabs, to help us understand God's end time purposes for the Jewish people returning to the land of Israel and being reconciled in their Messiah with the Arabs, and becoming a blessing in the midst of the whole earth.

5. To encourage us to watch, work and pray for the fullness of the Gentiles of all nations to come into the kingdom.

6. To help us better understand the signs of the end times so we can be as the Sons of Issachar, discerning the times in which we live, and knowing what we should do.

7. To encourage and teach us how to prepare for the coming of Messiah (the wedding of the Lamb); that we will be the wise (watchmen) virgins with oil in our lamps who will be invited to the wedding to be the wife of the Lamb throughout eternity.

If you need more understanding, teaching or encouragement in any one or more of these seven areas, this book is for you!

## Watch and Pray

The words *watchmen, watchman, watch, watching, watchful, watcher* and *watches* are mentioned 165 times in the Bible, but if you include words like *see* or *observe* or other words that have the same meaning as watch or watchman, you will find that this subject is mentioned over three hundred times. *Pray, prayer, praying, prayerful, prayers* are mentioned 295 times, yet possibly thousands of books have been written on prayer, and less than a dozen to my knowledge on watchmen. This may be the most exhaustive book written on the subject. Why are so few books written on this most important and yet neglected subject? I don't know the answer to this question, but believe it was precisely because of this need that the Holy Spirit inspired me to write this book.

On two occasions Jesus Himself prioritized watching over praying to show us its importance and significance. I believe watching is at least as important as prayer:

**Watch and pray so that you will not fall into temptation. The spirit is willing, but the body is weak (Matthew 26:41, Mark 14:38).**

**Be always on the watch, and pray that you may be able to escape all that is about to happen, and that you may be able to stand before the Son of Man (Luke 21:36).**

It is my conviction after years of study and experience that all believers are called to be watchmen. Therefore, this book is written to help prepare all those who know the Lord, whether a ten-year-old child, a pastor, businessman, worker, student or professor, Jew or Gentile, black or white, male or female, rich or poor. This book is written for all believers and has much meat that will help teach, train and equip you on how to become a watchman, as I have not seen any other thorough work on this vital subject for the end times.

## Nations Touched as Watchmen Obey

As you read this book you will see many examples of how God has worked through the proclamation, prayers and praises of His people.

One example was in 1986 in **Washington, DC,** where we had an ongoing 24-hour watch. Just before I moved to Jerusalem, the Lord called me to a forty-day fast, only three hours before I was to begin! I said, "Lord, could You give me at least a week or two notice?" My impression from Him was this was the appointed time, so I canceled numerous lunch and dinner appointments and began fasting. I was fasting for a breakthrough in the United States Supreme Court because the Chief Justice was pro-"choice" on abortion (in favor of killing unborn babies). Someone said the results of my fast would be seen on television, which I found hard to believe. But one hour after I ended the fast, forty days later, the Chief Justice of the Supreme Court resigned, and God gave a pro-life Chief Justice and at the same time another pro-life Justice was appointed to the Court, to everyone's surprise. This example showed me the importance of moving in instant obedience to the Holy Spirit and the good fruit—breakthroughs that can follow prayer and fasting.

Another example was in **Russia** in 1986-1992—seven times over seven years to do seven Jericho Marches around the Kremlin in Moscow, one every year. We saw tremendous breakthroughs: the year before we began only two hundred Jewish people had left Russia for Israel, but since then the walls of Communism came down and in the last ten years over 800,000 Jewish people have come home to Israel! There were numerous groups involved on 24-hour watches, praying and fasting as we went there, and many were praying all over the world.

Since 1990 we have seen God working in the area of **Jewish-Arab reconciliation** in Jerusalem continually undergirded by *Jerusalem Watch of the Lord* (our 24-hour prayer watch on the Mount of Olives in Jerusalem), and over seventy 24-hour watches worldwide. We have seen many breakthroughs as Jewish and Arab leaders are now coming together in Jerusalem, Israel and throughout the whole Middle East (from Israel and all the Arab nations). The walls of partition are breaking down through the Prince of Peace. Those Jews and Arabs being reconciled to and in Messiah are the spiritual first fruit of the Highway of Salvation from Egypt to Israel to Assyria (Isaiah 19:23-25). Spiritual breakthroughs have occurred in Israel from every Arab nation. Hallelujah!

Also, through the **Gulf War** (land and air war) in 1991 we had a continual 24-hour watch functioning on the Mount of Olives, and I was led to an extended fast over that time. We were locked in a sealed room with gas masks on during the air raids. But the Chief Watchman was watching over Israel, and His co-watchmen were standing with Him 24 hours a day in prayer. Miraculously no one was killed by the thirty-nine scud missiles that hit Israel over the number of months of the War. Praise God!

In 1994 we held the first *All Nations Convocation Jerusalem* in Israel continually undergirded by *watchmen standing on the walls* twenty-four hours a day. Praying pastors and prayer leaders came from **140 nations** to present their nations' prayer needs. God gave a special gift of repentance, reconciliation and much fruit in bringing together nations worldwide.

In 1996 the second *All Nations Convocation Jerusalem* was held with **188 nations** represented—the most nations gathered in Jerusalem for any event in history and more than the United Nations! Some likened it to a Messianic United Nations Convocation preparing for Messiah's reign in Jerusalem. Again this was undergirded by *watchmen on the walls* twenty-four hours a day—and there was an even greater gift of repentance, reconciliation and unity as we prayed for Israel and all nations.

Another example is of *Honduras Watch* in the City of San Pedro Sula, which has three thousand people involved in 24-hour prayer:

> For many months Nicaraguans planned the assassination of the President of Honduras. The places, the persons, the time, everything was meticulously arranged. Their goal was to assassinate our President and the two main Presidential candidates. This they were going to do to bring confusion within the nation, blame the army and so use this incident as a means of starting a Communistic revolution. Three days before this action was to take place, the Lord told me to call our prayer warriors to an all-night prayer meeting. We did. The next day the commander of this group came trembling before the authorities surrendering himself and confessing their diabolic plan. Hidden secrets like these can only be brought to light when God's people within a nation can agree to come together to pray. Prayer saved the life of our nation. —**Pastor Cloward Bennett**

The following testimony of Pastor John Mulinde is what God has done in **Uganda**:

> There are not very many times God has dealt with my life in the same way He did during the 1996 *All Nations Convocation Jerusalem*. The anointing and impact of the *Convocation* **has had a permanent effect not only in my life but also on my country.**

I went to Israel with a team of six other intercessors to represent our nation. By the time we went to Jerusalem we had been working on building a Network of prayer altars all over our nation and to turn each into a 24-hour prayer watch. Every district in Uganda is currently well covered with chain intercession. There is travailing for a God-sent revival to our land.

With such a background I arrived in Jerusalem with a heavy burden. "Lord," I said, "We have done all that we are supposed to do. Why hasn't Revival come yet? If there is any cost that needs to be paid, reveal it to us, Oh God, that we may pay it and see your outpouring."

The Lord began to talk to me during this *Convocation* and revealed things about our nation that I had never thought of. He said to me, "Before the Outpouring will come to you, you will have to purge your land thoroughly." I sought His face further and He revealed that our country was bound by a blood curse which was responsible for the unceasing bloodshed in our land. He revealed many other bondages our nation suffered, and called us to National Repentance.

I left Jerusalem with excitement, yet also with apprehension. The work was overwhelming. I returned to Uganda, and immediately began mobilizing the whole nation to prayer and repentance. After three months of hectic preparations, we held the National Prayer and Fasting campaign, and what God did in this meeting has left all of us astounded. The whole nation responded to the call including the President and his wife, Cabinet Ministers, Members of Parliament, the Mayor of Kampala, commanders of the Army and Police, leading businessmen and professionals, national religious leaders from all Christian backgrounds, and multitudes of believers from all the thirty-nine districts of Uganda. Participants also came from Kenya, Rwanda, Tanzania, Zaire and Burundi. Other teams came from the UK and USA and India, and Pastor Reuven joined us from Jerusalem, Israel.

We were blessed to see God work in the same power, anointing and conviction as He did in *All Nations Convocation Jerusalem*. The depth and sincerity of repentance was awe-inspiring, and the reconciliations worked were real miracles. Already many breakthroughs are happening in the nation and an undeniable change is sweeping over our land and region.

Now every district in Uganda is preparing similar conferences for repentance and reconciliation so that the whole nation will be thoroughly purged. The air of expectancy is high. Surely something has already started happening in Uganda.

When I look back at all this I give all the glory to God for taking me to Jerusalem for *All Nations Convocation Jerusalem*. It was there, under God's heavy anointing, that I clearly heard His voice, which determined the course of what is now happening to our nation. We were praying for nations in Jerusalem, and now ours is already being transformed by God's answers. Praise be to God Almighty. I thank God for Tom Hess and his team of organizers. I learned so many things from them. **—Pastor John Mulinde**

Many breakthroughs are coming as *watchmen are on the walls* individually and collectively. However, the *God of the Breakthrough* is not only using our watches to prepare the way for the Lord by bringing breakthroughs for individuals and nations. He is also using many watches worldwide to prepare us as worshiping watchmen, helping us develop intimacy with Him to be His Bride forever!

## Developing Intimacy as a Watchman

The following are two testimonies of watchmen developing intimacy with the Lord of the watch:

### "Be still and know that I am God (Psalm 46:10)."

This watch time was mainly focused on God. I was led to sing Psalm 104. Later, as I began to intercede, I was so aware that God *is* the source of all that is good (James 1:17). As I began to pray for the Church, I was aware of how He has preserved the Church through the ages, just as He has preserved His Word.

There was a very long period of silence. He spoke and said, *"Be still and know that I am God."* As I waited in His presence I could not pray or even think thoughts—there was just an awesome awareness of His presence. Two scriptures came to me, **"In repentance and rest is your salvation, in quietness and trust is your strength..."** (Isaiah 30:15) and **"The fruit of righteousness will be peace, the effect of righteousness will be quietness and confidence forever"** (Isaiah 32:17).

In these verses I see that God desires for us just to quiet ourselves before Him and gain strength from His presence with us. Sometimes I get caught up in thinking I have to be verbalizing prayer when today's time reminded me that heart-to-heart communion with Him is sometimes what *He* desires, and what I need to remind myself is that *He alone* is all and in all.

As I began to focus on Him, the Spirit of God led me to Psalm 136. I pondered as I read and then began to meditate on God's mercy that endures forever. For well over an hour I received from Him deeper revelation of Who He is. As I was meditating on His attributes, James 1:17 came to me, and I saw that the good things that come to us are not individual, isolated "gifts," but an outpouring or flowing to us, through Jesus, of Who He is.

I spent much time in repentance for our arrogance of heart, our taking Him for granted or simply ignoring Him, going our own way. This was a wonderful time of intimacy and renewal resulting from the time of repentance and brokenness before Him. **—Judy Adams**

## "Haven't You Forgotten Something?"

In June/July '76 I was just walking out of the front door of our home (Di was at work and the children at school) when I heard the Lord call me by name. I turned around and Jesus was standing in our lounge room looking in my direction. As I walked towards Him, He said to me, *"Haven't you forgotten something?"* I stood about three feet from Jesus as He looked deep into my eyes. I didn't know how to respond until I heard myself saying, 'Yes Lord, I haven't told you today that I love you.' His eyes were fixed on my eyes. I then said, 'I love you Jesus, I do love you, Lord.' With that Jesus said, **"You can go now."** I left to go to work.

As I thought through that experience, I realized that I had been faithfully spending time with the Lord in prayer and in the study of His Word, but I hadn't been spending time with Him in simply doing nothing else but expressing my love and adoration.

In 1982/83 the Lord seemed to require it of me that I spend the very early hours of the morning seeking His face—this went on for several months. It was during this season that Jesus appeared to me three times to do with the matter of living a life of intimate, loving devotion to Him as being my first and highest priority.

The first time I saw the Lord in this season He was weeping openly. I could see Him from His waist up. The tears were running down His face like water and soaking the front of the white garment He was wearing. The Lord's face was contorted in grief. I softly said, "Why Lord? Why?" meaning, "Why Lord are You weeping like this?" Jesus replied, *"My people don't love Me. My people don't love Me."*

This and subsequent like experiences caused me to see that the Lord is looking for a people to truly love Him just for who He is, and that He needs and longs for our love. The Lord began to teach me that all acceptable service, with lasting fruitfulness, flows out of an abiding First Love relationship with Him.

Then, in 1988, the Lord told me to lay down the ministry in unconditional surrender to Him. This turned out to be a real 'death' and the hardest thing I had ever done in obedience to the will of God. As I found the grace to obey the Lord, He began to show me that I had unknowingly given the ministry first place in my life and that He was not my First Love. I was so shaken and broken over this, because I had determined to fix it in my heart that Jesus would always be my first and best love. As I repented, the Lord spoke, and said, *"Son, do not sacrifice knowing Me for a ministry, as so many of My servants have done."*

In 1990/91 the Lord reinstated us in the ministry. When at home, I give every morning, Monday through Friday, to be alone with the Lord Jesus, and try consciously to obey His call to lay my head on His bosom and my ear on His heart—which call I believe has been coming to His servants, especially in the past three to four years. There has been such a real sense that deeper levels of intimacy with Jesus has released us to higher levels of effective warfare-intercession and other facets of ministry. Over the years we have tried to encourage the saints to be abandoned, passionate and fervent in their love for Jesus, and to keep a guard on their First Love. — **Pastor Noel Mann**

As I read the experiences of Judy Adams and Noel Mann, the Lord shows me that I need to put the "Lord of the work" much more before the "work of the Lord" in the remaining years of my life. The Lord is saying to me that as one of God's Watchmen, *"I am not calling you to save all the world, I only want all of you."*

*May we, as God's watchmen, put Him first before all we do. May He be our First Love, the all-in-all in our lives, and also may He fill all the earth with His glory! As we read the rest of this book, may God help us first to be prepared ourselves for Messiah's coming, and also may God work through us in all the ways He has purposed to prepare the way for His return.*

# PRAYER OF A WATCHMAN

*Abba, Father, **I bless You** as the Chief Watchman,*
***thank You** for the privilege of being called as a co-watchman with You,*
***ask You** to help me to get to know You more intimately,*
*and **love You**, the Chief Watchman, more dearly.*

*Father, as I read this book*
*help me to learn how to watch in all the aspects mentioned.*
*Teach me how to watch from examples of the*
*Biblical, Historical and Contemporary watches mentioned in this book.*
*Help me to learn how to overcome the watch of the enemy,*
*learn from the fig tree and all the trees,*
*watch the signs of the End Times and for the Coming of Messiah.*

*Father, I believe You to help me to be a faithful watchman.*
*Help me to watch and pray that I do not enter into temptation.*
*As I read this book, teach me to be Your watchman.*
*Help me to stand upon the watch in all the ways*
*that it means to be Your watchman in these Last Days, Lord God.*
*I thank You for the privilege of being "Your" watchman in the*
*City of Jerusalem, or wherever I may be in the nations of the world.*
*Help me to be a faithful watchman in all the ways to which You have called me.*

*I believe You, as the True Watchman,*
*to be watching through me, Lord God.*
*May I see eye to eye in Zion with You.*
*As I look into Your eyes that are blazing fire, may I see things through Your eyes.*
*Teach me to be Your watchman and know Your ways--*
*that I will walk in Your paths*
*that will lead to being prepared and preparing the way*
*for the coming of Messiah!*
*Thank You, Father.*

# Chapter 2

# God the Watchman

When I moved to Jerusalem in 1987, the Lord gave me this Scripture:

**I have posted watchmen on your walls, O Jerusalem; they will never be silent day or night. You who call on the LORD, give yourselves no rest, and give him no rest till he establishes Jerusalem and makes her the praise of the earth (Isaiah 62:6-7).**

He then directed me to do a Bible study on what it means to be a watchman. I had always thought that *watchman* was just another word for *intercessor*; but upon doing the Bible study, I realized that intercession is only one of twenty aspects of being a watchman. Then I saw that the most important watchman is our Chief Watchman, the Lord God of Israel, and we can only be watchmen because He is watching! We need to have an understanding that God, who is eternal, has always been, is and always will be watching and He is calling us to be co-watchmen with Him until He makes Jerusalem a praise in the earth, but also throughout eternity.

In these last days, and in a special way, God is watching over Jerusalem, Israel and His Church, all of which are the apple of His eye. He is calling His Church to stand with Him as watchmen in prayer, first for Jerusalem and their own nation as well as for other nations.

## The Watchman's Psalm

**I lift up my eyes to the hills—where does my help come from? My help comes from the LORD, the Maker of heaven and earth. He will not let your foot slip—he who watches over you will not slumber; indeed, he who watches over Israel will neither slumber nor sleep. The**

**LORD watches over you—the LORD is your shade at your right hand; the sun will not harm you by day, nor the moon by night. The LORD will keep you from all harm—he will watch over your life; the LORD will watch over your coming and going both now and forevermore (Psalm 121).**

This has to be called the *Watchman's Psalm*. In these eight verses there are five assurances that the Lord is watching over us. If the body of believers wholeheartedly believed that God is always watching us, we would be living much more holy lives before Him. May God give us greater revelation that He is always watching us.

## The Ever-Watching, Invisible God

Which would you be the most concerned about—the fact that your pastor is watching what you are doing, or that your parents are, or that your boss is, or that God is? Our first concern should be that God is always watching us. Sometimes we put more value on the presence of another human being than on the presence of the ever-watching, invisible God. We think that because someone is in the flesh, he is "really here," watching us. If we believe that someone's presence is more real, because he's in the flesh, than the presence of God, who is invisible, then we really don't believe that God is the Chief Watchman.

If we truly love and reverently fear God, we would reflect His holiness in our lives to such a degree that it wouldn't matter who sees us in any situation! When we know He is watching us, we will do only what pleases Him. **"When a man's ways are pleasing to the LORD, he makes even his enemies live at peace with him" (Proverbs 16:7).** God watches us because He loves us and wants the best for us. He wants us to flee from sin and run into His arms, so that He can watch over us in His bosom.

**He who dwells in the shelter of the Most High will rest in the shadow of the Almighty (Psalm 91:1).**

God is watching us, His eyes are upon us, and He wants us to be secure in Him, dwelling in the secret place of the Most High.

## God Watching Over His Word

**The LORD said to me, "You have seen correctly, for I am watching to see that my word is fulfilled," (Jeremiah 1:12)**

Our Awesome God, the Chief Watchman, is watching to see that His word is fulfilled! When did He begin doing this? I believe He began doing this in the beginning. We don't know exactly what He was doing before the beginning of creation, but God always existed, so He was always watching.

**In the beginning God created the heavens and the earth... And God said, "Let there be light," and there was light. God saw [was watching] that the light was good (Genesis 1:1, 3-4).**

He saw that the light was good! He spoke His word and then He watched that His word was performed! It is mentioned seven times in the account of creation—every time God created something, He was watching and said it was good:

He created the light; He was watching and it was good.

He created the land and the waters; He was watching and it was good.

He created vegetation; He was watching and it was good.

He created the sun, moon and stars; He was watching and it was good.

He created the creatures in the water, and the birds; He was watching and it was good.

He created the living creatures, the animals; He was watching and it was good.

He watched His word being performed, and said it was very good.

**So God created man in his own image, in the image of God he created him; male and female he created them (Genesis 1:27).**

God was watching all that He had made and said it was *very* good (v. 31)! God only creates good things because He watches over His word to perform it, and He is a good God. It was only because of sin entering into the world that evil came forth.

God was watching and even said what food would be best for us. In the beginning, before the fall, God said to Adam,

**"I give you every seed-bearing plant on the face of the whole earth and every tree that has fruit with seed in it. They will be yours for food" (Genesis 1:29).**

It is proven that people who watch what they eat and eat a diet of mostly fruits, vegetables, seeds and nuts are much healthier than those who don't. God is also watching us in the area of our sedentary lifestyle, that we are getting adequate physical exercise, as they did in the Garden of Eden.

God loves us so much that He is even creating miracles to heal us spiritually, emotionally, mentally and physically. He's watching over us and over the world. Because of His goodness, He will create new heavens and a new earth where sin will not abound. God, in His watching, will only allow evil to prevail for so long. One of these days very soon, when the fruit of the earth has come forth, He will say, "It is finished," and will completely burn up the existing heavens and earth. He'll be watching as He creates the new heavens and new earth. He says: **Behold I make all things new (Revelation 21:5 KJV).**

## God's Watch over Hagar and Ishmael

**The angel of the LORD also said to her: "You are now with child and you will have a son. You shall name him Ishmael, for the LORD has heard of your misery" (Genesis 16:11).**

This Scripture speaks of God watching Hagar, the mother of Ishmael. It says the angel of the Lord came to her. God was watching over Hagar, and He heard of her misery.

**She gave this name to the LORD who spoke to her: "You are the God who sees [watches] me," for she said, "I have now seen [been watching] the One who sees [watches] me" (Genesis 16:13).**

Isn't it amazing, the Lord was watching over Hagar? Sometimes we think it was a mistake that Hagar had a child; but God's ways are higher than our ways! God heard of her misery and was watching her.

We read in Isaiah 19 of God's end time purpose to open up the Middle East and create a highway from Egypt to Israel to Assyria. God will cause this region, which has been a curse, to be a blessing in the midst of the whole earth! I don't believe it's a mistake that Ishmael was born; God will reconcile the Arabs and the Jews in the Middle East and make it a blessing in the midst of the earth. There will be many problems until this is completed, but it's already beginning.

Not only was God watching over Hagar when He opened her womb, but she found herself watching the One who was watching her, the Awesome God, the Watchman.

## God's Watch Over Isaac—Jacob

God was watching over Isaac when he was being offered up by his father, Abraham. God continued to watch over Isaac throughout his life.

God was watching over Jacob when the Lord said to Jacob, **"I am with you and will watch over you wherever you go, and I will bring you back to this land. I will not leave you until I have done what I have promised you."** When Jacob awoke from his sleep, realizing that God had appeared to him, he said, **"How awesome is this place! This is none other than the house of God, this is the gate of heaven!"** Then Jacob vowed that, **"If God will be with me and will watch over me on this journey... then the LORD will be my God"** (Genesis 28:15-17, 20-21).

Again God was watching over Jacob, who was wrestling with Him, and Jacob said, **"I will not let you go unless you bless me."** God blessed him and said, **"Your name will no longer be Jacob, but Israel"... So Jacob called the place Peniel, saying "It is because I saw [was watching] God face to face, and yet my life was spared"** (Genesis 32:24-30).

So the Lord was watching over Jacob and changed his name to Israel; and Jacob saw the Lord face to face.

## God Watches Over Us, as We Watch Him

In our love relationship with the Lord, He watches us in a special way and we begin watching Him. Once I was watching (meditating) for about half an hour on Revelation 1:14-16, where it says,

**His eyes were like blazing fire... His voice was like the sound of rushing waters... His face was like the sun shining in all its brilliance.**

As I watched Him, I was changed by the Spirit of the Lord.

When Isaiah saw the Lord, He was high and lifted up, His train filled the temple and the angels cried "Holy."

*May God give us His revelation that He's watching us. May we recognize and understand, day by day, that He is omniscient, He is all-knowing, His eyes are going over the whole earth. He knows everything about us. He knows how many hairs we have on our head. He knew us before we were conceived in our mother's womb. He's watching over each detail and every aspect of our life.*

## God's Watch Over Israel

It's interesting that, in Psalm 121, the Lord said He's watching over us and also watching over Israel. When Jacob met the Lord, Jacob's name was changed to Israel. In Exodus 3, what happened to Moses when God called to him from the burning bush? The angel of the Lord appeared in flames of fire from within the bush. The presence of God was so strong, as God was watching him, that Moses hid his face because he was afraid to look at God (v. 6).

God's holiness and presence can be so strong that we're afraid to look at Him. But the Lord wants us to be conformed into His likeness and into His image. Thank God that the veil has been rent and we can behold the glory of the Lord in the face of Jesus Christ. As He's watching over us, we should be watching Him. God said to the elders and children of Israel, **"I have watched over you and have seen what has been done to you in Egypt"** (Exodus 3:16).

When the children of Israel were in Egypt, many thought God had left them. But He was watching over them, was going to deliver them out of Egypt and bring them into the land of promise, the land of milk and honey. Have you ever been in a situation where you felt God had left you, that He was no longer watching you? God has not left us; He's still watching us. Although we may go through some trials, God is watching, and He who watches over us never slumbers nor sleeps.

**The LORD your God has blessed you in all the work of your hands. He has watched over your journey through this vast desert. These forty years the LORD your God has been with you, and you have not lacked anything (Deuteronomy 2:7).**

God was not only watching over Israel in Egypt, but also in the wilderness. None of the diseases came upon them, they never got sick. A cloud went before them by day and a pillar of fire by night. They were grumbling and complaining and thought it was difficult. They could have gone into the land in eleven days. God was even watching over them in their rebellion. He kept them healthy and gave them manna from heaven.

He is patient with us! When He watches over us, if it weren't for His mercy, love, patience and long-suffering, He could destroy us for many of the things we've done. Thank God for His compassion, mercy, faithfulness and long- suffering. Our God is a good God. His mercy endures forever. But we also need to live in the fear of God, because His wrath can break out in a moment, as it did towards those who continually rebelled against Him in the wilderness.

As mentioned in Psalm 121, **"He who watches over Israel will never slumber nor sleep."** Again, in Deuteronomy 11:12, God says: **"It is a land that the LORD your God cares for; the eyes of the LORD your God are continually on it from the beginning of the year to its end."**

God is continually watching over Israel from the beginning of the year until the end; His eyes are continually looking over His land. God is watching over not only the people of Israel, but also over the land of Israel—that the Jewish people would serve as stewards of the land. **"He who scattered Israel will gather them and will watch over his flock like a shepherd" (Jeremiah 31:10).**

God scattered the Jewish people in A.D. 70, and now He is regathering them from the four corners of the earth. He will watch over His flock as a shepherd, and He who scattered them because of their disobedience and sin and rejection of Him is regathering them to the land. He was watching over Susan in Florida, and He spoke to her, "Come back to Israel." He gathered her back to Israel. She is now a vital part of *Jerusalem House of Prayer for All Nations.* All around the world God is watching over His word to perform it, to bring His people home. He'll return their land even if they try to give it away, and the suffering He allows will bring them to salvation. God's word will not return void, but will accomplish that which He's purposed.

> **But the eye of their God was watching over the elders of the Jews, and they were not stopped (Ezra 5:5).**

Ezra and Nehemiah were rebuilding the temple and their enemies tried to stop them. But the eyes of the Lord were watching over the Jewish people; they could not be stopped. If God's eyes are watching over you, He'll stop your enemies as well. As your heart is toward the Lord, He's watching over you more closely. We need to know that God wants us to turn our hearts toward Him in fuller measure, so He can watch over us more closely.

*David was a man after God's own heart. God was watching closely over David's life, because David's heart was after God. In these days of materialism and all kinds of distractions in the world, may God deliver our hearts from this present evil age and may we turn our eyes to Him.*

## God's Temple of Living Stones

The natural temple may again be built in Jerusalem. If God purposes to rebuild the temple, His eyes will be watching over the Jewish people in this work. Whatever He's purposed to do, He is watching very closely to perform it. Nothing and no one in the world can stop the rebuilding of the temple if God purposes to rebuild it. If God be for you, who can be against you? I don't know when the physical temple will be built, but I do know that another temple is being built—a much greater temple, a temple made without hands, a temple that Jesus shed His blood to build.

After His resurrection, Jesus breathed on His disciples saying, **"Receive the Holy Spirit" (John 20:22).** They became the temple of the Holy Spirit. Jesus Christ is the Chief Cornerstone of the temple. He is watching over His word to perform it. Jesus said, **"I will build my church, and the gates of Hades will not overcome it" (Matthew 16:18).**

The Chief Cornerstone is watching and building His temple out of living stones. The spiritual temple is being built of Jewish stones; Arabic stones; French, Chinese, Spanish, Russian, Belgian, Swiss, American, Papua New Guinea stones; stones from India, Bangladesh, Indonesia, Brazil; stones from every tribe, tongue and nation.

The Lord is watching over the nations to draw out a people from every tribe, tongue, people and nation into His living temple. Nothing can stop the building of this temple. One drop of the blood of Jesus is more powerful than all the forces of the enemy, than all the nuclear bombs in the world. We are victorious by the blood of the Lamb and the word of our testimony because God, the Awesome God, is watching over us. Even in death we are victorious. We are sheep sent to the slaughter. In all these things we are more than conquerors. Hallelujah!

## In Times of Blessing and Times of Trial

John says, in Revelation 1:9, that he is our brother **"In the suffering and kingdom and patient endurance that are ours in Jesus."** Because we go through difficulties, it does not mean that God has left us or no longer is watching over us.

When we think of Job, we sometimes think of a man who was very depressed because of all the difficulties God allowed him to go through. Job was a man whom God esteemed; but God allowed him to go through more difficulties than most people. I don't know whether or not there will be a rapture before the great tribulation, but we will go through more difficult times before the Lord returns.

> **You fasten my feet in shackles; you keep close watch on all my paths by putting marks on the soles of my feet (Job 13:27).**

Job, in this situation, thought the Lord was punishing him and he was very upset by all his problems and pressures. But the Lord was not punishing him; He was allowing Job to go though trials. The Lord was watching over all his ways and protected him in the midst of his problems. God did not allow him to die, although Job sometimes wished to die. God orders our steps today, as He did Job's.

Job remembered his better days, when it was easier:

> **How I long for the months gone by, for the days when God watched over me, when his lamp shone upon my head and by his light I walked through darkness! Oh, for the days when I was in my prime, when God's intimate friendship blessed my house, when the Almighty was still with me and my children were around me, when my path was drenched with cream and the rock poured out for me streams of olive oil (Job 29:2-6).**

In better times, it's easy to think that God is with us and that He's watching over us. Job, in the earlier passage, said that God was watching over him. In the later passage, however, I'm not sure he believed that God was still watching over him, because he said, "Oh for the days when God watched over me." God watches over us and is our intimate Friend through times of blessing and times of trial. His ways are higher than our ways and His thoughts are higher than our thoughts. He knows and wants the best for us. If we believe this, then we know, if our heart is completely turned towards Him, that He will watch over us and will take care of us, no matter what degree of trials He allows us to endure.

When the Apostle Paul was in prison with many difficulties, he sang the song, "**Rejoice in the Lord always, and again I say rejoice**" **(Philippians 4:4)**. These words were not written in a church pew, they were written in prison! May God help us to rejoice in the Lord always, and again He says "Rejoice!" knowing that He is always watching over us.

No matter what our emotions or circumstances, God has not forsaken us. He says, "**Surely I am with you always, to the very end of the age**" **(Matthew 28:20)**. There may be many difficulties between now and the end of the world, the worst difficulties in history, but the Lord says, "**Lo, I am with you [watching over you] always, even to the end of the age**" **(Matthew 28:20 KJV)**.

## Assurances of Our Awesome God, Our Chief Watchman

"**For the LORD watches over the way of the righteous, but the way of the wicked will perish**" **(Psalm 1:6)**. God says He will destroy the wicked, but will watch over the righteous.

"**He rules forever by his power, his eyes watch the nations**" **(Psalm 66:7)**. God is watching over all the nations. He puts down one king and lifts up another one. God is watching; He has everything under control.

"**Set a guard over my mouth, O LORD; keep watch over the door of my lips**" **(Psalm 141:3)**. The Lord is watching the words that we say and *we have to give an account for all the words that we speak, including idle words*. May God help us to speak the words we should as He watches over the door of our lips.

"**My eyes will be on [watching] the faithful in the land, that they may dwell with me; he whose walk is blameless will minister to me**" **(Psalm 101:6)**. If we're faithful, we will dwell with Him as His priests.

"**The eyes of the LORD are everywhere, keeping watch on the wicked and the good**" **(Proverbs 15:3)**. He is omnipresent, watching all things.

"**My son, keep your father's commands... When you walk, they will guide you; when you sleep, they will watch over you**" **(Proverbs 6:20,22).** The Lord and His commandments are watching over us when we walk and when we sleep.

"**My eyes will watch over them for their good**" **(Jeremiah 24:6).** He wants our best. His eyes and His hand of protection are always upon us.

"**For the eyes of the LORD range throughout [are watching] the earth to strengthen those whose hearts are fully committed to him**" **(2 Chronicles 16:9).** God is looking all over the world: all over Israel, the Arab Middle East, Asia, Africa, Europe, the South Pacific, the Americas—for individuals whose hearts are fully committed to Him. He's watching for people who want to be continually delivered from this present evil age, whose hearts are empty of the things of this world, who are poor in spirit, hungering and thirsting after righteousness, desiring only the Lord Jesus, who want to know Him more, who want to love Him more. When these people come forth, God will gather them unto Himself. He'll watch over them even more closely. He'll bless and use them in special ways. They may have many difficulties and trials, but God's blessings will be upon them, both in this life and in the life to come. God is no respecter of persons; He shows no favoritism (Acts 10:34-35).

Today you can recommit your life to the Chief Watchman, knowing that, as the Holy God, He is continually watching you and Israel, and as the all-knowing God, *His eyes will never leave you, as you and Israel are the apple of His eye!*

*May God bring us into a new dimension of the fear and goodness of God, and may we learn to fear and love our awesome* **GOD THE WATCHMAN** *with all of our hearts.*

# Chapter 3

# Jesus as a Watchman

## Some Who Were Watching for Jesus

Before the birth of Jesus, shepherds were in the fields watching over their flocks. An angel of the Lord came to them and they were terrified. The angel announced the birth of the Lord Jesus to those shepherds who were watching, because the Good Shepherd, Jesus, was coming to watch over His flock. In restoring the night watch today He is calling His pastor-shepherds also to be watching over their flocks by night.

The Magi were watchmen, watching the star that led them to find the Chief Watchman, the Lord Jesus. There were also two special individuals who were also watching for the coming of the Lord:

> **Now there was a man in Jerusalem called Simeon, who was righteous and devout. He was waiting [watching] for the consolation of Israel, and the Holy Spirit was upon him. It had been revealed to him by the Holy Spirit that he would not die before he had seen the Lord's Christ (Luke 2:25-26).**

He spent his time in the temple court, and when he saw the child Jesus, he took Him in his arms and said:

> **...my eyes have seen [are watching] your salvation, which you have prepared in the sight of all people, a light for revelation to the Gentiles and for glory to your people Israel (Luke 2:30-32).**

In these days, God wants us to be watchmen looking for the second coming of the Lord Jesus, even as Simeon was looking for His first coming. Not only was Simeon in the temple watching for the coming of the Lord, but there was another, a woman named Anna.

Her husband died seven years after their marriage. She was now eighty-four years old, and **"never left the temple, but worshiped day and night, fasting and praying" (Luke 2:37).**

She fasted day and night; she never left the temple. Apparently she alone was keeping a 24-hour watch for the first coming of Messiah! She drew close to the Lord as she watched for His coming. She was also looking, watching for the redemption of Jerusalem. Anna was blessed when the child Jesus was born.

Simeon and Anna are examples of faithful watchmen, as they were watching for the first coming of the Lord Jesus. We should be even more faithful to watch for the second coming, because Jesus will not come as the Lamb to be slain, but as the Lion to reign. He is coming as our Bridegroom. We will experience the greatest wedding in history with the ultimate altogether lovely and perfect Bridegroom.

*May God help us in the days ahead to be His faithful watchmen, like Simeon and Anna, looking and watching for His second coming, as they were looking and watching for His first coming.*

## Jesus Watching the Father

The first words of Jesus recorded in the Scriptures are found in Luke 2:49:

**"Why were you searching for me?" He asked. "Didn't you know I had to be in my Father's house?"**

His first commitment was to His heavenly Father. As we read the four gospels, we see that He speaks about His Father in heaven one hundred eighty-five times! I believe that when Jesus was upon the earth, He spent more time watching His Father in heaven than anything else did. The first thing He said was, **"I had to be in my Father's house"** (NIV); **"I must be about my Father's business"** (KJV). He did nothing unless He saw His Father doing it. May our eyes be upon our Father in heaven and may we do only that which we see Him do. Jesus died for our sins so that we could follow our Father in heaven.

**For we do not have a High Priest who is unable to sympathize with our weaknesses, but we have one who has**

**been tempted in every way, just as we are--yet was without sin (Hebrews 4:15).**

Jesus had the same temptations as we do, but because He was always watching, doing only what the Father told Him to do, He was victorious over sin. He went to the Mount of Olives at night and spent time with His Father; He delighted in having fellowship and communion with Him.

Jesus spent most of His time watching the Father. He also watched His enemy, Satan, not ignoring his devices. It's true that He watched the multitudes and had much compassion upon them, but His compassion was born of His relationship with His Father. Throughout the Old Testament we read about the compassion, the lovingkindness of the Lord. So the Lord Jesus wasn't just doing good things in order to meet people's needs. He was meeting only the needs of the people whom the Father put on His heart, the needs the Father told Him to meet. He brought forth one hundredfold fruit because He was obedient. Jesus didn't heal everyone, only the ones chosen by the Father.

**"After Jesus said this, he looked toward heaven and prayed" (John 17:1).** In other words, He looked toward heaven, watched the Father and prayed. This is an illustration of the way Jesus, as a Jew, prayed—lifting up His hands and looking toward heaven (Lamentations 2:19). I think it's representative of watching the Father. **"Our Father which art in heaven, Hallowed be thy name" (Matthew 6:9 KJV).**

Those of us watching the Father need to lift our hands and watch toward heaven. In the last days we are instructed to lift up our heads, because our redemption draws nigh. So when we're looking to heaven, we're focusing on watching the Father and anticipating Messiah's soon coming.

**Father, the time has come...I have brought you glory on earth by completing the work you gave me to do (John 17:1, 4).**

If we're going to follow the example of the Lord, we'll want to do only the things that He ordains. There are many good things to do, but if the Father has not initiated them, then they're dead works.

## The Temptation of Jesus

In Luke 4, Jesus enters His time of temptation. He had just been baptized, the Spirit took him into the wilderness, and He fasted for forty days. As Jesus began this fast, He was tempted by the devil, who came to Him in three different ways. Jesus stood with the Father; He was watching the Father through this fast.

We hear many voices which seem to be the opinions of other people, but as we look at the life of Jesus, He knew that either the Father or the enemy was speaking. When He said to Peter, "Get behind me, Satan," He was speaking to Satan, who was trying to work through a person. He spoke in the same way to the Pharisees and the Sadducees. So I believe there really are only two voices in the world: the voice of our heavenly Father or the voice of the enemy. It may come in many different forms, but if we're not hearing God's voice, then we're hearing the voice of the enemy. There are no neutral voices! Jesus said, "My sheep hear My voice," and He said, "I and my Father are one"—so we need to be attuned to the voice of our heavenly Father and be watching and listening only to Him. Jesus was also watching the enemy, and never was caught off guard!

In Matthew 4:1-11, there are three direct confrontations between the Lord Jesus and Satan, where Jesus overcame him, not with His own words, but with the Scriptures.

When Satan challenged Jesus to turn stones into bread, Jesus answered, **"It is written: "Man does not live on bread alone."** Next, Satan took Jesus to the highest point of the temple and suggested that He jump off, but Jesus did not follow the enemy, who even quoted Scripture to Him. Jesus said, **"It is also written: 'Do not put the Lord your God to the test.'"**

His victory was in quoting the word of God and standing against the enemy. He chose only to watch and hear His Father from heaven, and to stand against the works of the enemy.

Then Satan offered Jesus all the kingdoms of the world, which He refused. Jesus said to him:

> **"Away from me, Satan! For it is written: 'Worship the Lord your God, and serve Him only.'"**

So He did not yield to worldly temptations. There are really only two gods: the true God from heaven and the god of this world. Here Jesus was in direct confrontation with the god of this world and the father of lies (John 8:44). Jesus received the word from heaven and quoted the word of God.

The Muslims believe that world leadership was offered to Mohammed, who accepted. The Muslims also say that when Jesus comes again, the Imam, the leader of the Mosque in Jerusalem, will offer leadership to Jesus, but He will refuse, follow the Imam and become a Muslim priest.

Satan, the god of this world, offered Mohammed the kingdoms of this world and he took them, but the Bible says that the kingdoms of this world shall become the kingdoms of our Lord and His Christ, and He shall reign forever and ever.

**When the devil had finished all this tempting, he left him until an opportune time (Luke 4:13).**

I believe that when Jesus began the fast, Satan knew that there was power in fasting, so he tempted Him then, realizing that this fast could defeat his works (which it did)!

## Jesus' Death Was Intercession

As a Watchman, Jesus saw—realized—the only way man could be redeemed was through His death. *We thank You, Lord, that when You were on earth You not only showed us how to live, but You died as an Intercessor that we may live.*

**Therefore I will give him a portion among the great, and he will divide the spoils with the strong, because he poured out his life unto death, and was numbered with the transgressors. For he bore the sin of many, and made intercession for the transgressors (Isaiah 53:12).**

**He saw that there was no one, he was appalled that there was no one to intervene; so his own arm worked salvation for him, and his own righteousness sustained him (Isaiah 59:16).**

*Praise You, Jesus, that You ultimately fulfilled the cry of the Lord through Ezekiel in Chapter 22:30:*

**"I looked for a man among them who would build up the wall and stand before me in the gap on behalf of the land so I would not have to destroy it but I found none."**

*Thank You for overcoming death, hell and the grave and ascending into heaven as our Great High Priest after the order of Melchizedek. Thank You that as our Great High Priest You have been ever-living to make intercession from the heavens for us over the last two thousand years.*

In Hebrews 12:2-3, the writer in essence says we should follow Jesus' example in the difficult days before us.

**Let us fix our eyes on Jesus, the author and perfecter of our faith, who for the joy set before him endured the cross, scorning its shame, and sat down at the right hand of the throne of God. Consider him who endured such opposition from sinful men, so that you will not grow weary and lose heart.**

Jesus as a watchman saw what He needed to do in dying as an intercessor for us, but also saw the joy set before Him. We should walk even as He walked.

## Jesus, a Watchman After the Order of Melchizedek

### Melchizedek the Priest

**This Melchizedek was king of Salem and priest of God Most High. He met Abraham returning from the defeat of the kings and blessed him, and Abraham gave him a tenth of everything. First, his name means "king of righteousness"; then also, "king of Salem" means "king of peace." Without father or mother, without genealogy, without beginning of days or end of life, like the Son of God he remains a priest forever.**

**Just think how great he was: Even the patriarch Abraham gave him a tenth of the plunder! Now the law**

requires the descendants of Levi who become priests to collect a tenth from the people—that is, their brothers--even though their brothers are descended from Abraham. This man, however, did not trace his descent from Levi, yet he collected a tenth from Abraham and blessed him who had the promises. And without doubt the lesser person is blessed by the greater. In the one case, the tenth is collected by men who die; but in the other case, by him who is declared to be living. One might even say that Levi, who collects the tenth, paid the tenth through Abraham, because when Melchizedek met Abraham, Levi was still in the body of his ancestor (Hebrews 7:1-10).

## Jesus Like Melchizedek

If perfection could have been attained through the Levitical priesthood (for on the basis of it the law was given to the people), why was there still need for another priest to come—one in the order of Melchizedek, not in the order of Aaron? For when there is a change of the priesthood, there must also be a change of the law. He of whom these things are said belonged to a different tribe, and no one from that tribe has ever served at the altar. For it is clear that our Lord descended from Judah, and in regard to that tribe Moses said nothing about priests. And what we have said is even more clear if another priest like Melchizedek appears, one who has become a priest not on the basis of a regulation as to his ancestry but on the basis of the power of an indestructible life. For it is declared: *"You are a priest forever, in the order of Melchizedek."*

The former regulation is set aside because it was weak and useless (for the law made nothing perfect), and a better hope is introduced, by which we draw near to God.

**And it was not without an oath! Others became priests without any oath, but he became a priest with an oath when God said to him: "The Lord has sworn and will not change his mind: 'You are a priest forever.'"**

**Because of this oath, Jesus has become the guarantee of a better covenant. Now there have been many of those priests, since death prevented them from continuing in office; but because Jesus lives forever, he has a permanent priesthood. Therefore he is able to save completely those who come to God through him, because *he always lives to intercede for them.***

**Such a high priest meets our need—one who is holy, blameless, pure, set apart from sinners, exalted above the heavens. Unlike the other high priests, he does not need to offer sacrifices day after day, first for his own sins, and then for the sins of the people. He sacrificed for their sins once for all when he offered himself. For the law appoints as high priests men who are weak; but the oath, which came after the law, appointed the Son, who has been made perfect forever (Hebrews 7:11-28).**

Thank God that the **"Word became flesh and dwelt among us"**! The Lord Jesus came to earth from heaven to do at least two major things: one was to show us the nature and character of God and how to live, the other was to die for our sins that we might live. In His earthly ministry, as He dwelt in Israel, He showed us how to be watchmen. There is much we can learn from His life, as He was a watchman and a victor in His life here on the earth. Even in death He triumphed over death, hell and the grave.

Today in the heavens Jesus is our Watchman, our Prophet, Priest and King, and ever lives to make intercession for us as the Chief Watchman. Jesus, who is continually interceding for us, sees, knows, and is watching every detail of our lives. He knows our greatest needs and God's purpose for our lives, and is praying for this to be fulfilled, that we may lay hold of all we have been laid hold of for by Christ Jesus. Jesus is weeping because we don't really love Him. If we truly love Him we will want Him to be pleased with what He sees in our lives, thoughts, attitudes and actions every moment of every day, as He is constantly watching us. If we are faithful, we are preparing and being prepared to be His Bride for eternity.

## Lessons for the Disciples as Watchmen

> **Then Jesus went with his disciples to a place called Gethsemane, and he said to them, "Sit here while I go over there and pray." He took Peter and the two sons of Zebedee along with him, and he began to be sorrowful and troubled. Then he said to them, "My soul is overwhelmed with sorrow to the point of death. Stay here and keep watch with me" (Matthew 26:36-38).**

Jesus was always watching the Father, so He knew what was coming in each situation. His disciples were not as aware as He was, but in this example He was teaching them to be watchmen, and they totally failed. Then He returned to His disciples and found them sleeping. Jesus then said to them, and is saying to us today:

> **"Could you men not keep watch with me for one hour?" he asked Peter. "Watch and pray so that you will not fall into temptation. The spirit is willing, but the body is weak" (Matthew 26:40-41).**

When He said **"Watch and pray so that you will not fall into temptation,"** He very clearly stated the importance of watching, then praying.

Here Jesus ranked *watching* over praying, however it is at least as important as prayer. If His disciples had followed His instructions, it would have been impossible for them to fall asleep. You cannot be watching and sleeping simultaneously. Your eyes need to be open to be watching. The disciples didn't fall asleep once or twice, but three times!

What was happening? There were several things. Jesus, who then greatly needed their prayers, was teaching the disciples a lesson on being watchmen, and the enemy brought a spirit of slumber over them. Have you ever been interceding for something important and began falling asleep in a very crucial situation? When this happens, it's not necessarily that you're just tired, but the enemy tries to put you to sleep with a spirit of slumber. In those kinds of situations, the best thing to do is to stand up, walk around, start singing or shouting, and take authority over the spirit of slumber. Bind the spirit of slumber; command it to be gone from you in Jesus' name! Keep watching and praying and believing God for the fullness of the breakthrough.

We want to learn from the mistakes of Jesus' disciples. We want to watch and pray and stay awake, especially when the Lord is calling us to pray. There's a time to watch and a time to sleep. Jesus was sleeping in the boat when the storm was raging; but in the Garden of Gethsemane it was not a time to sleep, but a time to watch.

Their temptation was to sleep, and they yielded and fell asleep. Thank God that the Lord Jesus didn't fall asleep, but was our example of a watchman even to the point that "**His sweat was like drops of blood**" **(Luke 22:44)**.

His eyes were so much on the Father that He didn't allow anything to distract Him; He kept watching the Father. We may think that His relationship with the Father made it easier for Him, but we have the same potential of developing a relationship with the Father, because Jesus opened the way. We can be as close to the Father through Jesus as we want to be, but it will cost us everything, even as it did Jesus.

## Lessons from Jesus for Us as Watchmen

> **Therefore, brothers, since we have confidence to enter the Most Holy Place by the blood of Jesus, by a new and living way opened for us through the curtain, that is, his body, (Hebrews 10:19-20)**

As we spend time in fellowship and communion with the Father, we will continue to want just to be with Him. The world would try to distract us, but we've been delivered from this present evil age. Jesus' eyes were only on His heavenly Father. *May God help us to watch and to do only what He has initiated from Heaven.*

The words of Jesus Himself are:

> **"Be always on the watch, and pray that you may be able to escape all that is about to happen, and that you may be able to stand before the Son of Man" (Luke 21:36).**

We need to watch and pray so that we are not unprepared because of dissipation, drunkenness or the cares of the world. These are the words of Jesus speaking from His own experience. He was always on the watch, alert and watching. We need to follow His example, to be alert, always on the watch, and to pray in these last days so we will be delivered from this present evil age and able to stand before Him at His coming.

**For the accuser of our brothers, who accuses them before our God day and night, has been hurled down. They overcame him by the blood of the Lamb and by the word of their testimony... (Revelation 12:10-11).**

Satan is the accuser of the brethren day and night. Did you know that Satan keeps a 24-hour watch? He's not sleeping, so we should indeed be living in the spirit of fasting and praying 24 hours a day and not in a spirit of slumber, at ease in Zion. Thank God we overcome Satan by the blood of the Lamb and the word of our testimony. We have the victory through our Lord Jesus Christ!

God wants us to see Him, eye to eye, in Zion. He wants our eyes to look into His eyes. As we behold Him and look only into His eyes, we will continue to see through His eyes. Our God is a consuming fire. We may be like Shadrach, Meshach and Abednego in the fiery furnace, but the Lord Jesus was in the midst of the fiery furnace, and Revelation 1:14 says Jesus' eyes are like blazing fire. As Isaiah 31:9 says, Israel and Jerusalem will be like the fiery furnace. We're going to see the fire of God in increasing ways, especially in Jerusalem, but also wherever you live in the nations, because He is like a refiner's fire; and the Lord, by the fire in His eyes, will be purifying and refining us. We will be going through increasing fires in the last days, but we need to welcome the fires because they're the refiner's fire preparing us, as His bride, to be ready for His coming (Malachi 3).

# Chapter 4

# The Holy Spirit as a Watchman

## The Holy Spirit: a Watchman Since Time Began

The Person of the Holy Spirit is also a Watchman. The working of the Holy Spirit is first recorded in Genesis 1:2, where the Spirit of God was hovering over the waters, brooding over the waters at creation. Since the beginning of time, the people whom God created to be in the world have grieved, quenched and ignored the Holy Spirit, who is watching them and wanting to help them. Jesus said that the Father gives the Holy Spirit as our helper (John 14:16).

At the baptism of Jesus, **"the Holy Spirit descended on him in bodily form like a dove. And a voice came from heaven: "You are my Son, whom I love; with you I am well pleased" (Luke 3:22).** Jesus actually was baptized with the Holy Spirit. Also, John's Gospel points out concerning Jesus, **"That was the true Light which gives light to every man coming into the world (John 1:9 NKJV).**

We were not created to be dead in our sins; we were created to be born again by the Holy Spirit and to receive the light of God through the Holy Spirit. Everyone is born with the potential to receive the Holy Spirit; we each have a conscience, and when reaching out for the truth, will be born again and receive the Holy Spirit.

**We do, however, speak a message of wisdom among the mature, but not the wisdom of this age or of the rulers of this age, who are coming to nothing. No, we speak of God's secret wisdom, a wisdom that has been hidden and that God destined for our glory before time began. None of the rulers of this age understood it, for if they had, they would not have crucified the Lord of glory. However, as it is written: "No eye has seen, no ear has heard, no mind has**

conceived what God has prepared for those who love him"—but God has revealed it to us by his Spirit.

The Spirit searches all things, even the deep things of God. For who among men knows the thoughts of a man except the man's spirit within him? In the same way no one knows the thoughts of God except the Spirit of God. We have not received the spirit of the world but the Spirit who is from God, that we may understand what God has freely given us. This is what we speak, not in words taught us by human wisdom but in words taught by the Spirit, expressing spiritual truths in spiritual words (1 Corinthians 2:6-13).

The Holy Spirit searches all things; He watches over and for all things (v. 10).

## Watching to Convict the World

The Person of the Holy Spirit has come as a Watchman to convict the world of guilt in regard to sin and righteousness and judgment.

"Now I am going to him who sent me, yet none of you asks me, 'Where are you going?' Because I have said these things, you are filled with grief. But I tell you the truth: It is for your good that I am going away. Unless I go away, the Counselor will not come to you; but if I go, I will send him to you. When he comes, He will convict the world of guilt in regard to sin and righteousness and judgment: in regard to sin, because men do not believe in me; in regard to righteousness, because I am going to the Father, where you can see me no longer; and in regard to judgment, because the prince of this world now stands condemned" (John 16:5-11).

The Holy Spirit is the one whom God uses to draw us to Himself. He's watching for people who are open to Him, those whom He can draw to Himself. He said, "But I, when I am lifted up from the earth, will draw all men to myself" (John 12:32).

## The Spirit of Truth—Within Us

> "You may ask me for anything in my name, and I will do
> it. If you love me, you will obey what I command. And I
> will ask the Father, and he will give you another
> Counselor to be with you forever--the Spirit of truth. The
> world cannot accept him, because it neither sees him nor
> knows him. But you know him, for he lives with you and
> will be in you. I will not leave you as orphans; I will come
> to you. Before long, the world will not see me anymore,
> but you will see me. Because I live, you also will live"
> (John 14:14-19).

Here the Lord says it's better that He goes away so that the Holy
Spirit can come. Our closest, most intimate friend is the Holy Spirit.
Jesus left; He went to heaven. It's true that Jesus lives within us, but
He's saying it's better that the Holy Spirit is with us than if Jesus
personally were with us. The Holy Spirit is not just here in this room,
the Holy Spirit lives within us, and He watches us even from within.
He wants to be our most intimate friend.

## Watching the Holy Spirit—While He's Watching Us

Referring to the Holy Spirit, Jesus says:

> "The world cannot accept him, because it neither sees
> him nor knows him. But you know him, for he lives with
> you and will be in you. I will not leave you as orphans; I
> will come to you. Before long, the world will not see me
> anymore, but you will see me" (John 14:17-19).

How do we see Him? He's not visible! We see Him with the eye of
the Spirit—the eye of faith. We're watching Him and He is watching
us. He's a Watchman, watching over us. Jesus said that unless a man
is born again, he cannot see the kingdom of God. What is the
kingdom of God? It's righteousness, peace and joy in the Holy Spirit.
Because we were born again by the Spirit of God, we can see the
kingdom of God; we can "see" the Holy Spirit. We can be watching
the Holy Spirit as He goes before us, watching Him move, following
Him wherever He goes; and the Holy Spirit is watching us and

searching the deep things of God. He wants to work within us in increasing ways, and work through us in these last days.

## Intimacy with the Holy Spirit

The Holy Spirit can either become our best, most intimate friend—or our enemy. He is extremely gentle and sensitive, yet it's easy to grieve and to quench Him. If we're not sensitive to Him, He'll just lift from our midst and go away—so we need to treat the Holy Spirit with great respect, honor and sensitivity. I believe that God is looking for a people who are willing to watch the Holy Spirit, revere Him and treat Him the way He is meant to be treated.

The Holy Spirit wants to become our intimate friend, and that's the reason He has come into the world. People who have had intimate friendships with the Holy Spirit have been used significantly in history. St. John the Apostle, St. Francis of Assisi, Kathryn Kuhlman, had intimacy with the Holy Spirit, and the love of God worked through them. Many miracles were performed through them. This can be seen in many other people's lives, in the Scriptures as well as in history.

Even today God is working through many people, as they have fuller intimacy with the Holy Spirit. However, if the Holy Spirit is our enemy, He can be very harsh; it's extremely dangerous for Him to be our enemy. Although He can be very harsh, He can be very, very gentle and kind—and very much our friend. How can He become our friend? The first way is for us to receive the indwelling and baptism of the Holy Spirit. When we receive the Holy Spirit we're saying that we want Him to become our #1 friend. We're inviting Him into our lives to dwell within us. How much closer can a friend be than to live within us? He's the only friend who lives within us! Our wife or husband doesn't live *within* us. Even Jesus, in the physical realm, can't live within us.

## Living by the Spirit

**So I say, live by the Spirit, and you will not gratify the desires of the sinful nature (Galatians 5:16).**

First, we need to receive the Holy Spirit (Acts 2). Second, the Holy Spirit wants to be our closest friend. Third, He wants us to walk in the Spirit. Fourth, He wants us to be filled afresh each day with the Spirit. Some people feel that once they have received the baptism or fullness of the Holy Spirit, they're always filled with the Holy Spirit; but the Bible teaches that each day we need a fresh infilling (Ephesians 5:18). Fifth, Acts 5:32 says those who are led by the Spirit obey the Holy Spirit, so we need to obey the Holy Spirit. Jesus told His disciples that they were no longer His servants, but His friends, *if you do what I command* (John 15:14-15).

Also, God wants the Holy Spirit to manifest His fruit through us, the fruit of the Spirit. If we are friends with the Holy Spirit, if we are developing fellowship and communion with Him, then we'll allow His fruit to be manifested through our lives and He'll bring forth the fruit of the Spirit through us (Galatians 5:22-25).

## Grieving the Holy Spirit

If we have a true friendship with someone, we don't want to upset or grieve them. If we're friends of the Holy Spirit, we will not grieve Him—quench or resist the Holy Spirit—but will allow Him to flow through us and to have His way. If we rebel and grieve the Holy Spirit, He can actually turn and become our enemy and fight against us!

> **Yet they rebelled and grieved his Holy Spirit. So he turned and became their enemy and he himself fought against them (Isaiah 63:10).**

Acts 7:51 speaks of resisting the Holy Spirit. God is sometimes merciful even when we have resisted the Holy Spirit. He can have great mercy and patience with us; but on the other hand He can become our enemy. *May God give us hearts that are not resistant, but which flow and respond to the promptings of the Holy Spirit.*

> **Quench not the Spirit (1 Thessalonians 5:19 KJV).**

Ephesians 4:29-32 speaks of grieving the Holy Spirit through such things as unwholesome talk, bitterness and malice. Sometimes in meetings I've seen people do this; the Holy Spirit is moving very powerfully, and someone will say something that's totally out of the Spirit and the Spirit will be quenched. It shows how sensitive we need to be to the Spirit.

We can grieve the Spirit by sin. Jesus, in Mark 3:29, speaks of blaspheming the Holy Spirit. "Blaspheming the Holy Spirit" means to speak against the Holy Spirit, to say that He's not God and to ultimately come against Him. In Matthew 12:31, Jesus says that if we speak against the Son of Man we will be forgiven, but if we speak against the Holy Spirit we will not be forgiven. Now I can't say exactly when God decides that's going to happen to someone, but it certainly shows how God the Holy Spirit, working in the world today, is to be respected. Jesus is saying that He wants us to allow the Holy Spirit to have His way and to honor and respect Him. Sadly, not only those in the world, but also the Church throughout history, have quenched, grieved and come against the Holy Spirit.

I believe the twentieth century is THE CENTURY OF THE HOLY SPIRIT. It's interesting that in 1900, on New Year's Eve, literally at the turn of the century, there were people in Topeka, Kansas praying on a 24-hour watch, and God poured out the Holy Spirit upon them. They were baptized in the Holy Spirit and some began to speak in other tongues! So God has birthed this century as the Century of the Holy Spirit.

From the second century until this century there has been much grieving and quenching of the Holy Spirit. God has opened up this century to the outpouring of the Holy Spirit in an incredible way. Those of us who have been filled or baptized in the Holy Spirit still have to make sure that we're being filled afresh each day, obeying Him and allowing Him to have full reign in our lives.

Ananias and Sapphira lied to the Holy Spirit and were killed as a result (Acts 5:1-11). That shows us how serious it is to offend the Holy Spirit. I'm not quite sure why God hasn't wiped out many more people for lying to the Holy Spirit today. He's been merciful; but I believe that when we're moving in fuller dimensions of revival, God's presence is there in increasing ways, and it can become more serious to lie to the Holy Spirit. Deliberately turning away from the Holy Spirit... I don't know when that happens to a person, only God knows, but it shows us how grievous it is to turn away from the Holy Spirit after receiving Him. I've seen people who have totally gone away from God and yet He has brought them back. But there is a point beyond which a person can go, and not be brought back. It shows us the gravity of rejecting the Holy Spirit.

## Our Counselor, Our Guide, Our Watchman

> **For to us a child is born, to us a son is given, and the government will be on his shoulders. And he will be called Wonderful Counselor, Mighty God, Everlasting Father, Prince of Peace (Isaiah 9:6).**

> **"And I will ask the Father, and he will give you another Counselor to be with you forever—the Spirit of truth" (John 14:16-17).**

> **"But when he, the Spirit of truth, comes, he will guide you into all truth. He will not speak on his own; he will speak only what he hears, and he will tell you what is yet to come. He will bring glory to me by taking from what is mine and making it known to you" (John 16:13-14).**

Acts 9:31 shows the result of allowing the Holy Spirit to strengthen and encourage us:

> **Then the church... enjoyed a time of peace. It was strengthened; and encouraged by the Holy Spirit, it grew in numbers, living in the fear of the Lord.**

The Holy Spirit wants to lead and guide us. He knows everything about us. As He's guiding us He's watching over us as our Watchman. He leads us into all truth, protects us, is the one who is our Teacher, Counselor, teaches us all things, brings all things to our remembrance, and supplies all our needs. God can bring incredible things to our remembrance. The Holy Spirit is omniscient, knows all things; He is God, so He has the potential of bringing everything to our minds. He cares for us (1 Peter 5:7).

Dr. Lloyd Ogilvie, who recently wrote a book, *The Holy Spirit, The Greatest Counselor in the World,* says that for the last twenty to thirty years he has spent half an hour every morning and every evening fellowshipping with and taking counsel from the Holy Spirit. If pastors and spiritual leaders would teach their people to do this, it would help to eliminate much of their pastoral counseling, as God the Holy Spirit would directly counsel them.

The Lord also wants us to continue to walk with Him as little children. A man cannot see the kingdom of God unless He becomes as a little child. Luke 10:21 shows that Jesus, "full of joy through the

Holy Spirit," praised God that He hides many things from the wise and learned (people who are wise in their own minds), and He reveals them to little children. I don't believe that God reveals things only to little children, but that we need to have hearts and spiritual eyes and ears like little children in order to enter the kingdom and to receive the things of the Holy Spirit. We need to be humble before Him and receptive as a little child. At the same time, God is revealing many things by the Holy Spirit to little children. He loves to work in the children.

**From the lips of children and infants you have ordained praise (Psalm 8:2).**

Matthew 23:37 speaks of how the Lord Jesus, like a mother hen, wanted to brood over the City of Jerusalem. But Jerusalem was not willing (in the first century). So Jesus was crucified; He left. The Jewish people missed their hour of visitation. And the Holy Spirit wants to do the same thing today; He wants to brood over us individually and collectively, like a mother hen over her chicks.

I have been in meetings when the Holy Spirit was brooding over us--His presence was so strong it felt as though we were in heaven; and we were so sensitive to Him, because we didn't want Him to leave. It was as if the Dove came down on the meeting. This is what the Holy Spirit wants to do; He wants to brood over us individually and collectively. When our hearts are totally open and sensitive to Him, and He senses that we're reaching out to Him-- loving Him and welcoming Him—He will come upon us in a special way. It's heaven on earth when the Holy Spirit visits us and broods over us and we can fellowship with Him! It's a down payment of heaven.

So the more we are sensitive to Him and develop an intimate friendship with Him, love Him and commune with Him, the more He will manifest Himself to us and brood over us. He also wants to release the gifts of the Holy Spirit through us. May we allow the Holy Spirit to have His way, in increasing ways in and through our lives.

# Communing with the Holy Spirit

**The grace of the Lord Jesus Christ, and the love of God, and the communion of the Holy Spirit be with you all (2 Corinthians 13:14 NKJV).**

This Scripture speaks of the grace of the Lord Jesus and the love of God being upon us—the *grace* of the Lord Jesus and the *love* of God. But it refers to something more intimate when it mentions the Holy Spirit; it is the fellowship, the *communion* of the Holy Spirit. God has created us to commune with Him. Jesus gives us grace, God gives us love, and the Holy Spirit wants to commune with us—to fellowship with us, to share intimately and develop intimacy with us. *May God grace us to develop the fullness of intimacy with the Holy Spirit that He has purposed for us.*

The Holy Spirit is watching us, and He says that we who are born again by the Spirit of God have eyes to watch Him. Unbelievers cannot see Him, but we can see Him, because it says *he who has eyes to see, let him see* what the Spirit is saying to the churches! *May God anoint our eyes, so that we will see Him more clearly and fellowship with Him more nearly (intimately) in increasing ways, so that the Holy Spirit may truly have His way in us and through us.*

*My prayer is that the last decade of the twentieth century will be known as THE DECADE OF THE HOLY SPIRIT in an even fuller way than this century has been known as THE CENTURY OF THE HOLY SPIRIT. May we allow the Holy Spirit to have full reign in our lives individually and in His church collectively in this decade, preparing the way for Jesus to come to His church (His temple) in all His glory!*

The Lord is looking for a place to rest today on the earth, even as the dove was looking for a place to rest when it left the ark in Noah's day. *May we provide a resting place for Him as we commune and fellowship with the Holy Spirit and prepare the way for Him to come to His people for His people and with His people!*

In the First Century Jesus said the Jewish people were unwilling to be gathered by the Holy Spirit under His wings (Matthew 23:37). As we, together with the Jewish people, prepare for Messiah's coming, may we all be willing to be gathered together by the Holy Spirit, to commune with Him under His wings, to be prepared and sheltered by the Holy Spirit in the ark—our refuge and fortress.

**He who dwells in the shelter of the Most High will rest in the shadow of the Almighty. I will say of the LORD, "He is my refuge and my fortress, my God, in whom I trust."**

Surely he will save you from the fowler's snare and from the deadly pestilence. He will cover you with his feathers, and under his wings you will find refuge; his faithfulness will be your shield and rampart. You will not fear the terror of night, nor the arrow that flies by day, nor the pestilence that stalks in the darkness, nor the plague that destroys at midday. A thousand may fall at your side, ten thousand at your right hand, but it will not come near you. You will only observe with your eyes and see the punishment of the wicked.

If you make the Most High your dwelling—even the LORD, who is my refuge—then no harm will befall you, no disaster will come near your tent. For he will command his angels concerning you to guard you in all your ways; they will lift you up in their hands, so that you will not strike your foot against a stone. You will tread upon the lion and the cobra; you will trample the great lion and the serpent.

"Because he loves me," says the LORD, "I will rescue him; I will protect him, for he acknowledges my name. He will call upon me, and I will answer him; I will be with him in trouble, I will deliver him and honor him. With long life will I satisfy him and show him my salvation" (Psalm 91).

## COMMUNE WITH ME

Commune with Me, commune with Me.
Between the wings of the cherubim,
Commune with Me.

I worship You, I worship You,
Between the wings of the cherubim
I worship You.

Alleluia! Alleluia!
Between the wings of the cherubim,
Alleluia!

## THE WATCHMAN'S ANOINTING

**"You have an anointing from the Holy one" (1 John 2:20).**

In these last days, although 1 John 2:27 says the anointing abides with us, we also need to be freshly anointed daily by God the Holy Spirit—that we **"may be filled to the measure of all the fullness of God (Eph 3:19)**—to be His watchmen in the following ways:

## ANOINTING

| | | |
|---|---|---|
| 1. | for eyes to see | **Rev 1:12-17; Mt 13:16** |
| 2. | for ears to hear | **Rev 2:7** |
| 3. | for unity | **Ps 133** |
| 4. | breaks every yoke | **Isa 58:6** |
| 5. | to preach the good news to the poor | **Isa 61:1; Lk 4:18** |
| 6. | to bind up the brokenhearted | **Isa 61:1; Lk 4:18** |
| 7. | to proclaim liberty to the captives and release the prisoners and sight to blind | **Isa 61:1; Lk 4:18** |
| 8. | to proclaim the *Year of Jubilee* (double portion) | **Isa 61:2; Lk 4:19** |
| 9. | for vengeance of our God | **Isa 61:2** |
| 10. | to comfort all who mourn | **Isa 61:2** |
| 11. | to provide for those who grieve in Zion | **Isa 61:3** |
| 12. | to bestow beauty for ashes and the oil of gladness for mourning | **Isa 61:3** |
| 13. | the garment of praise instead of despair | **Isa 61:3** |
| 14. | teaches all things | **1 Jn 2:27; Jn 14:26** |
| 15. | brings all things to our remembrance | **Jn 14:26** |
| 16. | for death and burial | **Jn 12:7** |
| 17. | brings blessing | **Ps 133** |
| 18. | for breakthroughs | **Mic 2:13** |
| 19. | for grace and intercession | **Zec 12:10** |
| 20. | to cleanse from sin and idolatry, remove idols | **Zec 13:1-2** |

# Chapter 5

# Man as a Watchman
## (20 Aspects of Being a Watchman)

# Part I

## Every Believer Called to Be a Watchman

God has called every believer to be a watchman. Is a watchman a special ministry to which God has called certain people? I believe that every believer is called to be a watchman, but people have different spheres of responsibility.

A ten-year-old child is called to be a watchman because he has to give an account for his own soul. He has to watch over, and be responsible for, his own life. As a watchman, he's watching the Lord and watching over his own life. A husband is also a watchman over his family, over his household. Women are watchmen over their children, over their families. A businessman is a watchman over his business. Elders are watchmen—pastors over the church. Watchmen sit at the gates of the city; elders are watchmen over the city in a spiritual sense.

God has called some to be watchmen over cities and some to be watchmen over nations. Jeremiah and Isaiah were called to be watchmen over Israel and the nations. Some people are called to be watchmen in an international way. So this is not something that is limited to a few people; every believer is called to be a watchman. Everyone has to be responsible, but also to know his or her sphere of responsibility in being a watchman.

## What Is a Watchman?

I used to believe that being a watchman only meant being an intercessor. As I ministered in Jerusalem and traveled in the nations, I heard disagreement about what a watchman is. Some said a watchman is simply an intercessor. Others said, "No, he is a worshiper."

Others said, "No, he is a prophet." Still others said that he is someone who waits on and listens to the Lord. Actually, all are right.

True watchmen are those who watch God, the Chief Watchman—those who are attentive to Him with all their faculties and who consequently see things through His eyes and His Word. Such people clearly hear and obey God's voice, faithfully practicing all the aspects of watching as led by the Holy Spirit. They will be prepared for the coming of the Messiah, and will be faithfully preparing His way.

## Aspects of Being a Watchman:

### 1. Watching the Lord

This, to me, is the most exciting thing in my life, because the Lord is the most important One to watch! He created us to watch Him. It says in Revelation 1:14,16 that His face is like the sun shining in all of its strength; His eyes are like blazing fire. He wants us to look into His face, to look into His eyes and to behold Him. As we behold Him in the Spirit, we are changed into His likeness from glory to glory—into His likeness and into His image as we behold Him in the Spirit. Watching the Lord, I believe, is the most important thing we can do.

> **Listen! My lover! Look! [Watch!] Here he comes, leaping across the mountains, bounding over the hills. My lover is like a gazelle or a young stag. Look! [Watch!] There He stands behind our wall, gazing through the windows, peering through the lattice. My lover spoke and said to me, "Arise, my darling, my beautiful one, and come with me. See! [Watch!] The winter is past; the rains are over and gone" (Song of Songs 2:8-11).**

The Lord wants us to watch Him and to follow Him wherever He goes.

The Lord's Revelation to John reminds us that we should follow the Lamb wherever He goes, and love not our lives even unto death. If we're beholding Him and watching Him, just as the cloud arose and led the children of Israel, we are to follow the Lord as He moves forward. It says that His going forth is as certain as the dawn. The cloud continually moves, and if we are going to follow the cloud we must have our eyes on the Lord Jesus, because He is continually moving forward.

**My lover is radiant and ruddy, outstanding among ten thousand. His head is purest gold; his hair is wavy and black as a raven. His eyes are like doves by the water streams, washed in milk, mounted like jewels. His cheeks are like beds of spice yielding perfume. His lips are like lilies dripping with myrrh. His arms are rods of gold set with chrysolite. His body is like polished ivory decorated with sapphires. His legs are pillars of marble set on bases of pure gold.**

**His appearance is like Lebanon, choice as its cedars. His mouth is sweetness itself; he is altogether lovely. This is my lover, this my friend, O daughters of Jerusalem (Song of Songs 5:10-16).**

Hallelujah! The Lord is altogether lovely. Hallelujah! He wants us to watch Him and to follow Him wherever He goes, and love not our lives even unto death. Paul says in Philippians 4:8, that we should dwell upon **"whatever is true, whatever is noble, whatever is right, whatever is pure, whatever is lovely, whatever is admirable—if anything is excellent or praiseworthy [of good report]."**

Basically, we should dwell upon the Lord, for He is the utmost of all these qualities; He is all these different things upon which we should dwell. And so, if we are dwelling upon Him, there is only Jesus—He is everything. He is the essence of goodness, of purity, of loveliness, of honesty, of all these things. Jesus keeps in perfect peace those whose minds are stayed upon Him. He wants us to look continually at His face and to follow Him.

As we're approaching the Day of the Second Coming of the Lord, now more than ever we should have our eyes watching Him, and be following Him, the Lord of the Watch. We should have *eye contact* with Him in the Spirit, and be in love with Him. God doesn't want us to lose our first love—in fact, He wants our first love to be restored if we're losing it in any way. He wants us to be watching Him continually.

## 2. Watching His Word

We're to be meditating upon [watching] His Word day and night. Psalm 1:2-3 says that if we meditate upon His Word day and night, we will be like trees planted by the rivers of water, we will bring forth fruit in season, our leaves will not wither and whatever we do will prosper. The Lord is watching over His Word. His Word is settled in heaven and He wants to settle His Word upon the earth. As He's watching over His Word from heaven, He's looking for people to watch His Word on the earth—people through whom He can perform it—people who will be challenged for His Word to be performed through them. As we're watching His Word day and night, meditating upon His Word, we will see Him performing His Word in increasing ways through us.

John 15:7-8,16 says that if we abide in Him and His words abide in us, we will bear much fruit that remains. He wants us to watch His Word, that it will become spirit and life, to be written on our hearts and abide in us. The more we watch His Word and it becomes part of us, the more it becomes spirit and life in our lives.

I believe that people who are watching television more than the Word of God are living in idolatry. God wants us to turn off our televisions and to turn on the Word of God, to spend time watching His Word, that we will be washed by the Word and conformed into His image and likeness.

## 3. Watching in Thanksgiving

On New Year's Eve, 1990, the Lord showed me that this decade was going to be the decade of the greatest spiritual warfare in history. We're only part way through the decade and we've seen incredible spiritual warfare. By the time we get to the end of the decade, it will be much more intense. He said that we need to spend more time in thanksgiving and in praise and worship, because we enter His gates with thanksgiving, and as we do this, God will arise and His enemies, our enemies, will scatter.

When we begin to thank the Lord, we may be a bit depressed or a little discouraged, but if we spend time thanking the Lord, we're lifted out of our discouragement. We realize the nature and character of the goodness of the Lord. We realize the things that we are thankful for, in terms of the Lord Himself and what we see God doing. We need to count our blessings and to be thankful to the Lord, for He is good, to see the goodness of the Lord in the mighty deeds that He's doing before our very eyes. Then we enter His gates with thanksgiving and His courts with praise.

> **Enter his gates with thanksgiving and his courts with praise; give thanks to him and praise his name (Psalm 100:4).**

> **Devote yourselves to prayer, being watchful and thankful (Colossians 4:2).**

God wants us to be watchful and thankful. In other words, we should watch the things for which we are thankful, for different ways that we can be thankful for who the Lord is and for what He does, as well as for our brothers and sisters in the Lord.

## 4. Praise and Worship

God wants us to enter His gates with thanksgiving and His courts with praise, to move not only into praise, because God arises on our lips as we're praising Him, but also to move into intimate times of worship with Him. As we do this, we draw into fuller communion and intimacy with Him. This is what we are created to do, to enjoy God and to worship Him forever. This is our eternal purpose—to worship Him forever.

As we enter into the millennial reign of Jesus on earth and then on into eternity, there will be a time when there won't be a need for evangelization; but there's never going to be a time when we won't be worshiping! Worship is our eternal vocation, to worship God and to enjoy Him forever. When we're worshiping God, we're moving into the Holy of Holies—through the gates with thanksgiving, into the courts with praise. But when we're moving into worship we're abiding in Him in the secret place of the Most High. We're living in the Holy of Holies in intimate communion with Him.

He's calling us to move from thanksgiving to praise and to worship. So He wants us to be watchful for ways that we can praise Him. His character and nature are so tremendous that He wants us to watch the aspects of who He is. Then we can praise Him and move into deeper realms of worship and adoration of the Lord.

The four living creatures are described in Revelation 4 and 5. They had eyes all around them, were watching, and

**Day and night they never stop saying: "Holy, holy, holy is the Lord God Almighty, who was, and is, and is to come" (Revelation 4:8).**

Hallelujah! All they have been doing for thousands of years has been worshiping the Lord, day and night, on a 24- hour watch!

God is restoring 24-hour worship and 24-hour prayer world-wide, preparing for His coming in Jerusalem. We are worshiping with them even now. In one sense, the Lord Jesus never left the earth. He said, "Lo, I am with you always," and He just disappeared. But we're looking for the blessed hope, the glorious appearing (Titus 2:13). He's going to appear again. He's coming back to be with us visibly. Every eye will see Him; every eye will behold Him.

### 5. Pouring out Our Heart Like Water Before the Presence of the Lord

**Arise, cry out in the night, as the watches of the night begin; pour out your heart like water in the presence of the Lord (Lamentations 2:19).**

For many years I did not understand what this meant, thinking that the Lord would minister to me if I were available, any time He wanted. I never realized that I needed to pour out my heart before Him. I felt that if He wanted to minister to me, I was there and He could do so. I ended up getting ulcers.

That was about twenty-five years ago. I thought I was going to die from ulcers, but suddenly realized it was a two-way relationship, that God didn't create me just so He could minister to me, but He wanted me to pour out my heart like water before His presence. As we do that, something is released into us and God ministers to us, because He created us for communion with Him. He wants us to share the deepest needs of our being with Him, to pour out our heart like water before Him.

Praise God, I received the baptism of the Holy Spirit, and God totally healed me of ulcers as I started pouring out my heart before the presence of the Lord. If we would do this, there would be much less need for counseling. Some of us place all our burdens on our pastors. Praise God for pastoral counseling, but if we would go directly to the Lord and pour out our heart to Him, He would give us counseling.

## 6. Waiting Upon the Lord

This is most difficult for me. I grew up in a Western culture where everything is instant: instant mashed potatoes, instant microwave cooking, instant foods, everything is instant! If you come from Papua New Guinea, things aren't as instant as in the United States or Germany. I tell people who come from third world countries that they are more blessed than people from Western countries because they can learn the ways of God more easily. God can do things instantly. He can perform miracles and heal people instantly, but learning the ways of God does not happen instantly.

The children of Israel knew the *acts* of God, which can happen instantly, but Moses knew the *ways* of God, which are not learned instantly. It took Moses forty years in the desert to learn the ways of God. It takes time to learn the ways of God, because God's ways are higher than our ways, His thoughts are higher than our thoughts.

**Since ancient times no one has heard, no ear has perceived, no eye has seen any God besides you, who acts on behalf of those who wait for him (Isaiah 64:4).**

What does it means to wait upon the Lord? It's like strands being woven together into a rope. To wait on God means not to go before Him, nor to lag behind Him, but to go *with* God. Our spirit is one spirit with the Lord, joined to the Lord. He who is joined to the Lord is of one spirit. So if we're born again and we're joined to the Lord and are one spirit with Him, we're like a rope that's woven together with the Lord. If we try to go ahead or lag behind God, we can abort what God wants to do.

God wants us to live with an "open heaven"—a pipeline to heaven. If we're waiting on God, we're living with an open heaven. If we try to go ahead of God, we short circuit, we close the heavens. If we lag behind God, again we close the heavens. We need to learn the art of waiting upon God. That means, basically, that God is not looking for people to do good works for Him. He's looking for people through whom He can do His works.

God wants us to be channels of the Holy Spirit—for the Holy Spirit to work through our lives. If we learn the art of waiting on God, and we're sensitive to the Holy Spirit in such a way that we will not try to do good works *for* God, then this will allow the Lord to do His works through us, bringing forth one hundredfold fruit. It's very easy. Jesus said, **"My yoke is easy and my burden is light" (Matthew 11:30),** and in three years many things were accomplished through Him, bringing forth one hundredfold fruit. He didn't heal everyone. The compassion within Him could have led Him to heal everyone, but He did only what the Father told Him to do. He was allowing the Father to bring forth one hundredfold fruit through His life.

Many times God will show you something; He'll conceive something by the Holy Spirit. Then you'll have to wait for the birthing. That can be difficult, because when something's conceived, it seems as though it's already happened. But if you don't wait for the birthing, you'll cause a spiritual abortion.

In 1982 God showed me a vision to move to Israel, and in 1984 He showed me a vision of the House of Prayer. The first thing I did was go to a real estate agent in West Jerusalem, trying to find the House of Prayer. I had seen it in the spirit, and was saying "Where is it?" About three and one-half years later, in 1987, while walking across the Mount of Olives, I saw the House of Prayer; it wasn't even in West Jerusalem. I had been looking in the wrong place. It was now God's timing to birth what was conceived by the Holy Spirit.

## 7. Inquiring of the Lord

This is very important. David mentions about thirty times in the Psalms that he inquired of the Lord about this and that. David was always inquiring of God, while Saul was a man who did not inquire of God. Saul "did his own thing" (acted in the flesh). He did not take counsel with the Lord, which is why God rejected Saul. But God said David was a man after His own heart. David would always take counsel from the Lord, would always inquire of the Lord about what he should do. If we're going to be men and women after the Lord's own heart, we need to ask the Lord questions about what we should be doing.

All these areas are as important as intercession. In fact, we can't even know how to intercede unless we do them. Otherwise, we could be interceding out of our own mind and not out of the mind of the Spirit and out of the ways of God.

> **Someone calls to me from Seir, "Watchman, what is left of the night? Watchman, what is left of the night?" The watchman replies, "Morning is coming, but also the night. If you would ask, then ask; and come back yet again" (Isaiah 21:11-12).**

God is saying that He wants us, as His watchmen, to ask, to inquire. "If you would ask, then ask; and come back yet again." We need to be seeking God continually. Even if we don't get the answer the first time, don't give up; *keep inquiring of the Lord.* Sometimes it takes me awhile to get God's counsel, His answers. It could even be that the enemy is trying to stop the counsel of the Lord from coming to us. *We must keep asking God until we get the mind of the Lord.* We shouldn't ask God just once and assume that He doesn't want to give it or think the first thought we receive is the answer. We should continue pressing in to know the Lord, to know His counsel, until we have it in such a way that we're sure, that it's confirmed in different ways to us, that we truly have the mind of the Lord.

## 8. Listening to the Lord

This is one of the most important aspects of being a watchman. In fact, I tell many Pentecostals and Charismatics to be very grateful that God restored praise and worship, shouting, dancing and celebrating to the church. But at the same time, I believe God sometimes would say, "Why don't you just be quiet for awhile?" This is a two-way communication. God didn't create people just to intercede, dance, shout, jump and make a joyful noise. Praise God for all these things, they're great. But God created us for two-way communication, and what God speaks to us is at least as important as what we speak to Him.

I cherish different words that God has spoken to me. I'm sure that if God speaks something to me, it's at least as important, if not more important, than what I'm speaking to Him. If that's true, we should give God as much time, if not more time, to speak to us, as we take in speaking to Him. If we really believe this, we need to spend as much time listening to the Lord as we do interceding, dancing, shouting, rejoicing or whatever. It says seven times in the Book of Revelation, chapters 2 and 3, **"He who has an ear, let him hear what the Spirit says to the churches."**

If we hear accurately and clearly what God is speaking to us, only then do we know how to pray; only then do we know how to intercede, what to do. The art of listening to God is very important.

> **I will stand at my watch and station myself on the ramparts; I will look [watch] to see what he will say to me, and what answer I am to give to this complaint (Habakkuk 2:1).**

He wants us to be watchmen. He wants us to be on the watch, listening, being fully alert, our ears open. That should be our posture as listening watchmen, watching to see what God will say to us. We know that most times He speaks to us in a still, small voice, so we need to give adequate time, as His watchmen, to be listening to the voice of our Master. He says,

> **"My sheep listen to my voice; I know them, and they follow me... no one can snatch them out of my hand" (John 10:27-28).**

In the last days it's important that we hear the voice of our Master, because there is much deception, many false voices in the world today. This will increase more and more between now and when the Lord comes back, so we need to be sensitive and listening to His voice.

### 9. Keep Watch and Do Not Allow Your House to be Broken Into

**"Therefore keep watch, because you do not know on what day your Lord will come. But understand this: If the owner of the house had known at what time of night the thief was coming, he would have kept watch and would have not let his house be broken into. So you also must be ready, because the Son of Man will come at an hour when you do not expect him" (Matthew 24:42-44).**

The Lord wants us not to allow our house to be broken into. This could mean different things, but I believe it could be dealing with not just something physical but also our spiritual house. In fact, I am learning this lesson as my house where I personally live (not the House of Prayer) was recently broken into. I believe in these last days that the warfare is going to get more intense all the time, no matter where we are in the world. Those of us who live in Jerusalem can be assured that the warfare is going to get much more intense: "We ain't seen nothing yet." We're still dealing on a kindergarten level; we're just in boot camp. We'll have many other levels to go through between now and when Jesus comes back. In the natural, wherever we are in the world, especially in areas of more warfare, both spiritual and physical, we need to make sure that we're applying the blood of Jesus to the doorposts of our houses on a daily basis.

Several years ago, the Lord spoke to us to take communion on a daily basis, and that's been a great blessing. There's something in the protection of the blood of Jesus that, when done on a daily basis, is affirming the protection of the Lord in the covenant. I believe that the Lord wants us to apply the blood of Jesus to our vehicles, everything that we're dealing with, on a daily basis, that we would not allow our houses to be broken into in the natural.

But I also believe it deals with our own bodies. He wants us to apply the blood of Jesus to our bodies on a regular basis, affirming the covenant, the protection that we have over our bodies through the blood of Jesus, and not allow any demonic forces to enter into our houses or into our bodies. So I believe this is what is talked about in not allowing our houses to be broken into; protection for our own bodies, as well as the houses in which we dwell—on both levels. God's Word says that we should be watchmen, that we not allow our house to be broken into.

## 10. Watch and Pray that You Do Not Enter into Temptation

As the disciples went with the Lord toward Gethsemane, Jesus said to Peter, **"this very night, before the rooster crows, you will disown me three times."** Peter didn't believe it and declared, **"Even if I have to die with you, I will never disown you."** And all the disciples said the same (Matthew 26:34-35).

What happened next? They were all in the Garden of Gethsemane with the Lord Jesus. He took Peter, especially Peter, and the two others, the sons of Zebedee, James and John. He took them alone, away from the other disciples, because they were the three who were the closest to Him.

> **He began to be sorrowful and troubled. Then he said to them, "My soul is overwhelmed with sorrow to the point of death. Stay here and keep watch with me." Going a little farther, he fell with his face to the ground and prayed "My Father, if it is possible, may this cup be taken from me. Yet not as I will, but as you will" (Matthew 26:37-39).**

Three times Jesus cried out to the Father, asking if it were possible, that this be taken from Him; three times—the exact number of times He said Peter would deny Him. Basically, all three times Peter was already denying Him, because he fell asleep, he was sleeping, he was totally asleep. And Jesus said, **"Could you men not keep watch with me for one hour?"** (Matthew 26:40).

A biblical watch was three hours, but they couldn't watch for even one hour. Jesus was there by Himself in His greatest hour of need; all the disciples fell asleep. Then Jesus said to them,

**"Are you still sleeping and resting? Look [Watch], the hour is near, and the Son of Man is betrayed into the hands of sinners. Rise, let us go! Here comes my betrayer!" (Matthew 26:45-46)**

So even Peter denied Jesus—Peter, to whom the Lord said, **"on this rock I will build my church" (Matthew 16:18).** Peter denied Him three different times.

Peter said, **"I don't know what you're talking about,"** when they identified him as having been with Jesus. Later he said, **"I don't know this man."** And again he said, **"I don't know this man" (Matthew 26:70-74).**

Had Peter been watching, alert and not falling asleep when he was to be watching with Jesus, I believe he would not have denied Him when the time of trial came, because he would have been alert. He would have been victorious on the watch and would have overcome at the time when he denied Him. But when Peter was supposed to be on the watch with the Lord Jesus, a spirit of slumber came against him. The enemy tried to put him to sleep—and they all fell asleep.

When we're called to be on the watch and a spirit of slumber comes against us, we need to bind the spirit of slumber and stay on the watch. We can learn from the mistakes of the disciples of Jesus. At strategic times, when I should have been on the watch, the enemy would try to put me to sleep. A spirit of slumber would come upon me and I would find myself falling asleep when there was something very vital that God wanted me to be doing in watching. That's not the time to bow our head and close our eyes. It's a time to jump up, to bind the spirit of slumber. There are times we can bow our head and close our eyes. We often see paintings of Jesus with His hands folded and looking downward, but many times we read that Jesus raised His hands toward heaven and looked up into the heavens.

So if a spirit of slumber is coming against you, it's better to raise your hands toward heaven, look up into the heavens, walk around and pray. Stay awake and fulfill your calling as a watchman. In fact, you can't watch with your eyes closed. If you're going to watch, your eyes must be open; you can't fall asleep with your eyes open!

Many times Jesus prioritized watching over praying. **"Watch and pray so that you will not fall into temptation" (Matthew 26:41).**

He didn't say, "Pray and watch." He said, **"Watch and pray."** He prioritized watching, and I believe that in these last days God is calling us, as a priority, to be His watchmen. As He's calling us to be His watchmen in these different ways, we will know how to pray in fuller ways. We will be more alert to pray.

There was a time in my life when I was interceding so much that I was being hit by the enemy. I was so tired from interceding, I wasn't alert as a watchman. God wants us to be watchmen first. That's why I believe He prioritizes, saying **"Watch and pray."**

*May God help us to be His watchmen in all ways. May He help us to watch and pray that we do not enter into temptation.*

*Father, we believe You to help us to be faithful watchmen. Help us to watch and pray that we do not enter into temptation. We believe You for all these different aspects of watching. Teach us to be Your watchmen. Help us to stand upon the watch in all the ways that it means to be Your watchmen in these last days, Lord God. We thank You for the privilege of being Your watchmen here in the City of Jerusalem or wherever we may be in the nations of the world. Help us to be faithful. We believe You to be the Chief Watchman, watching through us, Lord God. May we see eye to eye in Zion with You. As we look into Your eyes, may we see things through Your eyes. Teach us Your ways that we will walk in Your paths. Thank You, Father. We bless You as the Chief Watchman, and we thank You for the privilege of being co-watchmen with You. In Jesus' Name, Amen.*

# Chapter 6

# Man as a Watchman
## (20 Aspects of Being a Watchman)

# Part II

### 11. Going Up to Zion

The eleventh aspect of being a watchman can be found in Jeremiah 31:6, which speaks of watchmen going up to Zion. There are two ways that watchmen go up to Zion: in the natural and in the spiritual.

## Naturally

God is bringing His people up to Zion. He calls all the Jewish people and the Christians to come up to Jerusalem to keep the Holy Convocations of Israel to the Lord: the Holy Convocations of Passover (*Pesach*), Pentecost (*Shevuot*) and the Fall Convocations of Trumpets (*Rosh HaShanah*), the Day of Atonement (*Yom Kippur*) and Tabernacles (*Succot*). In these days God is also calling the Jewish people from around the world to move to Israel and to "make *Aliyah*," which means "to go up to Zion," to be established and rooted in the land. Many others from around the world come to keep one or more of the three feasts.

So, in the natural, God is calling the Jewish people to come up to Zion, to settle in Israel, and Gentile Christians to come up to Zion, to celebrate the Feasts and to be His watchmen and intercessors.

> **"These I will bring to my holy mountain and give them joy in my house of prayer... for my house will be called a house of prayer for all nations" (Isaiah 56:7).**

God is drawing intercessors, watchmen, to Jerusalem—to His holy mountain, and giving them joy in His house of prayer. He is bringing them to Jerusalem House of Prayer for All Nations and other places to pray as His watchmen on the walls of Jerusalem. He says they are to give Him no rest and give themselves no rest until Jerusalem is established **"as a praise in the earth"** (Isaiah 62:6-7).

> **There will be a day when watchmen cry out on the hills of Ephraim, "Come, let us go up to Zion, to the LORD our God" (Jeremiah 31:6).**

We live in a day when the watchmen are calling out, **"Let us go up to Zion, to the LORD our God."** He is drawing the watchmen up to Zion from the four corners of the earth. The more we see the restoration of Israel in the natural and in the spiritual, the more we see God bringing both the Jewish people to Israel to make *Aliyah*, to ascend to Zion, and the Gentiles to intercede as His watchmen on the walls of Jerusalem.

Within the Psalms are the songs of Ascents (Psalm 120-134), sung as the people were ascending to the temple, "coming up to Zion." When you come to Jerusalem, you have to come "up," because it is a city on seven hills. You cannot come "down" or even "over" to Jerusalem. From wherever you come in the world, you are *ascending* to Jerusalem because it is a high place. It is the City of the Great King.

## Spiritually

> **But you have come to Mount Zion, to the heavenly Jerusalem, the city of the living God. You have come to thousands upon thousands of angels in joyful assembly, to the church of the firstborn, whose names are written in heaven. You have come to God, the judge of all men, to the spirits of righteous men made perfect, to Jesus the mediator of the new covenant, and to the sprinkled blood that speaks a better word than the blood of Abel (Hebrews 12:22-24).**

Praise God! Here the writer is talking about ascending in the Spirit! When we are born again by the Holy Ghost we come into the presence of the Lord. Jesus broke down the middle wall of partition; the veil of the temple was torn so that we could "ascend to Jerusalem," not only in the natural, but also in the Holy Spirit. Hallelujah! It says that if we are born again, we have spiritually **"come to Mount Zion."** Those of us who are living in Jerusalem have not only come to Jerusalem in the natural, but in the Spirit as well. God's Word says we are sealed in the Holy Spirit. That means we have **"come to Mount Zion"** and, praise God, we are partakers of the Heavenly Jerusalem, the City of the Living God. Thousands upon thousands of angels in joyful assembly are on Mount Zion. It also says we are sprinkled by the blood of Jesus, and that speaks a better word than the blood of Abel.

We need to pray for the Jewish people who are in Israel, as well as for the Arabs. Even though they have "come up" in the natural and are living in Zion, in Jerusalem, that they will receive Messiah and ascend in the Spirit. We need to pray that God will open the fountain and pour out His Holy Spirit, that they can come up and live in Zion, both in the natural and in the spiritual.

In creating *Shabbat* (Sabbath), God is inviting us to enter into His rest, not only in the natural but also to enter into His spiritual rest. Entering into His spiritual rest means coming up to Mount Zion in the Spirit, and resting in the presence of the Lord in His fullness of joy. **"For the LORD will rebuild Zion and appear in his glory" (Psalm 102:16).**

As the Jewish people come "up to Zion" naturally and spiritually, and the fullness of the Gentiles come up to Zion spiritually, then Zion will be rebuilt and Messiah will appear in His glory. May we be faithful watchmen to help prepare the way for this day!

## 12. Standing as a Watchman

One of the first times we see "stand" mentioned in the Scriptures is Moses' arrival at the Red Sea. The Egyptians were chasing him. I don't know what I would have done if I had been in his situation, but I imagine many things went through his mind. He probably thought: "Should I go to the right, to the left? Should I go up, down? What should I do?" All Pharaoh's horses, chariots, horsemen and troops were pursuing him and he didn't have many choices. So what did he do? He listened to the voice of the Lord. Then Moses assured the people,

**"Do not be afraid. Stand firm and you will see the deliverance the LORD will bring you today....The LORD will fight for you; you need only be still" (Exodus 14:13-14).**

Moses stood as a watchman. He stood still and saw the salvation of God. He was told to do nothing, simply to hold his arm out, and God would do everything! When he held his arm out over the Red Sea, God supernaturally blew across the sea, it parted and He led the children of Israel out of Egypt.

Today God wants us to understand in fuller ways what it means to stand as a watchman. Four times, Ephesians 6:11-14 speaks of standing:

> **Put on the full armor of God so that you can take your stand against the devil's schemes... stand your ground... after you have done everything, to stand... stand firm.**

In these last days we need to learn to stand, because the warfare will be increasingly more intense every year between now and when Jesus returns, whether we are in Jerusalem or wherever we are in the world. But especially in Jerusalem, we need to learn to stand with the Lord.

The Lord showed me a few years ago that I was to stand with Him for Jerusalem. God is already standing for Jerusalem! But He is looking for people who will stand with Him for His purposes for Jerusalem. We need to learn how to stand because there will be many times, in increasing ways, when *all we will be able to do is to stand.* As we stand with Him, His purposes are being fulfilled in Jerusalem.

The enemy tries to make us run. The pressure gets intense, things get difficult and he tries to chase people out of Jerusalem. But the Lord says, "Do not run, stand with Me for Jerusalem!" When everything looks impossible, all we can do is to stand. We cannot stand on our emotions, feelings, or circumstances. We can only stand on the promises of God, the Word of God, when we stand with the Lord for Jerusalem. God wants us to stand as watchmen.

I believe fasting is another aspect of standing. Isaiah 58 speaks about God's chosen fast. If God is truly calling us on a fast, we should ask Him, not just decide to fast. When I decide for myself, I usually last one or two meals. But if we ask the Lord to call us to His chosen fast, we can fast for a week, or twenty-one days, or forty days. If God calls us on a fast, we will have the grace to fast, no matter how long. If we try to do it on our own strength, it's just a good idea and we will not have His grace for it.

There are many types of fasts. When they all fasted in Nineveh, in response to God's word through Jonah, what happened? God changed His mind! He turned the situation around. I believe that fasting is a way of standing and saying, "God, I cannot do it, but I am believing you for the breakthrough. I believe your Word that is settled in heaven is settled on the earth."

In the book of Daniel, the Lord gave Him a word, but it took twenty-one days before the breakthrough came. What was Daniel doing during the twenty-one days? He was fasting and standing for the breakthrough. When we are fasting, we are saying to God, "God, I am standing for Your breakthrough; I cannot do it, but I am believing You to intervene as the God of the breakthrough." Is that not what happened with Daniel? God's word was settled in heaven; and after the twenty-one days, His word was settled on the earth.

As watchmen, we need to stand with the Lord for His breakthroughs in the last days.

## 13. Entering into Victory Warfare!

This is an exciting story:

> Gideon arrived just as a man was telling a friend his dream. "I had a dream," he was saying. "A round loaf of barley bread came tumbling into the Midianite camp. It struck the tent with such force that the tent overturned and collapsed."
>
> His friend responded, "This can be nothing other than the sword of Gideon son of Joash, the Israelite. God has given the Midianites and the whole camp into his hands." When Gideon heard the dream and its interpretation, he worshiped God. He returned to the camp of Israel and called out, "Get up! The LORD has given the Midianite camp into your hands." Dividing the three hundred men into three companies, he placed trumpets and empty jars in the hands of all of them, with torches inside.

"Watch me," he told them. "Follow my lead. When I get to the edge of the camp, do exactly as I do. When I and all who are with me blow our trumpets, then from all around the camp blow yours and shout, 'For the LORD and for Gideon.'"

Gideon and the hundred men with him reached the edge of the camp at the beginning of the middle watch, just as they had changed the guard. They blew their trumpets and broke the jars that were in their hands. The three companies blew the trumpets and smashed the jars. Grasping the torches in their left hands and holding in their right hands the trumpets they were to blow, they shouted, "A sword for the LORD and for Gideon!" While each man held his position around the camp, all the Midianites ran, crying out as they fled.

When the three hundred trumpets sounded, the LORD caused the men throughout the camp to turn on each other with their swords. The army fled to Beth Shittah toward Zererah as far as the border of Abel Meholah near Tabbath (Judges 7:13-22).

It was the middle watch of the night when Gideon said **"Watch me"** and they blew their trumpets, smashed their jars and proclaimed the victory that caused all the Midianites to scatter and flee. The Midianites were frightened and the anointing of the Lord entered the situation. We need more victory warfare like this. The Lord, who always causes us to triumph, has given us the victory through our Lord Jesus Christ, and He wants us to proclaim it through victory warfare. The story of Gideon is a tremendous example.

## 14. Shouting Joyfully, Proclaiming

How beautiful on the mountains are the feet of those who bring good news, who proclaim peace, who bring good tidings, who proclaim salvation, who say to Zion, "Your God reigns!" Listen! Your watchmen lift up their voices; together they shout for joy. When the LORD returns to Zion, they will see it with their own eyes.

**Burst into songs of joy together, you ruins of Jerusalem, for the LORD has comforted his people, he has redeemed Jerusalem. The LORD will lay bare his holy arm in the sight of all the nations, and all the nations of the earth will see the salvation of our God (Isaiah 52:7-10).**

Hallelujah! God's watchmen **"lift up their voices; together they shout for joy."** God wants us to give a joyful shout. Hallelujah! They **"burst into songs of joy together"** as God turns the situation around and begins to restore Jerusalem! God is pouring out the joy of the Holy Spirit in a fresh way in these last days, and He wants to restore the joyful shout. The kingdom of God is righteousness, peace and joy in the Holy Ghost (Romans 14:17).

In Psalm 100:1-2, it says we should **"Shout for joy to the LORD all the earth. Worship the LORD with gladness; come before him with joyful songs."** The joy of the Lord is our strength. He wants us to have joy in our songs, and to shout for joy. Shouting for joy reminds us of Pentecostals, but God is restoring all things. Amen. He is restoring the joyful shout, and when we shout for joy, God arises and the enemy is scattered! God inhabits the praises of His people, and when we are shouting for joy under the anointing of the Holy Spirit, it is another way of being God's watchmen and seeing God arise in the midst of a situation, scattering our enemies.

## 15. Making Intercession

When God called Ezekiel as a watchman, He said that if He could find just one man who would stand in the gap, He would intervene. Ezekiel responded to the call and was the one man who stood in the gap. God intervened through his response.

**"Again, I tell you that if two of you on earth agree about anything you ask for, it will be done for you by my Father in heaven. For where two or three come together in my name, there am I with them" (Matthew 18:19- 20).**

We may think that multitudes of people are needed to come together for God to intervene. It is better to have a few people in agreement than a multitude not in agreement! Many times Jesus sent the multitudes away and had just a few people together—as when He revealed Himself on the Mount of Transfiguration and again when He was in the Garden of Gethsemane with only Peter, James and John. He took just a few aside with Himself. Often, when God intervenes, He uses fewer rather than more people. This was the situation with Gideon's army. There were thirty-two thousand people, and God told most of them to leave. Finally, only three hundred were left. He is not looking for multitudes; He is looking for people who are in agreement with Him.

God is looking for intercessors who will stand with Him for His purposes to be fulfilled. An intercessor is someone who will stand between the Lord and the person or situation that needs intercession, believing God for His intervention.

Jesus is both our Chief Watchman and Chief Intercessor. After He shed His blood in the city, He ascended from the Mount of Olives into heaven and is ever living to make intercession for us. He made intercession by His death, burial and resurrection, so that He could stand in heaven for the last two thousand years interceding for the believers, for the salvation of the nations, and for the salvation of His own people. He is our example.

Intercession is a very important aspect of being a watchman, because Jesus the Intercessor, ever living to make intercession, dwells within us. If we want to walk as Jesus walked, and follow His example, intercession should be our prime ministry.

There are certain areas of intercession that are priorities. In our day, especially in Western nations, people spend too much time praying for material things: "God, give me a new car... I need a television... a microwave oven." The majority of prayers in the New Testament were for *unity, spiritual awakening, and encouragement for the body of believers*. There were also prayers for different needs of the church and the body of believers, that they would be built up, strengthened and prepared for Jesus' return. It's been said that seventy percent of all the prayers in the New Testament are related to the body of believers.

*Praying for the body of believers* is a major priority. We need to pray for our own family, our church, believers in our city and believers throughout the world. When the church is really living in revival, the world will be changed, as we have seen when deep revival has occurred many times in history.

The second most needed area is *prayer for unbelievers*. This is why Jesus came into the world: to save sinners, whether they are our neighbors or people on the other side of the world.

A third area is *prayer for Israel, for the Jewish and the Arab people, for the other nations of the world, and for the governmental leaders of the nations*. We need to pray for all those who are in authority (1 Timothy 2:1-2):

1.  We must pray for Israel's salvation and restoration, both in the natural and in the spirit (Psalm 14:7), and for her governmental leaders.

2.  We must also pray for the salvation of the nations, for the fullness of the Gentiles to come into the kingdom of God. Then God will lift the veil that is over the eyes of Israel and bring the Jewish people to salvation (Romans 11:25,26).

There are many, many things for which we could pray; but I believe if we are sensitive to the Word of God and to the Holy Spirit, we will find that most of our prayers should be aligned with the main flow of the prayers that are in the Scriptures. I have been in some prayer meetings where ninety percent of the prayers have nothing to do with what God has shown us in Scripture to pray. But, praise God, may He help us to be intercessors according to His Word and purposes, intercessors after His own heart in these last days.

## 16. Reporting What He Sees

**This is what the Lord says to me: "Go, post a lookout and have him report what he sees. When he sees chariots with teams of horses, riders on donkeys or riders on camels, let him be alert, fully alert." And the lookout shouted, "Day after day, my lord, I stand on the watchtower; every night I stay at my post" (Isaiah 21:6-8).**

Praise God, Isaiah was a faithful watchman for Israel. A watchman should report what he sees. In other words, if God shows us something, there is a purpose in His showing it to us, His watchmen, and we need to discern that purpose.

Generally it will be for intercession. God may show us something, but that does not mean we are to broadcast it or to speak it to the whole church. Nor do we say nothing about it, but we need discernment to know to whom to report it. For example, if God gives you a word or shows you something, it may be just for yourself, your family, a friend, or your home fellowship group. You need discernment. It may be for a specific person, your whole congregation, or your city. If God gives you something for a specific person, you need to share it with him. If it is for your congregation, share it with your pastor. It may be for your nation. Isaiah and Jeremiah were prophets for their nation, and God gave them the word of the Lord to share with the whole nation and with other nations.

We need to get God's discernment, God's wisdom, not only on the word itself, but also with whom it is to be shared. If it is shared in an inappropriate manner, we are out of order, and can do more harm than good. If it is shared correctly, we are faithful watchmen, taking the word to the place that God has purposed. So God wants us to report appropriately what He shows us, whether it is in a vision or a dream or through the Scriptures, whatever God is showing us as we are standing on the watch. On Saturday evenings, in our Community 24-hour Prayer Watch, we report what we have seen by sharing what God has shown us in the watch during the previous week.

## 17. Staying Awake Physically and Spiritually

We need to learn from the mistakes of Jesus' disciples, who fell asleep three times. We need to get up, bind the spirit of slumber, walk around, and stay on the watch. Many times, when God is trying to show us something clearly, that is when the enemy is trying to put us to sleep. That has happened to me too many times over the past twenty-five years. I have missed things from God because I've fallen asleep on the watch when God wanted to speak something clearly. But, praise God, hopefully we will learn from our mistakes.

**"Behold, I come like a thief! Blessed is he who stays awake [who stays on the watch] and keeps his clothes with him, so that he may not go naked and be shamefully exposed" (Revelation 16:15).**

This is one of the seven beatitudes of the Book of Revelation. If we put on the Lord Jesus Christ, are clothed with Him and prepared for His coming (because we are continually staying on the watch), then God says we are blessed in a special way. He wants us to be awake, not only physically but also spiritually. God has set watchmen on His walls; they will take no rest day or night until Jerusalem is established as the praise of the earth (Isaiah 62:6-7). This means God wants us always to be on the watch and praying until Jesus returns.

## 18. Sounding the Warning

When God speaks a prophetic word to a watchman, the watchman must be faithful in bringing the warning. This is where Jonah got into trouble. God spoke to him and he did not obey, so he ended up in the belly of a whale. Finally the whale spat him out and Jonah was obedient to speak the word of the Lord to Nineveh. The whole situation turned around because of his ultimate faithfulness to the Lord.

> **"Son of man, I have made you a watchman for the house of Israel; so hear the word I speak and give them a warning from me. When I say to a wicked man, 'You will surely die,' and you do not warn him or speak out to dissuade him from his evil ways in order to save his life, that wicked man will die for his sin, and I will hold you accountable for his blood. But if you do warn the wicked man and he does not turn from his wickedness or from his evil ways, he will die for his sin; but you will have saved yourself"** (Ezekiel 3:17-19).

Even if people do not heed the word of the Lord that we give, we still have to give it. Most times we do not really know how it will turn out, we just need to be faithful. God is calling us to faithfulness, as His watchmen, in warning whomever He may show us. This can happen in a spiritual as well as a natural context.

God is calling many watchmen for the house of Israel to warn the Jewish people to leave the nations of the world and come back to Israel. These watchmen are fishers. God called me to do this when I wrote the book, *Let My People Go*. I am to warn the Jewish people in the nations that God says, **"Though I completely destroy a nation**

**where my people have been scattered, I will not destroy Israel. I will discipline her with justice, but will not destroy her" (Jeremiah 30:11).** There are seven hundred scripture verses calling the Jewish people home. God wants us to warn the Jewish people in the nations that their destiny is in Israel.

There were prophets all over Germany and Poland warning the Jewish people to leave before the Holocaust, but only 10% left. Because they did not heed the prophetic word of warning, 90% were destroyed in the Holocaust. Even now, God is raising up many prophetic voices throughout the nations to warn the Jewish people to come home to Israel before increased shakings or judgments come upon the nations of the world. God has called us to be watchmen for the house of Israel in the nations, warning the Jewish people to come home.

He has also called watchmen to proclaim the word of the Lord to the Jews and Gentiles, that they would come to know God. He is also calling us to give prophetic words of warning to other believers that they would be delivered out of snares and sin. Proclaiming the gospel to the unsaved is a way of warning them so they may be delivered from hell and come into salvation. God is calling us to be watchmen who sound the warning in many ways, whether it is warning our child that he needs to turn away from sin, warning another believer, warning the Jewish people to return to Israel, or warning unbelievers to repent and return to God.

> **"But if the watchman sees the sword coming and does not blow the trumpet to warn the people and the sword comes and takes the life of one of them, that man will be taken away because of his sin, but I will hold the watchman accountable for his blood. Son of man, I have made you a watchman for the house of Israel; so hear the word I speak and give them warning from me" (Ezekiel 33:6-7).**

Most important is that we personally are hearing God's voice, as we each must give an account before Him whether or not we were faithful in warning as watchmen (Romans 14:12).

## 19. Strengthening What Remains

Jesus, speaking to the church in Sardis, said,

**"Wake up! Strengthen what remains and is about to die, for I have not found your deeds complete in the sight of my God. Remember, therefore, what you have received and heard; obey it, and repent. But if you do not wake up, I will come like a thief, and you will not know at what time I will come to you" (Revelation 3:2-3).**

What does it mean to strengthen what remains? God is shaking that which can be shaken, but He wants to strengthen what remains. When God is pruning, cutting off branches, it actually gives more strength for the other branches to come forth. We go through times of shaking, times of pruning, when God wants to strengthen what remains. We are strengthened by the Word of God and by the Holy Spirit.

God is working through refining processes in our lives, and He wants our deeds to be complete in Him. He wants us to be delivered from dead works and to allow Jesus to work through us. As it says in John 15:7-8, the chapter about pruning, if we abide in Him and His words abide in us, He will bring forth much fruit that remains. God wants to strengthen what remains by allowing His Holy Spirit and His Word to work in and through us.

## 20. Watching for the Coming of the Lord Jesus

Luke 12:22-40 shows us an interesting relationship between "worry" and "watching." In the first half of this section, Jesus instructs His disciples, "Do not worry," and in the second He tells them to be watchful. There is a parallel between worrying and watching. If we are truly watching for the coming of the Lord, we are not worrying. If we are worrying, we cannot be watching for the coming of the Lord.

**Then Jesus said to his disciples: "Therefore I tell you, do not worry about your life, what you will eat; or about your body, what you will wear. Life is more than food, and the body more than clothes. Consider the ravens: They do not sow or reap, they have no storeroom or barn; yet God**

feeds them. And how much more valuable you are than birds! Who of you by worrying can add a single hour to his life? Since you cannot do this very little thing, why do you worry about the rest?

"Consider how the lilies grow. They do not labor or spin. Yet I tell you, not even Solomon in all his splendor was dressed like one of these. If that is how God clothes the grass of the field, which is here today, and tomorrow is thrown into the fire, how much more will he clothe you, O you of little faith! And do not set your heart on what you will eat or drink; do not worry about it. For the pagan world runs after all such things, and your Father knows that you need them. But seek His kingdom, and these things will be given to you as well.

"Do not be afraid, little flock, for your Father has been pleased to give you the kingdom. Sell your possessions and give to the poor. Provide purses for yourselves that will not wear out, a treasure in heaven that will not be exhausted, where no thief comes near and no moth destroys. For where your treasure is, there your heart is also" (Luke 12:22-34).

Numerous times in this passage, Jesus says, "Do not worry." If we watch the birds and the lilies of the field, and see that God takes care of them, we realize that He will take care of us as well. If we have that kind of faith and dependence on the Lord, we will be ready for His coming. It is interesting that Jesus exhorts the disciples not to worry, then goes directly into the subject of watching for the coming of the Lord. We can learn from the birds; we can learn from the lilies of the field not to worry but to watch for the coming of the Lord.

"Be dressed ready for service and keep your lamps burning, like men waiting for their master to return from a wedding banquet, so that when he comes and knocks they can immediately open the door for him. It will be good for those servants whose master finds them watching when he comes. I tell you the truth, he will dress himself to serve, will have them recline at the table and will come and wait

**on them. It will be good for those servants whose master finds them ready, even if he comes in the second or third watch of the night.**

**But understand this: If the owner of the house had known at what hour the thief was coming, he would not have let his house be broken into. You also must be ready, because the Son of Man will come at an hour when you do not expect him" (Luke 12:35-40).**

The first thing is that we should be dressed, ready for service. We should put on the whole armor of God and put on the Lord Jesus Christ so that we are ready for service at His coming. Next, we should be watching for the master, because he will return for the wedding banquet, and we must be ready when he comes. Then, we should be ready so that the door may immediately be opened for him. Finally, it will be good for those servants whose master finds them watching when he comes.

Do you want to be watching when the Lord Jesus comes? If you are worrying, you are not watching. You are preoccupied with the cares of the world. But if you are not worrying, if you are like the birds and lilies, just trusting in Him, you are watching for the coming of the Lord and it will be well for you. Of those whom the returning master finds watching, Jesus says, "I tell you the truth, he will dress himself to serve and have them recline at the table, will come and wait on them." Jesus, when He comes back, will be dressed to serve. As the bridegroom, He will be serving the bride. For those who are found ready, Jesus says that even if He comes in the second or third watch of the night, they have made sure they are ready.

We should be ready, watching for His coming, ready for His coming, even if He comes at the second or third watch of the night. Even if He comes at nine in the evening, or at midnight, we should be ready, prepared for His coming. This is one of the reasons He says we should not go to sleep at night without settling things with our brothers and sisters, if there is a problem between us. We should not allow the sun to go down before the problem is resolved, because if we have an unresolved conflict with our brother or sister and the Lord comes back in the middle of the night, then we are not ready for

His coming. The Lord wants us, when we go to bed at night, to leave nothing unresolved with Him and with our brothers and sisters so that we are "on the watch," prepared for His coming.

Let us remember His warning, **"But understand this, if the owner of the house had known at what hour the thief was coming, he would not have let his house be broken into. You also must be ready, because the Son of Man will come at an hour when you do not expect Him."**

It says clearly that the Lord is coming at an hour that we do not expect. That means we always have to be ready, because we will not be expecting His coming. Only those who are really prepared for His coming and are watching Him day and night will be ready and prepared for His coming. Therefore, we should always be on the watch and we should always pray. Hallelujah, may God help us to learn not to worry but instead to watch the birds and the lilies; and even as they are trusting in God, may we trust in Him and be watching and prepared for His coming. Praise God!

## Biblical Watches

Jesus did not say, "Could you not pray with me for one hour?" but He said, "Could you not keep watch with me for one hour?" (Matthew 26:40). If we are going to be disciples of Jesus, we should minimally be keeping a one-hour watch.

Although God is calling us always to be on watch and to pray, He also calls us to keep specific watch times, when we are more fully focused as His watchmen. Watches can be for any individual watch, for corporate watch groups or for watch groups that are part of 24-hour watches.

Watch groups can consist of as few as two or three people or as many as God would call to practice the twenty aspects of watching together, as led by the Holy Spirit. If there is a larger number, it is important that there is an experienced pastor, leader or facilitator.

While watch groups can meet for any amount of time, we recommend three or four hours, which are the Biblical New and Old Testament watch times. If circumstances limit this, a half-watch would be ninety minutes or two hours in length. Night watches are usually either four, eight, or twelve hours between 6 a.m. and 6 p.m. as the Lord would call you. Following are eight approaches to consider.

## Eight Biblical watch times:

1. A one-hour watch seems to be a daily minimum from Jesus' perspective. He says, **"Can you not watch with me for one hour?" (Matthew 26:40).**
2. A two-hour watch. One half of the Biblical Old Testament Watch. This is being used as the two- hour/twelve-gate 24-hour worship watch in Jerusalem (Revelation 21:13-14).
3. A two-hour and 24-minute watch. Give one-tenth, a tithe of your day to be with Jesus on the watch (Malachi 3:8-10).
4. A three-hour Biblical New Testament watch. Daily, weekly or periodically (Mark 13:35).
5. A four-hour Biblical Old Testament watch. Daily, weekly or periodically (Judges 7:19).
6. An eight-hour night watch. The last four-hour watches of the night.
7. A twelve-hour night watch. The three four-hour (Old Testament), or four three-hour (New Testament) watches of the night, from 6 p.m. to 6 a.m.
8. A twenty-four hour watch. (Isaiah 62:6-7). See Chapter 9 and Appendix A for examples.

Following are suggestions of how you can incorporate the previous 20 Aspects of Watching into your watch time daily or otherwise. Consider dividing your watch time, however long it may be, into the following four areas of watching the Lord, watching the Word, watching in intercession, and watching and waiting. Be led by Holy Spirit:

A. Watching the Lord

    1. Watching the Lord
    2. Thanksgiving
    3. Worship and praise
    4. Pouring out your heart like water before the Lord
    5. Stay awake spiritually and physically
    6. Watchmen going up to Zion
    7. Shouting joyfully, Proclaiming

B. Watching the Word

    8. Read and meditate on Scripture

    a.  Consider one chapter of Revelation, Song of Solomon each day of month

    b.  One chapter of Psalms or Proverbs daily (read through two times a year)

    c.  One chapter of New Testament and Old Testament daily, depending on length of your watch

9. Strengthen what remains

C. Watching in intercession

10. Intercession
11. Keep watch, not allowing your house to be broken into
12. Watch and pray that you will not enter into temptation
13. Standing as a watchman
14. Entering victory warfare

D. Watching by waiting

15. Waiting on God
16. Inquiring of the Lord
17. Listening to the Lord
18. Reporting what he sees (in right way and time)
19. Sounding the alarm (warning at the right time)
20. Watching for the coming of Messiah

*Father, we thank You for Your Word. Father, we believe You that Your Word will bring forth one hundredfold fruit in our lives. We believe You to teach us to be watchmen in every aspect of what that means. In all these twenty aspects, Father, may we be Your faithful watchmen. Help us to be faithful, to learn from You, the Chief Watchman. Thank You that You said that You watch over Israel, that You never slumber nor sleep. You watch over us as Your believers. Thank You for Your faithfulness as the Chief Watchman. Teach us to be with You and to be faithful watchmen in increasing ways, in Jesus' Name. Amen.*

# Chapter 7

# Biblical Examples of 24-Hour Watches

God has been watching from the beginning. We read about those whom He called to watch with Him, as recorded in both Old and New Testaments, as well as in Church history.

God is restoring His watch in our day, and calling us as His watchmen to participate with Him. He is restoring 24- hour praise and prayer. We are seeing this in over one hundred nations around the world.

The main Scripture that the Lord has given for this is Isaiah 62:6-7:

> **I have posted watchmen on your walls, O Jerusalem; they will never be silent day or night. You who call on the LORD, give yourselves no rest, and give him no rest till he establishes Jerusalem and makes her the praise of the earth.**

## Adam, the First Watchman

The Lord was watching over the Garden of Eden. He took man and put him into the garden to work it and to take care of it—or to "watch over" it (Genesis 2:15). God told Adam that he should take care of the garden, but there was one thing he was not to do; he was not to eat of the tree of the knowledge of good and evil. God created everything good, but was trying to protect him from (potential) evil. God was watching over him and wanted him to be a good watchman. But Adam failed in his mission of being a watchman. The serpent came to Eve and told her that if she ate from the tree of the knowledge of good and evil she wouldn't die. The serpent said to Eve:

> **For God knows that when you eat of it your eyes will be opened, and you will be like God, knowing good and evil (Genesis 3:5).**

Eve tempted Adam and they both ate the forbidden fruit. Adam's disobedience enabled sin to separate man from union with God. Because Adam failed in being the watchman over the Garden of Eden, he was banished from the garden and God established a watch—against him!

> **So the LORD God banished him from the Garden of Eden... After he drove the man out, he placed on the east side of the Garden of Eden cherubim and a flaming sword flashing back and forth to guard [watch over] the way to the tree of life (Genesis 3:23-24).**

Because Adam was not a faithful watchman, his responsibility of watching over the Garden of Eden was taken away from him and he could not partake of the tree of life. This is an example of man's first 24-hour watch in the Bible. Adam had to watch 24 hours a day so that he wasn't tempted by Satan. This teaches how we are not to follow the example of Adam, but to learn from Adam's mistake, because God wants us to be His faithful watchmen.

## Noah as a Watchman

God saw (was watching) and said He was going to wipe all mankind off the earth because of corruption, but Noah was watching and listening, and knew what God was about to do, and found favor with God. God showed him to build an ark of salvation. After all mankind was wiped out by the flood, again Noah was watching, saw the dove return with the plucked olive leaf, (saw) knew the judgment was finished, and the eight of them could leave the ark and have a new beginning.

## Abraham as a Watchman

Abraham was also a watchman, as he went out not knowing where he was going, but was looking (watching) for the city which had foundations, whose architect and builder is God. He found the earthly Jerusalem, the gateway to the heavenly city, Jerusalem.

## Moses as a Watchman

Moses at the Red Sea was a real example of a watchman. I'm sure in his flesh he wanted to do many things, but he stood still and saw (watched) the salvation of God and also (watched and) followed the cloud in the wilderness.

## Old Testament Watches

In the Old Testament there are six different watches, three in the night and three in the day. **"Arise, cry out in the night, as the watches of the night begin; pour out your heart like water in the presence of the Lord" (Lamentations 2:19).** This speaks of the first watch of the night. From the Jewish perspective, the day begins at sunset, about 6:00 in the evening. Here it speaks of the first watch, when the watches of the night begin.

In Jerusalem, in our House of Prayer, we have communion together at about 6:00 in the evening because we're ending one day and beginning a new day. We thank the Lord for what has happened during the past day and look forward to the new day that's beginning.

The middle watch is the second watch of the night (10 P.M. to 2 A.M.).

> **"Watch me," he told them. "Follow my lead. When I get to the edge of the camp, do exactly as I do. When I and all who are with me blow our trumpets, then from all around the camp blow yours and shout, "For the LORD and for Gideon."**
>
> **Gideon and the hundred men with him reached the edge of the camp at the beginning of the *middle watch*, just after they had changed the guard. They blew their trumpets and broke the jars that were in their hands (Judges 7:17-19).**

Our ministry actually was born out of night watches twenty-three years ago. Every Friday night we held twelve hours of prayer and worship from 6:00 P.M. until 6:00 A.M.--and revival broke out! Again, when God birthed *Jerusalem House of Prayer for All Nations* in 1987, we held corporate night watches on Fridays for several years. Although we have continued to maintain a 24-hour prayer watch, God again is calling us to the corporate night watches on Friday nights!

The next watch is shown in Exodus 14:23-24:

> **The Egyptians pursued them, and all Pharaoh's horses and chariots and horsemen followed them into the sea. During the last watch of the night the LORD looked down [watched] from the pillar of fire and cloud at the Egyptian army and threw it into confusion.**

(And that was the end of the Egyptians.) This happened during the last watch of the night, from 2:00 in the morning until 6:00, at sunrise.

Many times in the Bible, time is reported according to which watch of the day or night it is. God is restoring 24-hour worship and prayer, and maybe the time will come when people ask us the time, we won't say it's 4:30 in the afternoon but we'll say it's the last watch of the day! That was the Biblical expression, because they were accustomed to keeping their watches.

## Prophets as Watchmen

In the Old Testament, the prophets functioned as watchmen over Israel. An example is Jeremiah 6:17: "**I appointed watchmen over you and said, 'Listen to the sound of the trumpet!' But you said, 'We will not listen.'**"

Jeremiah was appointed as a watchman over the house of Israel, and because they didn't listen, disaster came upon the people. "**I am bringing disaster on this people, the fruit of their schemes, because they have not listened to my words and have rejected my law**" (Jeremiah 6:19).

God has used the prophets to warn the people that if they would repent and turn to Him, He would restore them. But if they did not listen to Him, then calamity would come to the nation.

## Watchmen on the Walls and at the Gates

Watchmen in the Old Testament were posted on the city walls and gates to scan for runners with messages for the king. As a watchman today, you may receive a message from heaven that's coming from the King to tell to the people. Watchmen also guarded the city walls day and night against enemy attacks or sieges. Saul had lookouts—people and places from which the people were watching:

> **Saul's lookouts at Gibeah in Benjamin saw the army melting away in all directions. Then Saul said to the men who were with him, "Muster the forces and see who has left us" (1 Samuel 14:16-17).**

Watchmen also were responsible to warn the citizens of impending attack. If a siege was coming against the city, they were to blow the trumpet. By the sounding of the trumpet the people were warned and would join together and prepare for the attack.

The watchmen were to keep the walls safe from the enemy day and night. They called out the hourly condition, as a sentry would tell the people that the city was safe. A watchman was especially valuable in a time of siege, when the city was under attack. This also applies if we're faithful watchmen today. We'll be on the alert when the enemy is trying to come against us. If we're alert, we'll discern his strategies and we'll be able to head him off.

Biblically, it was believed that the providence of God was such that no watchman could protect the city unless God Himself kept guard. "**Unless the LORD builds the house, its builders labor in vain. Unless the LORD watches over the city, the watchmen stand guard in vain" (Psalm 127:1).** We know that God is the Chief Watchman. Unless He's watching, our watching is in vain.

## The Watches of David and Solomon

David vowed not to rest until He found a dwelling place for the Lord (Psalm 132:4), and God's watchmen were told not to rest until Jerusalem is established as the praise of the earth (Isaiah 62:6-7).

> **I will allow no sleep to my eyes, no slumber to my eyelids, till I find a place for the LORD, a dwelling for the Mighty One of Jacob (Psalm 132:4).**

David was watching and refused to sleep until he could find a place for the ark to rest, until he could find a dwelling place for God. That's what God is looking for, a place to dwell on the earth. He wants us to be His watchmen so that He can come and dwell in our midst and be on the watch to protect His presence from the enemy who would try to come against His purposes.

Another watch in the Scriptures is the watch begun by David and Solomon:

> **May your eyes be open toward this temple day and night, this place of which you said you would put your Name there. May you hear the prayer your servant prays toward this place. Hear the supplications of your servant and of your people Israel when they pray toward this place. Hear from heaven, your dwelling place; and when you hear, forgive (2 Chronicles 6:20-21).**

Solomon asked the Lord to have His eyes open, to be watching the temple day and night. God answered the prayer of Solomon: **"My eyes and my heart will always be there" (2 Chronicles 7:16).** In effect, God answered Solomon's prayer by saying, *"I'll always be watching the temple, My eyes will always be upon the temple."*

God filled the temple with His glory, and Solomon called forth many musicians, as David had done before him. Although David didn't have the temple, he had many musicians who had come with him when he brought the ark into Jerusalem. David then put the musicians in charge of the music after the ark came to rest in Jerusalem. These musicians were worshiping the Lord day and night. David began this praise and worship watch and was preparing the way not just for the ark, but for the temple that Solomon was to build.

> **These are the men David put in charge of the music in the house of the LORD after the ark came to rest there (1 Chronicles 6:31).**

After the ark was brought to its place in the inner sanctuary of Solomon's temple,

> **The priests then withdrew from the Holy Place. All the priests who were there had consecrated themselves, regardless of their divisions (2 Chronicles 5:11).**

There were 120 trumpeters, many singers, people with cymbals, with harps and with lyres. They were worshiping the Lord—God's presence was in the temple. At one point His presence was so great that they had to stop worshiping; they couldn't continue (vv. 12-14). But God answered Solomon's prayer to watch over the temple day and night and Solomon raised up people to watch the Lord day and night, to worship Him, sing unto Him and magnify the name of the Lord. This was a very special time, when the temple of Solomon was finished. It is probably one of the most beautiful pictures in the natural of the body of believers that God is building today.

There were three Levitical groups that contributed to the musicians—the priests, the singers and the gatekeepers. They are referenced in Nehemiah 12:45-47 and 2 Chronicles 29:25-26.

## The Watch of Ezekiel

The watchmen are servants of the most high God who possess a certain authority to speak the decrees of God, servants who form a heavenly counsel, who listen to God's word and then act as divine messengers to bring forth the revelation through human beings.

Ezekiel was another watchman of the Lord. Ezekiel 1:26-28 relates Ezekiel's vision when he saw the Lord, "like glowing metal, as if full of fire." And when he saw (was watching) the Lord, he fell down on his face. Then the Lord (watching Ezekiel) called him as His watchman:

> **"I have made you a watchman for the house of Israel; so hear the word I speak and give them warning from me" (Ezekiel 3:17).**

He was then told that if a watchman does not speak forth the warning to dissuade them from their evil ways in order to save their life, then the wicked persons will die, but the watchman is also accountable for their blood. However, if the wicked hear the warning and turn away, they will die but he (the watchman) will be saved.

Ezekiel was tied up in ropes and unable to speak. He then was told to lie on his left side for three hundred ninety days and on his right side for forty days, representing the years that the northern and southern part of Israel had been in rebellion. For more than a year, even though he couldn't speak, he was a witness representing the sin of the house of Israel. The people watched and saw that. He was actually on a watch during that time, believing God that the people of Israel would repent and turn from their sins.

God told Ezekiel that if He could find one man who would stand in the gap, or would stand on the watch, then He would intervene (Ezekiel 22:30). Ezekiel was the man, standing on the watch, standing in the gap. He was an example of one individual as a watchman. The whole nation had gone astray so there wasn't a corporate watch going on as in the days of David and Solomon. God's preference is for there to be a corporate watch, many people worshiping and praying around the clock, but if a nation goes into exile, goes into sin, God may raise up just one man to be the watchman, as He did Ezekiel.

## The Watch of Daniel

Daniel was another example of an individual watchman who stood in the gap and repented for the nation. Daniel, as a righteous man and as God's watchman, cried out to God and repented on behalf of the nation of Israel. He said, **"We have sinned and done wrong. We have been wicked and have rebelled; we have turned away from your commands and laws" (Daniel 9:5).** And God heard his prayer.

## Watching the Fall of Babylon

Isaiah 21:6-12 tells about the destruction of Babylon. Much is said about being a watchman. We are told to post a watch, to be alert. Day after day the watchman stood on the watchtower and the Lord spoke to him. The Lord gave him the answer, **"Babylon has fallen, has fallen! All the images of its gods lie shattered on the ground!"**

We read in Revelation 18 and 19 that Babylon is going to fall again, so we need to be God's watchmen, individually and corporately, in these last days. The Babylonian system of this world is going to collapse, is going to fall; it's already beginning. God is shaking Iraq, the literal Babylon. He is in the process of shaking the United States, the daughter of Babylon, and its economic center in New York. He is also shaking the Babylonian religious systems centered in Rome (as we are moving in restoration back to Jerusalem), but also all aspects of Orthodox, Protestant, Evangelical and Charismatic Christianity that are not based upon the Word of God.

If we are God's watchmen, we'll have eyes to see what is happening and we, as Christians, need to be awake and alert. We also need to warn the people in the world to come out of Babylon, to be born again into the kingdom of God, to be delivered from this present evil age. As God's watchmen we can warn the Jewish people to come out of Babylon and encourage them to come back to Israel, back to Jerusalem to ascend to Zion naturally and spiritually in these days of restoration.

God wants us to be His watchmen in discerning the times of Babylon falling, walking in daily repentance of any influence of Babylon in our lives and prepared for the fall of the world's Babylonian political and religious systems. God wants us to be ready to call others to repentance and to call the Jewish people back to their homeland and Messiah.

## The Watch of Nehemiah

Another watch in the Old Testament is that of Nehemiah during the rebuilding of the temple in Jerusalem, after the Jewish people came back from Babylon. *Babylon fell, and they came home!* After learning that the wall of Jerusalem was broken down and the gates burned with fire, Nehemiah sat down and wept. He mourned and fasted and prayed before the God of heaven. He asked that the Lord's ear be attentive and His eyes be open to hear the prayer of His servant who was praying before the Him day and night. Nehemiah was keeping a watch before the Lord day and night in prayer (Nehemiah 1:4-11). And God intervened.

Nehemiah established a watch as they built the temple. He prayed to God and posted a guard day and night to meet the threat of those trying to destroy Jerusalem (Nehemiah 4:9). So Nehemiah rose to the occasion and started a 24- hour watch. We see how God worked through Nehemiah. In Nehemiah 12 we learn how he set singers and musicians on the watch.

## Rejoicing on the Watch

In Isaiah 52:7-8, the Lord talks about watchmen lifting up their voices and shouting for joy because He is about to return to Zion. So there's a time for the watchmen to rejoice and be glad and to proclaim the goodness of the Lord; and that's in days of restoration. The watchmen for Israel today should be rejoicing as they proclaim to the nations that the Jewish people are coming home. The following verse, found in both Isaiah 35:10 and 51:11, has also been used in a contemporary song of celebration.

**The ransomed [redeemed] of the LORD will return. They will enter Zion with singing; everlasting joy will crown their heads. Gladness and joy will overtake them, and sorrow and sighing will flee away (Isaiah 51:11).**

## Watching for Jesus

Consider Anna who was in the temple watching, praying and fasting day and night for about fifty years, looking for the redemption of Israel, for the Lord Jesus to come.

The watch In the Old Testament (six 4-hour watches) was based on the Hebrew calendar, while in the New Testament it was based on the Roman calendar, with four watches of the night and four watches of the day (eight 3- hour watches). Jesus gave instructions:

**"Therefore keep watch because you do not know when the owner of the house will come back--whether in the evening, or at midnight, or when the rooster crows, or at dawn" (Mark 13:35).**

The first watch begins in the evening at sunset and ends at nine; the second one ends at midnight; the third ends when the rooster crows, at three in the morning; the fourth watch ends at dawn. In Mark 13:35, when Jesus was talking with His disciples about keeping watch, He didn't say, "six in the evening, nine, twelve or three," but He said which watch of the day or night it was. As in Old Testament times, they were accustomed to the concept of 24-hour watches, of praying around the clock.

In Mark 6:47-48, Jesus was walking on the water of the Sea of Galilee:

> **When evening came, the boat was in the middle of the lake, and he was alone on land. He saw the disciples straining at the oars, because the wind was against them. About the fourth watch of the night he went out to them, walking on the lake.**

Jesus was walking on the water at about 3:00 A.M. They were so used to the concept of watches, day and night, that's the way they referred to the time.

## Watching with Jesus in Gethsemane, at the Ascension, and in the Upper Room

Our foremost example of being a watchman is the Lord Jesus, on the watch in the Garden of Gethsemane. As the disciples fell asleep, three times Jesus called to them to stay on the watch, but they continually fell asleep.

Another example of a New Testament watch is Jesus' ascension, before the very eyes of His disciples. While they were looking into the sky (watching Him), He was going to the Father. But they were told that the same Jesus they watched, the One who was being taken, would come back in like manner (Acts 1:9,10) and we should look (be watching) for **"the blessed hope—the glorious appearing of our great God and Savior, Jesus Christ" (Titus 2:13).**

Then followed the example of being watchmen in the Upper Room. For ten days the disciples were praying day and night, watching the Lord. Even though Jesus' disciples failed on the first watch just before He left, they were faithful on the second watch just after He left.

> **When they arrived, they went upstairs to the room where they were staying. Those present were Peter, John, James and Andrew; Philip and Thomas, Bartholomew and Matthew; James son of Alphaeus and Simon the Zealot, and Judas son of James (Acts 1:13).**

These were all the disciples of Jesus; they had abandoned Him a few weeks before. This time they were faithful on the watch. Not only the disciples, but **"They all joined together constantly in prayer, along with the women and Mary the mother of Jesus, and with his brothers. In those days Peter stood up among the believers..."** (Acts 1:14-15). Then, **"When the day of Pentecost came, they were all together in one place"** (Acts 2:1).

For ten days they had been praying constantly, around the clock. They were on the watch; they were watching for the Holy Spirit to come and they were faithful watchmen this time. They had learned from their mistakes.

> **Suddenly a sound like the blowing of a violent wind came from heaven and filled the whole house where they were sitting.... All of them were filled with the Holy Spirit and began to speak in other tongues as the Spirit enabled them (Acts 2:2,4).**

This is one example of a 24-hour watch, but believers were praying around the clock throughout the New Testament.

## Watching in the Throne Room

Revelation 4 and 5 tell about the throne in heaven. Basically, what's going on around the throne in heaven is a 24-hour watch. The Lord is watching from His throne and the living creatures are around the throne, worshiping the Lord day and night. They have eyes that are looking in all different directions; they even have eyes under their wings. They are looking at the Father, looking all over the earth. If you are a watchman, you have eyes only to watch. He who has eyes let him see (watch).

And what do these four living creatures say? They say, **"Holy, holy, holy is the Lord God Almighty, who was, and is, and is to come" (Revelation 4:8).** They are saying that now, and have been from the beginning. Jesus has yet to come back, and I don't know what they'll be saying when He does, but for thousands of years, 24 hours a day, they have been saying, *"Holy, holy, holy is the Lord God Almighty, who was, and is, and is to come."* This means the second coming is of utmost importance!

The twenty-four elders are also worshiping day and night. They fall down before Him who sits on the throne, worshiping Him. They lay their crowns before the throne and say,

> **"You are worthy, our Lord and God, to receive glory and honor and power, for you created all things, and by your will they were created and have their being" (Revelation 4:11).**

The Lamb is standing in the center of the throne. Around Him are the four living creatures and the elders. He has seven horns and seven eyes, which are the seven spirits of God sent out into all the earth. The four living creatures and the twenty-four elders fall down before the Lamb. Each one has a harp and is holding a golden bowl.

The role of the elders is worship and intercession. The harp represents worshiping God and the golden bowls contain incense— the prayers of the saints. So when we're worshiping God, He remembers our worship and our praise continually. When we're interceding, our prayers are being put into the golden bowls in heaven. When the bowls of incense are full, when the fullness of the prayers have been offered in heaven, a new song is sung:

> **"You are worthy to take the scroll and to open its seals, because you were slain, and with your blood you purchased men for God from every tribe and language and people and nation" (Revelation 5:9).**

Through the worship unto the Lord and through the intercession of the saints that is stored up before the Father throughout history, the time is coming when the seals of heaven will be opened and the fullness of the people will be gathered into the kingdom of God. Here we have a beautiful picture of the fullness of what's happening in heaven regarding 24-hour worship and intercession. This is the 24-hour watch in heaven—with the Lord Jesus standing in the midst of the throne.

Then were seen and heard ten thousand times ten thousand angels encircling the throne, the living creatures and the elders and loudly singing: **"Worthy is the Lamb, who was slain, to receive power and wealth and wisdom and strength and honor and glory and praise!" (Revelation 5:11-12).**

## Watching on Earth, as It Is in Heaven— in the Last Days

When Ezekiel and Isaiah saw into heaven, they saw what was taking place. Those in the tabernacle, the temple that was established by David and Solomon, saw what was happening in heaven. Recorded in the Book of Acts, the disciples touched upon the events in heaven when they were in the Upper Room. Again in the last days, God wants us to touch what is going on in heaven. The Lord wants us to be worshiping and interceding 24 hours a day on earth as it is happening in heaven. As Jesus prayed to His Father on the Mount of Olives, where I live, *"Thy kingdom come, Thy will be done on earth as it is in heaven."*

In this decade, *All Nations Convocation Jerusalem* is an example of a similar ten-day watch, where National Delegates from almost two hundred nations were in a 24-hour watch of worship and prayer continually for ten days in Jerusalem, being a House of Prayer for Israel and All Nations. This was coordinated by *Jerusalem House of Prayer for All Nations* in 1996, where praying pastors and prayer leaders came from 188 nations—and also in 1994, attended by delegates from 140 nations. We also had twenty-four hours of worship for twenty-four days on Mt. Zion, and we continually have twenty-four hour worship and intercession on the Mount of Olives.

As we are living in days of restoration and approach the year of the coming of the Lord, God has birthed 24-hour praise and prayer watches in Jerusalem and He is progressively birthing them in all nations. This is the culmination of all of history, in the years and decades in which we live. Since we believe that Jesus is coming back soon, it's time to allow worship and prayer to be manifested in all the nations of the earth as it is in heaven. *His kingdom come and His will be done on earth as it is in heaven!*

Every creature in heaven and on earth and under the earth and on and in the sea was heard to sing: **"To him who sits on the throne and to the Lamb be praise and honor and glory and power, for ever and ever!" (Revelation 5:13)** Then the four living creatures said **"Amen,"** and the elders fell down in worship (Revelation 5:14).

# Chapter 8

# Historical 24-Hour Watches

## The Bangor, Ireland Watch, A.D. 555

Let us look at some examples of watches that have occurred in church history since the time of the Temple. In the year 555, four hundred eighty-five years after the Temple was destroyed in Jerusalem, a 24-hour prayer watch of Christians began in Bangor, Ireland, which is very close to where Belfast is today. This 24-hour praise and prayer watch was based upon the system of Temple praise, devotion and prayer in Jerusalem, stressing both praise and intercession. Some Scriptures they used include:

> **And you will sing as on the night you celebrate a holy festival (Isaiah 30:29).**
>
> **Praise the LORD, all you servants of the LORD who minister by night in the house of the LORD (Psalm 134:1).**
>
> **Blessed are those who dwell in your house; they are ever praising you (Psalm 84:4).**

There were between two and three thousand people living together in that community. The main rule was: "Let the many keep awake in community a third of all the nights of the year in order to read aloud from the Book and to expound judgment and to sing blessings together." Alternating each 24-hour period, a third of the community would be praying, reading the Scriptures and worshiping night and day in shifts. Some would be sleeping and others would be worshiping; they were watching and praying around the clock. This continued for several hundred years.

They prayed for the sins of all Christian people, for persons to be consecrated to God in the various places of ministry, for those who give alms, for the kings of the earth, for peace for the kings and for their enemies.

The fall of the Roman Empire in the west occurred around this time, and the Dark Ages descended on Europe. During the sixth to the ninth centuries, through the Bangor community's strength and continual devotion, they sent out missionaries who took the gospel to evangelize throughout Europe.

They were diligent watchmen. One of their morning prayers was, *O God, our God, before You we must be watchful at daylight. Rouse our souls from deep sleep. Free them from drowsiness that we may be rightfully mindful of You.*

During the time of the prayer watch, this area was the center of revival for all of Europe, because heaven was manifested in their midst. They were worshiping and praying and interceding for hundreds of years. After the prayer watch ceased, many things went wrong. Sadly, there are many problems in Belfast, Ireland today. May God restore the watch in this divided region—city, nation and worldwide to His glory!

In 1994, a 24-hour prayer chain began in Belfast. A report on this watch in Northern Ireland can be found in the Appendix.

## The Knights of St. John Watch, 1080

Another watch of the Lord began in Jerusalem through the Knights of St. John in the year 1080, just before the Turkish Muslims tried to come against Jerusalem. The Knights of St. John also established many hospitals and needed their own soldiers to defend them. Theirs was a Christian order established on simple Christian vows: *"To stand against the enemies of the faith, to preserve the unity of the faith, and to defend our lords[1], the sick and the poor."* Out of this, 24-hour watches were birthed.

As a result of the Turks entering Jerusalem, the Knights of St. John moved to Rhodes where they built a large fortress. There the Turks came against them because their ships needed to sail past the fortress. The Turks sent seventy thousand men against the fortress of two thousand Knights of St. John. Two thousand withstood seventy

---

1.    The heads of feudal estates; those in authority over the people.

thousand. God was with them! So while Christian Europe was fighting each other and Islamic forces could have totally taken Europe, God used the two thousand Knights of St. John to stop seventy thousand Turks!

The leader of the Knights of St. John was a Frenchman named de Aubusson, and God used him to stop Islam from taking Europe in the 1400's. At one time an arrow pierced the lung of this French leader and all were convinced he was dead, because he was hit and wounded from many different directions. But God intervened and supernaturally raised him up. Shining armor was seen over him and the two people who were with him. At the height of the battle, when it was at its worst, the Turks saw him arise—and they fled. They knew God was with the Knights of St. John!

About forty years later the Turks returned with *two hundred thousand soldiers* to try to defeat them, and there were still only two thousand Knights of St. John! Again they held their ground. Many of the Knights of St. John were killed, but the Turks were stopped and almost destroyed. On Christmas Eve, the leader of the Turks, the Sultan, met with the leader of the Knights of St. John and agreed to stop the war against them. The Sultan said the Knights could go anywhere they wanted and he would take them with his own ships. He gave them gifts and helped them to relocate to Balfour. The Sultan thought they were gone, never to return.

In another forty years the Knights of St. John rebuilt their fortress, this time on Malta. Again the Turks attacked them, with even more men than before. Again they held their ground! God again used them powerfully to stop Islamic forces in Europe. It has been said that if it weren't for the Knights of St. John, Europe would have been taken by Islam. Today many Christian countries are fighting wars for Islam rather than being defenders of the Christian faith.

This is a tremendous lesson for us in these last days in two different ways:

First of all, *if we stand our ground and God is with us, we can overcome any obstacle.* I believe that God wants to raise up, throughout the world, more men like these leaders, because Islam is on the rise again.

Secondly, *we not only need to stand in the natural, but especially in the spirit;* we need to do spiritual warfare, believing God to draw the

Muslims into the kingdom of God. This is why we need to know what it is to watch, to stand and to resist.

The Knights of St. John were a tremendous example of watching, standing and resisting the enemy. They weren't the aggressors, they just stood their ground. And God defended them as they stood their ground. God arose and their enemies were scattered!

## Messiah's Watch on the Mount of Olives, 1200's-1500's

In Temple times, a procession circled the altar each day of the *Sukkot* festival (Feast of Tabernacles), saying, *"Pray! O Lord, save, I pray! Pray! O Lord, give success, I pray!"* On the seventh day, *Hoshana Rabba* ("the Great Hoshana"), seven circuits were made around the altar.

Beginning in the thirteenth century, when there had been no Temple for hundreds of years, the Jewish people would climb the Mount of Olives and circle its summit in a great procession of song and ceremony during each day of the Feast of Tabernacles. On the seventh day, the day of *Hoshana Rabba*, the procession would circle seven times around the summit of the mount, with its beautiful view of Mount Moriah and the temple site. They were believing for, watching for, and preparing for Messiah's coming!

It was a widespread custom for the Jewish people to stay up during the night before *Hoshana Rabba* and read the whole Pentateuch (the first Books of Moses) or the Books of Deuteronomy and Psalms. This was to ensure that those who did not complete the required reading during the year would do so at this time. It was also a time just after *Yom Kippur*, the Day of Atonement. Official announcements were proclaimed, communities received blessings, and public excommunications were issued. The people also prayed for rain for the New Year.

*Hoshana Rabba* was thought to be the last day man could receive forgiveness for his sins. They believed that the verdict of man, passed on the Day of Atonement, was sealed. The prayer of this day opened with the words, "the power [or, the truth] of Thy salvation cometh," which dealt with the splitting open of the Mount of Olives (Zechariah 14:4) and the resurrection of the dead. **"On that day His feet will**

**stand on the Mount of Olives, east of Jerusalem, and the Mount of Olives will be split in two from east to west" (Zechariah 14:4).**

The Jewish people were watching for, longing for the coming of Messiah, that He would descend from the upper heavens and sit upon His throne in Jerusalem. A legend of Jerusalem is that the Holy One would blow the trumpet seven times and the following seven things would happen (reminiscent of Ezekiel 37:7-11):

At the first blast, the whole world will quake.
At the second blast, the soil will crumble.
At the third blast, their bones will join together.
At the fourth blast, their limbs will become warm.
At the fifth blast, their skin will cover them.
At the sixth blast, spirit and soul will enter their bodies.
At the seventh blast, they will stand on their feet, clothed in their garments.[1]

In ancient times the words *Hosea Na* (Save, we pray!) were linked into one word, *Hosanna* (Matthew 21:9; Mark 11:9). The word served as a response or call after every section of prayer. The Jews carried willow branches, similar to palm branches carried by the Messianic believers in the first century and today when they say, ***"Hosanna to the Son of David!"***

The observance of *Hoshana Rabba* continued for hundreds of years and then stopped. In 1987 God birthed *Jerusalem House of Prayer for All Nations* on the Mount of Olives and now, beginning our tenth year, we continue to watch for Messiah's coming and have been trying to keep Messiah's Watch 24 hours a day. (More information about *Jerusalem Watch of the Lord* introduces Chapter 9 on Contemporary 24-hour Watches.)

Along with many Jewish people, we are believing for, watching for, and preparing for the Son of David (Messiah) to come to the Mount of Olives to bring true peace and redemption to the world. As Jews and Gentiles, may we have our sins forgiven through Messiah, and watch and work together for His coming to His Mount of Olives and to His City of Jerusalem. Hosanna to the Son of David!

---

1.  Zev Vilnay, *Legends of Jerusalem*, vol. 1 (Philadelphia: The Jewish Publication Society of America, 1973), 294, quoting *Beit ha-Midrash* (ed. Yellinek), II (1853), 58.

## The Moravians—Herrnhut ("The Lord's Watch"), 1727

Another example in Church history began in 1727, in a little town in former East Germany, close to the border of Czechoslovakia and Poland. The first Protestant movement of the Holy Spirit was in Czechoslovakia. In the fifteenth century, Jan Hus was burned at the stake because he took a stand for the truth. Following that was a major revival, and the Moravian Church was born in Czechoslovakia in 1467, exactly 500 years before the reunification of Jerusalem in 1967. Later persecuted by the Roman Catholics, the Moravians fled into Germany.

By 1722, three hundred had joined together in a community called Herrnhut, under the leadership of a German by the name of Count Zinzendorf. The community consisted of people from all the different Protestant sects of that day—Lutherans, those from reform movements, and Messianic believers. There were many problems because of all these different backgrounds, and they were about to give up. But in 1727 the Holy Spirit came upon them as they were in prayer, showing them to start praying and worshiping 24 hours a day. This 24-hour watch, "The Lord's Watch" (Herrnhut), continued for about 120 years.

Their first commitment was toward the Jewish people. They comforted, prayed for and saw many Jewish people come to know the Lord, and were the first movement in history to stand for Israel. In fact, the Scripture God gave them to start their prayer watch was Isaiah 62:6-7,

> **I have posted watchmen on your walls, O Jerusalem; they will never be silent day or night. You who call on the LORD, give yourselves no rest, and give him no rest till he establishes Jerusalem and makes her the praise of the earth.**

So they were praying for their Jerusalem, Herrnhut, for the physical city of Jerusalem and the nation of Israel to be reborn, for salvation of the Jewish people and for the salvation of the nations of the world.

Their second commitment was to the unity of the body of all believers. While there were many divisions and factions within their community in the early days, they were committed to the unity of the whole body and worked with all the other churches and denominations.

Their third commitment was to 24-hour prayer. As they prayed around the clock on different shifts, their vision expanded beyond their own community and needs. By spending more time in prayer, they had time to pray for things beyond their own and local needs. They began to get a world vision! They prayed for the nations.

This led to what became their fourth commitment, sending the first non-Catholic missionaries to the nations. Since the first century, only Catholics had been sent out as missionaries. The Moravians in Czechoslovakia, Luther, Calvin, none of these had sent out missionaries. This community of Herrnhut was the first Protestant missionary movement in the history of the Church! They sent missionaries to Africa, to the Americas, to the Eskimos in Greenland, and to the east—to the four corners of the earth. Three hundred missionaries were dispatched in sixty-five years.

Initially they had only about three hundred people—and many went out as missionaries. They challenged the other denominations who then joined in sending out missionaries, believing God to bless this work. They understood that **"The fire must be kept burning on the altar continuously; it must not go out" (Leviticus 6:13).**

The fire on the altar must always be burning, 24 hours a day, so they needed to keep 24-hour prayer going continuously. They were the Temple of the Holy Spirit, and could not allow the fire on the altar to go out.

They began with 24 men and 24 women, each praying an hour a day, around the clock. Their numbers grew, and 24- hour prayer continued for about one hundred twenty years. Tremendous blessing, both in the spirit and in the natural, came to this area. John Wesley visited them, saying he wished he could have spent the rest of his life there, because the glory of the Lord was covering the place as the waters cover the seas! Although he was genuinely converted and filled with the Holy Spirit through the ministry of this community, he was called to Europe, England and America to preach the gospel, which led to the Great Awakening in Europe and America.

This little town of twenty thousand people, built in 1722, is still called Herrnhut. In English it means "The Lord's Watch." Their understanding was that the Lord is always watching them, and that they are always to be watching the Lord. Their commitment as watchmen and to 24-hour prayer was so great they gave their town this name.

After the prayer watch ceased, much went wrong in Germany, Czechoslovakia and Poland: the First World War, the Second World War, the takeover by the Nazis, and then the Communists. This whole area has been devastated and is one of the most impoverished areas of Poland, the Czech Republic and Germany.

I was there for the first time in 1987, and the Lord showed me that He was going to rebirth the prayer watch and to start watches, initially in twenty-four nations of the world. That vision has already been fulfilled. There are now over one hundred nations of the world where 24-hour praise and prayer continues on an ongoing basis.

*God is restoring the age-old foundations* in Jerusalem and the Middle East at the same time as in Herrnhut, Germany and neighboring countries. Hallelujah! We live in the days of the restoration of all things. The Lord is restoring 24-hour watches all around the world. I'm believing the Lord for a 24-hour watch in every nation of the world before the end of this century—prayer watches where people will be praying and worshiping continually before the throne.

In June of 1993, I had just come from a meeting where, for the first time, Arab and Jewish leaders from throughout the Middle East had come together—spiritual leaders from the nations of the highway mentioned in Isaiah 19: Egypt, Israel, and Assyria. I went from there to Czech and it was the first time the leaders of that region came together, from Czech, Herrnhut, Germany and Poland, on the border of these countries.

On a more recent visit to the area of Herrnhut, I was blessed to see that God has restored the 24-hour prayer watch in that region. In fact, God has moved within the Moravian Church in the Czech Republic and now more than 50% of the church is born again and baptized in the Holy Spirit. Joined by the brothers in Herrnhut, the watch has been reestablished and God is moving again, even in the region where the watch first began.

For further information on restoration of this watch, please see the report in Chapter 9 from the Moravian Church in Liberec, Czech Republic (in the Euroregion Nisa—the same region, very close to Herrnhut.)

## Topeka, Kansas - New Year's Eve Watch, 1900

On New Year's Eve of 1900, literally at the turn of the century, there were some brothers and sisters praying in Topeka, Kansas (within the heartland of the United States) on a 24-hour prayer watch coordinated by Charles Parham. On New Year's Eve, the Holy Spirit fell. They started speaking in other tongues. This spread to Azusa Street in Los Angeles, California and then around the world. This was the beginning of the twentieth century, what many call the Century of the Holy Spirit, because many hundreds of millions of people have received Jesus and the Holy Spirit in increasing waves throughout this century. As God birthed this "Century of the Holy Spirit" out of a 24-hour prayer watch, He is ending this century by birthing 24-hour watches in Jerusalem and in nations all over the world!

## Historically, Presently, and in the Years to Come—God Is Calling Us to Pray for Jerusalem, Our Cities and Nations

I have posted watchmen on your walls, O Jerusalem; they will never be silent day or night. You who call on the Lord, give yourselves no rest, and give him no rest till he establishes Jerusalem and makes her the praise of the earth (Isaiah 62:6-7).

There are two cities for which God has called everyone to pray. One of these is Jerusalem.

Pray for the peace of Jerusalem: "May those who love you be secure. May there be peace within your walls and security within your citadels." For the sake of my brothers and friends, I will say, "Peace be within you." For the sake of the house of the LORD our God, I will seek your prosperity (Psalm 122:6-7).

God also calls everyone to pray for another city:

> **Also, seek the peace and prosperity of the city to which I have carried you into exile [your city]. Pray to the LORD for it, because if it prospers, you too will prosper (Jeremiah 29:7).**

God may call people to pray for many cities, many nations, but there is the irreducible minimum of praying for the nation of Israel and the city of Jerusalem as well as the nation and city where we live. So all these watches that God is birthing throughout the world should see their priority to pray for Jerusalem and Israel and for their own city and nation. Many are also praying for other nations, as we are also called to be a House of Prayer for All Nations.

In the following chapter and in the appendix are different models and examples of contemporary 24-hour watches and watch groups God has established at the end of this twentieth century. God is involved with praise and prayer watches. He is birthing them, He wants us to be involved and He wants to work through us!

# Chapter 9

# Contemporary 24-Hour Watches and Watch Groups

The following are twelve Watch Models that are being kept in Jerusalem and in different parts of the world. Some of these incorporate all twenty aspects of watching as mentioned in chapters 5 and 6 of this book. Others have a more distinct focus of one or more of these aspects. Please ask the Lord of the Watch to show you how He would be calling you to keep the watch individually and corporately in your area. Additional Watch Models and suggestions on how to start a 24-Hour Watch or Watch Group are included in the Appendix.

1.  **All Nations and Peoples Community Model:**
    *Jerusalem Watch of the Lord/Jerusalem House of Prayer for All Nations,* Jerusalem, Israel

2.  **City/Regional Model:**
    *24-Hour Watch,* Moravian Church, Liberec, Czech Republic

3.  **Contemplative Model:**
    Jerusalem-*Watch of the Lord*-Kansas City, Missouri/Kansas, USA

4.  **Intercession/Spiritual Warfare Model:**
    *Watchman Intercessors Network,* Kampala, Uganda

5.  **Local Church Model:**
    *Biblische Glaubens - Gemeinde,* Stuttgart, Germany

6.  **Ministry Model:**
    *Indian Evangelical Team,* Punjab, India

7.  **Missions Model:**
    *24-Hour Permanent Prayer Watch, Valley of Blessing,* Sao Paulo, Brazil

8.  **National (Israel) Model:**
    *Jerusalem House of Prayer for All Nations* - Philippines

9.  **National Model:**
    *US/DC Prayer Watch,* Washington, DC, USA

10. **Night Watch Model:**
    *Watch of the Lord*, Charlotte, North Carolina, USA (Corporate Friday Night Watch)

11. **Unreached Peoples Model:**
    *Jericho Center,* Colorado Springs, Colorado, USA (Watch in formative stage)

12. **Worship Watch Jerusalem-City Model:**
    *Jerusalem Watch of the King,* Jerusalem, Israel

### JERUSALEM WATCH OF THE LORD
### A Ministry of
### JERUSALEM HOUSE OF PRAYER FOR ALL NATIONS
### JERUSALEM, ISRAEL

On October 1, 1987 God called Tom Hess from ministry in Washington, DC to Jerusalem, Israel with the mandate from the Lord to establish *Jerusalem Watch of the Lord.* Out of this grew the multifaceted ministry of *Jerusalem House of Prayer for All Nations.*

The foundational Scripture and vision for *Jerusalem Watch of the Lord* was based on Isaiah 62:6,7:

> **I have posted watchmen on your walls, O Jerusalem; they will never be silent day or night. You who call on the LORD, give yourselves no rest, and give him no rest till he establishes Jerusalem and makes her the praise of the earth.**

While *Jerusalem Watch of the Lord* is the foundation in our Lord of the ministry of *Jerusalem House of Prayer for All Nations,* the servant community, *Messianic Community of Reconciliation,* is the heart of *Jerusalem Watch of the Lord* and tries to keep the Watch filled 24 hours a day, even in the times when other watchmen from the nations are not present! We have a large house on the Mount of Olives where our Community, which averages twelve members from throughout the nations, worships, prays and works full time. They are housed on the lower floor, while the top two floors can house up to thirty watchmen from the nations!

Watchmen have come individually from over two hundred nations and as groups from over forty nations, all to join in worship and prayer with our Community for one week or more. Visiting and Community watchmen cover one or more hours individually each day on the 24-hour watch and all join together for one hour before dinner for corporate prayer watches! Most also participate in a 2-hour worship watch (see Model #12, Worship Watch).

As we completed our tenth year in Jerusalem on October 1, 1997, we can say this has not been easy, as the enemy would try to distract us from our watches in any way possible; but by the grace of God, as the Lord of the Watch, He has kept the watch going through the Intifada, the Gulf War and the bombings in Israel, as faithful watchmen have joined us from nations all over the world.

The *Messianic Community of Reconciliation* also serves *Jerusalem House of Prayer for All Nations* in coordinating meetings of leaders from the different regions to pray from the Mount of Olives, Jerusalem, Israel, the Arab Middle East, the *10/40 Window* nations and all nations!

Praise the Lord for all the breakthroughs we have seen! The walls of Communism have fallen in Russia, the C.I.S. nations and Ethiopia. Over 800,000 Jews have come home to Israel from these nations. Major breakthroughs have taken place and we're seeing the first fruits of Jews and Arabs being reconciled through Messiah to God and one another from all Arab nations and Israel. There have also been numerous breakthroughs in many nations of the world.

We also coordinate 24-hour prayer and fasting among twelve congregations in Israel, each covering a month of the year. The focus is on the reconciliation and salvation of Jews and Arabs in Jerusalem, Israel and the Middle East.

We are now in relationship with 24-hour watches in over one hundred nations and are praying that 24-hour watches will be established in over two hundred nations of the world before the end of the year 2000, to pray for the peace of Jerusalem (Jews and Arabs), their nations and all nations. We are available to serve you in any way to develop 24- hour watches, to pray for and encourage unity and spiritual awakening in your nation, and to help you build a highway to Jerusalem, the City of the Great King.

As watchmen here on the Mount of Olives, we also pray that we will be prepared as the Bride for the coming of the Bridegroom, making ourselves ready, watching and praying for His coming and for the marriage supper of the Lamb. Very soon we will experience His coming, the most dramatic event since the creation of the world. May we always be on the watch and pray, making sure we are pure before Him and have oil in our lamps, ever looking for the blessed hope and glorious appearing of our Lord and Savior Jesus Christ to put His feet on the Mount of Olives (Zechariah 14)! Pray that we will be prepared for His coming, faithful to help prepare a glorious place for His feet (Isaiah 60:13).

You are encouraged to pray about coming as an individual or bringing a group from your nation for a week or more, participating with us in *Jerusalem Watch of the Lord* on the Mount of Olives.

The Lord may be leading some to seek information about joining *Messianic Community of Reconciliation*, serving for a period of six months or longer at *Jerusalem House of Prayer for All Nations* on the Mount of Olives.

God is also preparing to birth watches in other places in Israel, including Haifa (Mt. Carmel), Beersheba, and Tel Aviv. We truly live in the days of the restoration of the Watch of the Lord, both in Jerusalem, Israel, and the nations of the world.

## 24-HOUR PRAYER WATCH - MORAVIAN CHURCH
### LIBEREC, CZECH REPUBLIC

We belong to a congregation that is part of the Moravian Church, a church with a wonderful history and currently in the process of renewal. We are thankful to God our Father; He is faithful and keeps His promises. The history of the Moravian Church goes back to the post-Hussite War period. It was founded in 1467 in Kunvald, and its domain was mostly Bohemia and Moravia. After 1620, however, it was forced to leave those countries. That was the official end of the work of the Moravian Church here. At the beginning of the eighteenth century some Moravians set off to Saxony under the influence of the zealous Christian David. They founded the town of Herrnhut in the Earl of Nicholaus Ludwig

Zinzendorf's dominion on June 17, 1722. The town lies just 35 km to the northeast of Liberec.

Herrnhut soon became a refuge to more and more emigrants not only from Bohemia and Moravia but also from Poland and some parts of Germany. The conflicts of several cultures and confessions reached its peak in the spring of 1727. Then the young Earl established an order for the life in Herrnhut in May, 1727, and spiritual restoration followed. This peaked in August of 1727 in several powerful Holy Spirit-filled meetings, establishing the 24-hour Prayer Watch lasting over 100 years, and also in a mission beginning in 1732 and reaching a great part of the world. Nevertheless, there has not arisen any bigger church in this region; the converted and the Spirit-filled Christians became missionaries (about 200 from one small village).

After over one hundred years of continual prayer came a lukewarmness and spiritual recession. It was as late as the 1920's when some German brothers attempted to renew the Moravian Church congregations in Bohemia. They succeeded mainly in the Sudeten Land but more with the German inhabitants. After World War II, the work in the Moravian Church was extremely difficult. All Germans had to leave the country and the Communistic oppression began. It lasted almost forty years. In 1987, first the Rucky family and then the Krasny family came to minister to the church. From 1987 to 1989 the church membership base rose from 35 to 120 people.

The following period meant harder spiritual warfare for Liberec and the surrounding area, prayer devotion and acceptance of this region. In that time we had strong attacks from occultic people; we led the spiritual warfare and the Lord gave us the victory. The sins committed in the past were confessed, and God's word was proclaimed over the city and its institutions. We really recognized and experienced the power of prayer. In that time (1989-1990) we renewed what we had from history—the 24-hour Prayer Watch. Presently the promises of the outpouring of the Holy Spirit and the growth of the Lord's work covering the area of the region were received. What we experienced in the spiritual area we also could see in the natural political area. We started to look for any contacts with German and Polish churches, and we started to cooperate together.

Then the politicians made an agreement among the Germans, Poles and Czechs in our area and established an association of towns and villages called Euroregion Nisa (Nisa is the river that begins in Czech and forms the border between Germany and Poland).

In 1990 we held several evangelistic meetings, and about twenty thousand people heard the gospel. By 1992 the membership rose to more than five hundred people. In 1993 we planted new congregations within a radius of 50 km by separating from the Liberec church and we called new young pastors to serve there. The watch in Liberec also expanded.

In 1991 we established *The Diakony Lamb*, which takes care of elderly people and physically and mentally handicapped children. In the future they want to work with abandoned and maltreated children, with women thinking about abortion, with single women with children, with the homeless, with alcoholics and drug addicts. Many other programs have been established: in 1992 the Christian School of Johan Amos Comenius; in 1993 the Business Department; in 1994 a daily study at the Mission School of Nicholas Ludwig Zinzendorf; and in 1995 the Foundation Euronisa to financially support the projects dealing especially with problems in social and educational areas.

In the last several years God has promised wonderful things for this region. The 24-hour Prayer Watch was established, and 24 Prayer Houses promised. There was also prophetic insight into the past, and grafting into the Moravian prayer and mission revival. Consistent with these, all the Christian churches in the Czech Republic were challenged to engage in fasting and prayer for the country. Another prophecy spoke about this region becoming a bridge between the West and the East. The impact of this region may be not only on Slavonic countries, but we hope that we will reach the countries under Islamic influence, too. God's promises concerning the opening of the borders came ten months before the foundation of Euroregion Nisa. The opening of the new border crossing really followed. This was actually a renewal of a hundreds-year trade path leading from south to north up to the Baltic Sea. A highway construction project from Prague to Berlin going through the

Euroregion Nisa was designed. We believe this highway is holy (Isaiah 19), and it will serve the purpose of preaching the Gospel.

At the present time it is much more difficult to reach the people because our whole society is based on our country's economic development and all the people are busy making money. So now we have about four hundred members in four independent daughter-churches, with three small satellite churches. We work in home groups and believe that the promised revival will come. We are also rebuilding our church house, and it is a very difficult time for us. But God is faithful in all His promises. He has given us a lot of His mercy and grace, as well as a big responsibility to seek His face and to fulfill His promises.

**—Petr Krasny**

JERUSALEM
## WATCH OF THE LORD
### KANSAS CITY

## The Jerusalem-Kansas City Connection: The Seed

On October 1, 1991, the seed of 24-hour prayer was sent forth from Jerusalem as a summer staff member of the *Jerusalem House of Prayer for All Nations* returned home to Kansas City. On February 22, 1992, the Lord sovereignly connected the seed carried from Jerusalem to a Kansas City (Missouri and Kansas, USA) ministry, planting it in the good soil He had prepared. The tiny seedling sprouted on October 1, 1992, exactly one year after leaving Jerusalem. What began as 24-hour prayer each Thursday expanded to continuous, seven-day-a-week praise and prayer on December 8, 1992, when the Lord issued His call for the fullness of the *Watch of the Lord*.

## The Watch Strategy

As the Lord called His watchmen to labor with Him, He told us to bring our armor and our bows, but He would bring the arrows— the prayers. Each watchman prays one hour weekly in his or her own home, forming a continuous, corporate "prayer closet."

## The Bride of Christ Being Made Ready

Through the call to labor with God in prayer, the Bride of Christ is being drawn to a more intimate relationship with Him. We are being called to set aside our own agenda as we wait in His presence so that we can know His heart more fully. Through the Word of God, the Holy Spirit increases our understanding, faith and love, enabling us to respond in prayer and worship to what He reveals to our hearts. Our time spent with the Lord follows the pattern of "The Bridal Process," a model for our lifetime walk with the Lord, as well as our one-hour watch with Him:

**We come to Jesus, with childlike hearts, responding to His call**... as little children came to Jesus, and were not to be hindered (Mark 10:13-16).

**We turn from our own ways and focus on Jesus, learn to follow Him, learn to hear His voice**... as the sheep follow the Good Shepherd, close by, obedient to Him (John 10:1-18, 25-30).

**We sit at the feet of our Lord, without agenda, wait expectantly, meditate on His Word, and hear what is on His heart**... in the pattern of Mary of Bethany who listened attentively at the feet of Jesus (Luke 10:38-42).

**We come to know Him more intimately as we share our hearts and needs with Him. We learn more of His ways, finding them greater than our ways, resulting in a higher level of faith**... as the faith of Mary, Martha and their friends was raised when Jesus called Lazarus from the tomb (John 11:1-44).

**We respond in greater faith, pouring out a sacrifice of devotion**... as Mary poured out the expensive perfume, anointing the feet of Jesus, ministering to the One who poured Himself out for us (John 12:1-8).

**We look back at our time with the Lord, record those things which are to be preserved, identify what is to be shared with others, and continue to praise God**... as the disciples had been blessed by Jesus, watched as He ascended to heaven, returned to Jerusalem with great joy, and continued to praise God (Luke 24:46-53).

**We go on with a fresh infilling of the Holy Spirit, to accomplish what God has purposed through us, in Him**... as His Church, the Bride being prepared, was released and empowered to go forth at Pentecost (Acts 2; Ephesians 5:25-27).

## The Watch Results

Noting Isaiah 21:6, **"Post a lookout and have him report what he sees,"** each watchman is encouraged to submit a simple log after each watch, reporting the Lord's direction in prayer and any insight that is to be shared. The logs contain a wide variety of spiritual and secular concerns. Prayer topics reported invariably include our local cities, states and nation, Jerusalem, Israel, the Arab Middle East, and the other nations; pastors and other spiritual leaders, unity of the Body of Christ; issues of truth, wisdom, faith, strength, repentance, holiness and humility; revival, evangelism, families, suffering and violence.

There is usually a primary theme drawn from the watchmen's monthly logs. During 1993-94 it was Pastors, Spiritual Leaders and Revival; in 1995, Suffering, Violence and Seeking the Lord; throughout 1996-early 1997, Truth; and from mid 1997, Humility. At the close of each month a summary of the previous month's logs is sent to each watchman with a compilation of the prayers and scriptures involving the primary theme reported—a further testimony that we are not alone but are linked together, arm in arm, in a vast army of the Lord of Hosts.

Results from a responsive expression of prayer are perhaps more difficult to measure than those from prayer for a predetermined need. We are, however, seeing greater unity within the Body of Christ in the Kansas City area, as well as a yearning of the individual believer for greater intimacy with Jesus. Significant issues have been exposed, resulting in personal and corporate repentance. There is less evidence of gang activity, and the number of homicides has fallen dramatically. We thank the Lord for His enduring mercy which is ours through the cleansing blood of Jesus!

## Return to Jerusalem

In 1995, after three years of tender care under the Lord's right hand, a tithe of His Kansas City watchmen responded to His call to return to Jerusalem, bringing an offering of praise to Him for His faithfulness. Our primary offering was the week-long coverage of 24-hour praise and prayer at *Jerusalem House of Prayer for All Nations* on the Mount of Olives. *May this offering be one of many that bring honor and glory to the Lord!*

—Katherine Kirk

### WATCHMAN INTERCESSORS NETWORK
### WORLD TRUMPET MISSION
#### KAMPALA, UGANDA

Our call to prayer stemmed out of a life of agony and pain. Through the repressive regimes of Idi Amin and Obote II, Uganda reeled under the blows of tyranny. Murder, whole village massacres, robberies and torture were the order of the day. Many times we witnessed pregnant mothers having their bellies cut through and the contents spilled out. Many times men were killed in hideous torture as their families watched, mothers raped before their watching children, babies thrown into the air and shot as they came down. Human life was no better than a dog's life.

Our population suffered silently. Those who could not bear it fled into exile, while all other nations simply closed their missions in Uganda. We were left at the mercy of those forces, and little did we realize that behind those conditions were satanic powers tearing our nation apart. A time came though, when we had to cry out, "Enough is enough!"

That's when prayer really began. It was not formal prayer, but deep, desperate, agonizing prayer. After two years of consistent intercession we got the desired changes. Now we can raise our heads again and not feel ashamed of Uganda.

But we had not fully learned our lessons. As soon as peace came, prayer ceased, and everyone went back to his own program. Very soon we were awakened by another enemy destroying our society; a combination of evils was tearing us apart. This included a very serious AIDS (H.I.V.) epidemic, many families divorcing in frustration and pain, lots of children ending up in prostitution because of being orphans without help, or students without enough to care for their daily needs. Others joined crime gangs while the infants ended up on the streets as street kids. Child rebellion was rising alarmingly. Criminal acts, violence, drug abuse and suicides were now becoming the order of the day.

In all this, the people turned to the church as a refuge. They sought answers to life's problems from the institution that stands for the almighty God. But the church was also bound in hopeless divisions, complacency, petty skirmishes and worldly attitudes. Humanism and other religious fundamentalism were having an upper hand over the gospel, and there seemed to be no hope for our situation.

It was during this period, as we sought God for direction, that He revealed to us a breakthrough truth that eventually birthed the present 24-hour watches we have. God showed us that all these influences in society, be they in Uganda or in any other nation, are the work of satan bent on destroying the human race and sanity. These forces contribute to blinding people against the gospel of our Lord Jesus Christ. This darkness can be broken **if** the church will give itself to prayer—deep travailing prayer, with aggressive spiritual warfare. We should then cry out for the outpouring of the Holy Spirit—for whatever God will do will have to come through the anointing of the Holy Spirit gained through deep intimacy with God, which only prayer can build.

As we began to pray in this direction, the Lord revealed yet another dynamic truth to us. He took us to Isaiah 62:6,7. The Lord said to me, "I don't want just a few people to hold a few occasional prayer meetings every now and then. I want intercessors who will stand as Watchmen over their cities, communities and nations—people who will pray without ceasing—people willing to pay the cost to see their lands delivered from the powers of darkness." And He promised that as people will make that commitment, He would anoint them with a fire of travail in their hearts, and this would keep them praying unceasingly.

The Lord also directed us to set up "prayer altars" in every Christian home, in every church, every community and city. Fill the land with prayer altars; fill the world with prayer altars. Then centers should be opened where members of various prayer altars would come in united prayer on a 24-hour basis. I started alone, spending my nights on the floor of my office, praying with travail. With time, more people joined me and we moved to the church. We began holding prayer sessions at various times of the day in addition to night vigils. Gradually, the gap between the different sessions narrowed until we achieved our first 24-hour watch centre in 1995 at *Trumpet Centre* in Kampala. In all this, I had to keep at the forefront, in full participation. If the vision bearer doesn't do this, the whole effort fails.

In mid-1995 we began building the *Watchman Intercessors Network* all over our nation and today we have four other centres nearing the 24-hour accomplishment, while thousands of others are at the stage of regular prayer sessions at different times of the day. In a year's time we shall have over one hundred such centres with 24-hour watches. We are seeing cities, communities and whole regions changed with prayer-power. We are seeing greater signs and wonders, diseases healed, higher faith, multitudes of souls coming to the Lord, church division eradicated, and the changing of morals in society.

In short, this thing works. It works beyond any man's imagination. We are now convinced that nothing is impossible if there are enough people willing to seek the Lord until a breakthrough is accomplished. We believe the words of Christ as very true (Luke 11:10):

**Whoever asks shall receive...**

**whoever seeks shall find...**

**whoever knocks shall have the door opened unto him.**

—John Mulinde

## BIBLISCHE GLAUBENS-GEMEINDE
### STUTTGART, GERMANY

*Could you stay awake with me one hour?* Yes, we can, day and night, around the clock! In autumn 1994 we started a prayer chain which has been going on without a break from the day it began. Our church had already practised 24-hour prayer chains for special events from time to time. With the inspiration of the Holy Spirit this developed into a vision of a permanent nonstop prayer chain in autumn 1994.

Up to now about two thirds of our church membership, as well as Christians from other churches, have been involved in this strategy. The focuses of our strategy vary from time to time. At the moment, one of our main concerns is to pray for a prayer revival: this is also the reason why we have called this year's prayer strategy *Prayer Revival 96.*

Everyone ready to participate promises to dedicate one hour a week (or less if necessary) to the Lord, always sticking to the time that he has chosen, either at daytime or during the night (i.e. every Tuesday at 8:00 P.M.). The participants are to sign a prayer list. Each person who commits one hour of prayer to the Lord receives a handbill giving the individual prayer issues:

**Be... faithful in prayer! (Romans 12:12c)**
**"However, when the Son of Man comes, will he find faith**
[for enduring prayer] **on the earth?" (Luke 18:8b)**

*Thanksgiving, praise and worship to our Father:*
**"Glorified be thy name..." (Matthew 6:9).**

*Requests and intercession regarding Prayer Revival:*
on a personal basis                    in your family
in the church                              in the whole Body of Christ
**"Pray continually..." (1 Thessalonians 5:17).**

*All-around well-being of the church:*
church leadership                      unity and love
everyone in the will of God         move of the Holy Spirit
growth in all parts                     finances
missionaries/evangelism            new churches (branch churches)
**"All believers were one in heart and mind..." (Acts 4:32).**

*Our town, state, nation:*
politicians                                  people in leading positions

schools, training centres                       other churches and fellowships
deliverance from     occult influences           media scene
**"Also, seek the peace and prosperity of the city..."
(Jeremiah 29:7).**

*Current events:*
Israel                                      needs and sicknesses
world politics                          important requests
**"With all prayers and supplications pray at all times in
the Spirit..." (Ephesians 6:18).**

Parallel to the prayer strategy, our pastor regularly taught and preached on prayer. By this the church received practical help in personal prayer life and, above all, their faith was edified, vision for a prayer revival was enhanced, and people became motivated to pray. Here are some practical instructions for the realization of a prayer strategy:

The strategy cannot run without constant support from the leadership. People have to be encouraged, reminded, and motivated to keep it going. The latest news should be given from the pulpit. As the pastor is the person mainly responsible for this initiative, he should be the one to add current prayer requests to the strategy during church services and meetings.

The chain itself requires regular prayer support. We invite the Spirit of Prayer to help us pray for every participant's protection. One person responsible for the organizational part of the prayer strategy has a special prayer desk where, on Sundays, participants sign the prayer list and practical information is provided on request. Also, it is the place for any feedback.

Every participant signs up to do his individual hour during the daytime or at night. One hour can be "occupied" by several people. This presents a crucial advantage if one participant happens to be unable to do his prayer time. Everyone is invited to pray, which means that the strategy is not reserved for "members only," but is open to anyone fulfilling the prerequisite of praying ten minutes daily (e.g., by saying The Lord's Prayer).

Prayer is to be done at home, in private. There is no central prayer room. Usually people pray on their own, but there are also married couples, prayer partners, or groups praying together.

There is no condemnation for those who missed their hour of prayer. We encourage them to continue. At any rate, we want to avoid setting people under pressure through their prayer ministry.

Since the start of this uninterrupted strategy in 1994 we have seen great breakthroughs and visible changes as a result of consistent prayer of the church:

The personal prayer life of many people has been changed;

Our missionaries have been clearly blessed;

In our newly established churches we observe a strong move of the Holy Spirit;

A new quality of unity, especially with other churches from our region, can be seen;

With regard to church structure, strategies and evangelism, our church has experienced very specific guidance from the Holy Spirit.

Be encouraged to utilize our strategy in some form, as directed by the Holy Spirit—it is definitely worth the effort!

—Gabriele Brauer

## INDIAN EVANGELICAL TEAM
### PUNJAB, INDIA

## A Background:

It is believed that Christianity reached the Indian Shores in A.D. 52 through St. Thomas, one of the twelve disciples of Christ. Although almost two thousand years have passed by, the largest democracy in the world has a Christian population accounting for a mere 2.4%. The majority of these Christians are located in specific pockets of this vast and diverse nation. Even now in India, Christianity is a minority religion—a group of people still considered untouchable, and outcasts following a foreign religion.

Therefore Christians in India are easily discouraged. I often have been sad at this turn of events. I wanted God to work among the top level and shake them up and I wanted Christians to be in the high offices. I wanted India to be filled with the knowledge of Jesus Christ, and for Christian believers in India and all over the world to be blessed and walking in victory.

## The Birth of a Vision:

While in Korea attending the Church Growth Seminar held by Rev. Paul Yonggi Cho I learned that there were 52 members of Parliament in his church, and this did not include the many high ranking officials and dignitaries, including the wife of the then-president of Korea. I found out the reason behind this—it was Prayer. I said to myself, "If that can happen in Korea because of prayer, then I know the answer for India." The Lord told me that He is not a respecter of any person, and if the Indian Church will pray, He would do the same thing in India. I returned to India with the burden to pray for the revival of my nation from the top level to the lowest, and not remain limited to the lower level, as has been happening for decades.

Obedience to His voice gave birth to a 24-hour prayer chain on the 1st of August 1991 at 0000 hrs at Pathankot, Punjab, India at the base headquarters of our mission, *Indian Evangelical Team* (I.E.T). Pathankot is the meeting point of the three northernmost states of India—Jammu & Kashmir, Punjab and Himachal Pradesh.

## The Fire Spreads to Delhi:

The victorious results led us to start another prayer group at Delhi on the 31st October 1994. Each member of this group of warriors dedicates a minimum of a quarter of each day to shake the throne of God almighty on behalf of the nation and those in need. We are asking God to provide us with the facility to have the prayer hours extended to 24 hours. We shall shake this nation with prayer!

## How We Pray:

In a land where most homes do not have a telephone, most of the people write to us. We receive hundreds of letters every day from all over the world requesting us to pray for various needs. Many contact us through the fax and some through E-mail. There is a group of over ten dedicated men and women, from different linguistic states at our headquarters, some of them Bible school graduates, who pray over these letters. Then as the Holy Spirit guides them, they reply to these letters, comforting the sender with the Word of God. These prayer requests are then passed down to the prayer group at Delhi, who pray over these prayer requests for one week before sending them over to the chain prayer group at Punjab where two ladies are constantly in prayer. They pray over these needs for thirty days. Rarely do we have to wait for the thirty days, as messages of victory start pouring in.

We have a list of every mission and its leaders in India, and of every cabinet minister and other high-ranking administrative and political officials in the government of India. The prayer group prays for each of them every day. And we pray for the nations of the world, especially for India and it's evangelization.

In 1993 after visiting *Jerusalem House of Prayer for All Nations*, God put in my heart to start praying for the nation of Israel. Our prayer group started to pray earnestly for Israel, its peace, for the return of the Jews to their promised land, and for the revelation of their Messiah.

## Impossibilities Become Possibilities:

We have experienced the dynamic results of prayer. Continual offering of the incense of prayer makes even God hurry. People have been reporting victory, peace and comfort. People are healed of cancer, tuberculosis, arthritis—and the list goes on. I know that our prayers have been bringing victory. The Church in India is now experiencing the result of prayer. Five years ago it was difficult to imagine churches of different factions coming together for even an evangelistic effort. The I.E.T prayer group started to pray, against hope, and we saw a breakthrough.

Prayer has had a great effect on our nation. In the last national election, May 1996, the fundamentalist Hindu political party—the B.J.P—came to power. It had the best ministers on its cabinet— perhaps the most efficient, clean and wise that can be found in India. But, every Christian was terrified. The statement of the President of B.J.P. during his election campaign to make India a Rama Rajya (a kingdom of Rama, the Hindu god) sent shivers down our spines. The Church prayed. We prayed. Initially nothing seemed to happen. We persisted, and on the 13th day the B.J.P government fell. Prayer brings victories!

## Future Vision:

To the best of my knowledge this is one of the only three existing 24-hour prayer groups in India—the other two being in Madras and in Nagaland. I pray that there will be such prayer groups in every region—at least one in every state in India. By prayer alone we can change the history of our nation and the world.

**—P. G. Vargis**

*(Editor's note: God has used Pastor P.G. Vargis to begin over six hundred churches in North India.)*

### 24-HOUR PERMANENT PRAYER WATCH
### VALLEY OF BLESSING, SAO PAULO, BRAZIL

The *Valley of Blessing* came to be through a vision given by God in the mid-1970's. It was at a time of powerful spiritual revival that the vision of a Bible School surrounded by activities such as ministry for children, for the elderly, self support projects, conference centre, etc. was given. Included was a building just for prayer that would be the Permanent Centre For Prayer.

It was a long conception time. For seven years we prayed and worked so that the *Valley of Blessing* could be established. We needed a big miracle. The miracle happened in 1981 when a group of pastors and businessmen from Sao Paulo organized an enterprise that bought a big property (45 hectare), in the outskirts of the city. A residential area was developed in half the property, and with the money that came from the selling of the plots of land the whole property was purchased. We commenced building at the end of 1982.

Part of the vision was a Permanent Centre for Prayer, a building where there would be prayer, every day, every hour until Jesus' second coming. In fact, the Lord gave us the privilege of separating a plot of land right in the centre of the Valley, and the Prayer Centre was built in the middle of the woods. The woods are now becoming the Prayer Garden.

In those days our financial resources were very small, and it was with great difficulty that we hired a tractor to prepare the site for building. After the tractor finally came and worked for a few hours, it stopped and could not be started again. We clearly felt the enemy's hand, showing that the work would not be easy. In fact, we struggled a great deal to build the Prayer Center. To finish it, we could not hire another tractor, so on a Sunday around thirty people worked from morning to afternoon and prepared the site. But we had learned! We set up a tent near the place, and during the whole day two or three people were praying while the others did the job. We really felt the presence of the angels helping us. I was really amazed that by 5 P.M. the work had been completed. A bigger miracle happened when the builder arrived to verify if the land was leveled. To our surprise it was almost perfect. Prayer works, was what we felt.

As soon as the basic part of the building was finished and the first room was covered, we started our prayer vigil. At the beginning, just 3-4 hours were scheduled and every person came for half an hour. Soon we increased the period to five, six or seven hours. We continued until we had the whole day covered—always in a shift system.

Finally, the Prayer Centre was finished, the first building in the *Valley*. It was really beautiful. We believe that the Father's heart was pleased. The path in the middle of the woods makes the walk very special. Here and there one can read phrases like the following:

"PRAY WITHOUT CEASING,"

"FAITH HONORS GOD, GOD HONORS FAITH,"

"OH LORD HEAR MY PRAYER."

The person arrives at the Prayer Centre already edified!

The doors of the Prayer Centre do not have locks, so at any time it is open for prayer. The person finds himself in a big hall, the floor with big steps, no chairs, no pulpit or any other piece of furniture. The environment invites the person to kneel down or sit on the carpet (another miraculous provision from God). There is no place for sermons or lectures, as it is for prayer. On the main wall is a huge map of the world, reminding each one that this is a *HOUSE OF PRAYER FOR ALL NATIONS*. As a community, we always intercede for the world, and especially for our eighty missionaries who are scattered in fifteen countries of the world through our mission agency, *Antioch Mission*.

The main hall accommodates one hundred fifty people, and from this hall are seven cells for individual prayer, in one of which we have our 24-hour prayer vigil. Although there are always people praying in the other ones, in this cell there is a book which each person signs, to say that he was there during his time. Sometimes someone misses the time, and there may be some small delays, but most of the time the chain goes without stopping, and there is always someone in prayer.

There is a person in charge of the prayer chain, to make sure that the chain does not stop. If someone needs to miss their "slot," they advise this person so they can be replaced. We have come to realize that we need to be motivated and taught to pray. It is a necessary discipline in our devotional life, as in our work and our studies. If we do not discipline ourselves, we cannot maintain a solid program of prayer.

All the students of our Bible School take part in the prayer chain, as do all the workers in the *Valley*. We have all come to learn that EVERYTHING CAN BE CHANGED BY PRAYER. Sometimes there are nights of prayer or mornings with God. People also come from outside the community to spend the day praying. Others come for two or three days of fasting and prayer.

The *Valley of Blessing* will be thirteen years old this year. When people visit us and see everything that has been accomplished in so little time, they are amazed. The various parts of the original vision God gave us are in place, and much is being accomplished. Our church has grown considerably and is becoming a missionary church. What is the secret for this and other blessings? Just one—the continuous prayer. God honors His word. He fulfills what He says. Prayer works. It is God who gives grace to maintain this vigil. We depend on Him to continue the program. We pray for this. We pray that God will raise, among our successors, men and women who have the grace of God to continue praying. If we stop, the *Valley of Blessing* will miss the spiritual beauty that it has today. But, by receiving power from God to continue and enlarge our prayer program, we will become a stronghold against the enemy. Please pray that we will have grace, wisdom and strength to continue.

**—Pastor Jonathan Santos**

## JERUSALEM HOUSE OF PRAYER FOR ALL NATIONS - PHILIPPINES

ISRAEL is a land which once again God has brought to the center stage, and the eyes of the entire world are focused upon her. As Filipinos, we believe that we have a continuing dependence upon the past, present and future of Israel. *JERUSALEM HOUSE OF PRAYER FOR ALL NATIONS-PHILIPPINE CHAPTER* has a goal to establish prayer support for the different local churches, and to serve as a bridge of peace and understanding between the Nation of Israel and the Philippines.

At present, we have 168 prayer watches all over the Philippines; twenty-five prayer watches at the National Capital Region; twelve in Luzon and eighty-seven in Mindanao. The daily prayer focuses for the peace of Israel (Psalm 122:6), **"Pray for the peace of Jerusalem: may those who love you be secure,"** are for the abolition of abortion (Exodus 20:13); for the fulfillment of the GREAT COMMISSION (Matthew 28:19); for all those in authority in Israel (1 Timothy 2:1-2); for persecuted and needy Jews and Christians (Hebrews 13:3); for the Arab community in Israel, Middle East and all parts of the world (Genesis 17:20); and for the return of the Jewish people to their land and to God (Ezekiel 37). We believe that the linking of prayer and God's House will help accomplish God's plan for Israel.

In 1993, Sister Fely Tan, Founding Chairman of *Jerusalem House of Prayer for All Nations-Philippines,* took the challenge of being in charge of the prayer mobilization in the Philippines. Thus, from May to September, 1993, Sister Fely, along with twelve other brethren from different churches, went on a nationwide Israel Prayer Mobilization trip to mobilize churches to pray for the peace of Jerusalem. God, who is faithful and true, graciously blessed the team's efforts tremendously.

In February 1994, Pastor Tom Hess came to the Philippines for the first time. I was then the Spiritual Director of *Take the Nations For*

*Jesus Global Ministries, Inc.* and was asked to be the National Chairman of *Jerusalem House of Prayer for All Nations-Philippine Chapter.*

My goal is to encourage and stir up the hearts of people to pray for the peace of Jerusalem and to visit Israel at least once a year, to participate in *All Nations Convocation Jerusalem* (a ministry of *Jerusalem House of Prayer for All Nations,* which is held from *Rosh HaShana* to *Yom Kippur*), a week-long 24-hour prayer watch, (*Jerusalem Watch of the Lord*), and the celebration of the Feast of Tabernacles.

The Word of God in Genesis 12:3, **"I will bless those who bless you, and whoever curses you I will curse; and all the peoples on earth will be blessed..."** sank deep into my heart and has become the foundation of our work in Israel.

It is indeed a privilege for us Filipinos to have a part in the work of God in Israel. We are seeing God's end time plan unveiled before our eyes. People and churches who had the burden and persever-ance to pray for the peace of Israel have been receiving answered prayers in their personal lives, and in their churches as well. The promise of God in Genesis 12:3 is coming into fulfillment in the lives of those who responded to God's call to bless Israel in whatever ways God instructed them.

The vision that the Most High God placed in my heart is to anticipate this time and to prepare the way for the Lord's coming by challenging the Philippine Christian churches, making them aware of God's plan for Israel, and why we as Filipinos should pray for Israel and to send more, consistent delegates to come on each year's prayer tour. It is indeed a great and demanding task, but He who began the good work in us will be faithful, and enable us to carry it to completion.

**GLORY TO THE MOST HIGH GOD!**

—**Rev. Rolando S. Blas**

## National Model

### US/DC PRAYER WATCH
### 24-HOUR PRAYER FOR THE US AND
### THE CAPITAL CITY, WASHINGTON, DC

In 1988 a group of national Christian leaders organized one week of 24-hour prayer in a strategic public location in Washington, DC. The results were astounding. They felt the Lord wanted them to continue some kind of ongoing prayer for the nation, but did not completely apprehend or fulfill the call. These same leaders gathered nine years later during the summer of 1997 to repent for their disobedience, and then felt led to issue a call to prayer.

*The US/DC Prayer Watch* is a national call to 24-hour prayer for the United States, with a special focus on Washington, DC—the nation's capital and a world capital city that is strategic in God's global purpose. This prayer watch includes all the nations represented by embassies in DC and has given special attention to the nation of Israel. Because every state and U.S. territory, as well as every nation of the earth, is represented in the city, spiritual awakening could quickly spread throughout the U.S. and around the world.

The goal of the watch is to mount a continuous 24-hour canopy of prayer from across the nation, which will overlap with and reinforce 24-hour prayer from DC-based churches, pastors, prayer groups and individuals. A central prayer calendar is being filled with the names of individuals and prayer groups who commit to watch and pray during the same specific hour each week, or at least one specific hour each month.

A brochure was printed explaining the watch, which included a sign-up form. The brochure was printed in one dark color on white paper to make photocopying and printing easy. A post office box was secured for the responses, along with a fax number and e-mail address. The organizers of the *US/DC Prayer Watch* felt that this watch had to be a very pure call to prayer, and could not be used to promote any ministry or individual. Therefore, no names appear on the brochure other than that of the *Prayer Watch* itself. Some of the strongholds over Washington, DC which are battled both within the church and without are power, control and pride. This pure call to prayer was in itself a strategic offensive against these powers.

A symphony of prayer for America is beginning to be heard. Many believers, churches and ministries are now responding to Jesus' invitation to tarry and watch with Him in prayer, fasting and in 24-hour prayer watches as never before.

**—US/DC Prayer Watch**

## WATCH OF THE LORD
### (Eight-Hour Friday Night Watch)
### CHARLOTTE, NORTH CAROLINA, USA

In 1995, Mahesh and Bonnie Chavda and a handful of others began meeting spontaneously to seek the Lord in prayer. The Holy Spirit began revealing corporate intercession as a missing link between the renewal and the harvest. The *Watch of the Lord* represents a restoration of something very dear to the heart of our Savior: PRAYER. In these desperately wicked times there must arise a corporate surge of prayer to move the hand of God. When the nation of Israel was in spiritual desolation the prophet Joel called a corporate fast to last through the night (Joel 1:13-14). Thousands of watchmen worldwide are now meeting corporately each Friday night to spend the night in prayer, fasting, and worship. One prophetic picture gives understanding to the primary revelations concerning the watch: A BEAUTIFUL BRIDE IN ARMY BOOTS!

The first primary revelation the Lord gave concerning the *Watch of the Lord* was His desire that we become the **corporate BRIDE OF CHRIST**. During the early days of the watch the Holy Spirit showed that prophetically we are as Ruth lying at the feet of Boaz, her kinsman redeemer. On the encouragement of Naomi, a type of the Holy Spirit, Ruth laid at the feet of Boaz in submission all night. As a result Boaz extended grace to her, and became her husband (Ruth 3:1-13). The Holy Spirit is presently drawing people all over the world to spend the night with the Lord, loving and cherishing Him, as a bride cares for her husband. Just as Ruth said to Naomi we are saying to the Holy Spirit, *"All you say we will do" (Ruth 3:5)*. We come to the watch ready to spend eight concentrated hours loving on our Bridegroom, Jesus. In this concentrated worship the Lord is showing up in extraordinary ways. We are experiencing His response to our love, worship, and adoration.

We are also the **ARMY OF THE LORD**. In Nehemiah we find God's army rebuilding the wall for the sake of protecting the people of God. Today the Spirit is calling those who will hear to come to the wall of prayer. Those hearing this call are willing to work through intercession in order to repair the breaches and burned gates of the wall that have resulted from generations of general prayerlessness, and to fight the hordes of the enemy that are trying to destroy the church through those breaches (Nehemiah 4). The Spirit is searching for soldiers of prayer who will not break ranks, change course without proper orders from the Captain, or flee the scene of the battle (Neh. 4:7). He wants soldiers that fight as one mighty unit, damaging the enemy, not one another (Neh. 4:8). Watchmen are mounting an offensive attack at night, encroaching upon the enemy's territory, the night hours that have previously been so tightly in Satan's possession. We are as an army of watchmen entering the windows of the night like silent thieves, taking back what the enemy has stolen (Joel 2:9). *"Proclaim this among the nations, 'Prepare for war! Wake up the mighty men! Let all the men of war draw near, let them come up... let the weak say, I am strong!'"* (Joel 3:9).

In the *Watch of the Lord* we come together as a corporate body each Friday night from 10:00 P.M. to 6:00 A.M. on Saturday to spend eight concentrated hours in prayer and worship. While fasting from food and sleep we focus on issues that the Holy Spirit reveals prophetically, and obey Him in prayer. We also fast from chitchat and earthly fellowship in order to give the Lord and His purposes our full attention. We give people the freedom to leave if they must, or nap during the course of the watch. Children are welcome to participate in the watch, and have received tremendous blessings there (Joel 2:16). When they are ready to sleep they retire in sleeping bags on the floor. Watch groups vary their worship according to what is available to them. Some have only one worship leader; others are able to use several worship leaders for the night as a relay team; others use recorded music. Events of the watch include intercession, prophetic praise and worship, communion, sharing of prophetic insight received during the watch, and personal ministry to those in attendance. The focus of the watch is not for venting personal needs, but to seek first the kingdom of God. In seeking Him, our personal needs are being met supernaturally (Matthew 6:33)!

Mahesh and Bonnie invite you to seek the Lord regarding participating long-term, in your city, in the *Watch of the Lord*. Many of the current watch groups operate under the guidance of a pastor, and many others are led by people just like you who have received a personal call from the Lord to start a watch night service. Some are participating in the watch as a group, some as a single family unit, and others as individuals. The important issue is to obey the call of the Spirit to the night watch. We cannot begin to tell you of the rich spiritual treasures you will receive from being a part of the watch! *"Blessed is he who watches..." (Rev. 16:15); "... so we built the wall, and all the wall was joined together unto the half thereof, for the people had a mind to work" (Neh. 4:6).*

### —Mahesh Chavda Ministries International

### JERICHO CENTER
### (In Formative Stage)
### COLORADO SPRINGS, COLORADO, USA

This center is based on a recognition of the unusual challenges regarding the ultimate evangelization of the remaining dark places of the earth (especially the world's 1,739 clearly defined unreached people groups). It also recognizes the increasing role of concerted prayer that will be necessary to penetrate these regions, and the need to provide a "covering" for those ministries specifically targeting these areas. The directors are from six international ministries in Colorado Springs (Campus Crusade for Christ, Disciple a Whole Nation, Every Home for Christ, International Students Inc., Mission America, and Youth With a Mission), under the leadership of Dr. Dick Eastman of Every Home for Christ. Together they have been prayerfully pursuing the building of a prayer facility in Colorado Springs, The Jericho Center. This center would operate in direct cooperation with the World Prayer Center to be completed in February of 1998.

The Jericho Center, because of its strategic focus on a practical penetration of regions of the world yet to be evangelized, will be established based on the following purpose, vision, and mission statement:

Our Purpose - To facilitate the strategic partnering of ministry resources and initiatives to serve the Body of Christ in achieving closure of the Great Commission.

Our Vision - To see ministries working together synergistically on a local, national, regional, and global scale through joint-venture initiatives focused towards closure of the Great Commission.

Our Mission - In order to accomplish our vision, we will commit to:

Mobilize Prayer-

Mobilize and Sustain 24-Hour Prayer Shields for Ministers, Ministries, Strategic Initiatives, and Geographic Locals.

Integrate Strategy Development-

Facilitate the Collective Integration of Mission Strategies to Achieve Manifold Wisdom and Ensure Initiatives Success.

Joint-Venture Initiatives-

Improve Stewardship of Kingdom Resources through the Strategic Alignment and Collaborative Implementation of Joint-Venture Initiatives.

Track and Realign Initiatives-

Support, Track and Evaluate Initiatives and Facilitate Realignment when necessary to Achieve Maximum Impact.

World Prayer Center Collaboration-

Collaborate with the World Prayer Center in the Collection, Analysis, Assessment, and Dissemination of Prayer Intelligence.

Collaborate with the World Prayer Center in establishing 24-Hour Houses of Prayer for All Nations in Gateway Cities Globally.

We are in the time of an accelerated and increased harvest. Along with the church world-wide, God has been raising up strategic and fruitful parachurch ministries globally, like huge harvest combines, for the last fifty years (CCC, EHC, YWAM, Navigators, Wycliffe, non-western mission agencies, etc.). And now with the breathtaking worldwide movement of prayer which has accelerated in the last twenty years, we are seeing increased holiness, power and boldness infused into these structures, like high octave fuel being pumped into the harvesting combines. We are also seeing new levels of unity and strategic partnerships to complete the Great Commission worldwide.

Imagine with us the impact of the Kingdom of God in any city or region of the world where the Body of Jesus Christ worldwide, the Church (modality), and the Parachurch (sodality) cooperate and coordinate their existing efforts at ever-increasing levels of unity, with one central motivation: to see Jesus glorified. Yes, you have it, His dream would come true in a short time; worshippers among every tribe, tongue, people and nation.

—**Wesley Tullis**

## JERUSALEM WATCH OF THE KING
### JERUSALEM, ISRAEL

In 1996 we coordinated twenty-four days of twenty-four-hour worship in Jerusalem, beginning on *Rosh Hashanah*, the Jewish New Year, which was a very special time with the King in His City. We now believe it is God's time to begin an ongoing twenty-four-hour Praise and Worship Watch called *Jerusalem Watch of the King*. The Watch commenced October 1 of 1997, on *Rosh Hashanah*, the beginning of the Jewish New Year, which was also the official beginning of Israel's *Year of Jubilee*. The foundational Scriptures are Isaiah 62:6-7; Psalms 9:11,14; Psalms 24:7-10; Revelation 4:8-11; Revelation 5:11-14; Revelation 21.

*Jerusalem Watch of the King* consists of continual twenty-four-hour worship surrounding the city and the throne of the Great King of Jerusalem. There are two-hour daily worship watches joined with twelve different gates on the North, South, East and West walls of the old and new Jerusalem. There are responsible Gatekeepers— Worship Watch facilitators—for each locations. This model corresponds with New Jerusalem where there will be twelve gates. Those who are being called to join the watch from various parts of Jerusalem will be within a short distance from one of the Worship Watch locations. We are worshiping as watchmen with a view and expectancy of the day the New Jerusalem will come down from Heaven and the Tabernacle of God will be with men (Revelation 21).

In addition to being the King of Jerusalem, our Bridegroom will bring us into intimacy with Him as His bride (Revelation 19:6-7). We believe He is also calling us to be on the front lines as praisers (Judah sent out first) standing with Him in the end time battle for Jerusalem and for her salvation as all nations come against her (Zechariah 12:10; 13:1-2; 14:2-3).

We believe this Watch is Holy to the Lord and King of Jerusalem and that it is part of the answer to the Lord's Prayer when He prayed "Our Father which art in heaven, holy is your name, your kingdom come... on earth as it is in heaven." For thousands of years in heaven they have been continually worshiping, saying, "Holy, holy, holy is the Lord God Almighty, who was and is and is to come."

The fact that God is birthing this watch now in Jerusalem may mean that it is also time for our praises to continually rise to His throne in heaven from the earth. This will prepare the way for the veil to be lifted from the Jewish people in Jerusalem so they can receive their Messiah who is coming back soon to take up His throne in Jerusalem as her King. We need to be priests who are fully consecrated to the Lord and King of Jerusalem. We believe that this Watch should be Holy unto the Lord. As He says, we should be holy as He is holy. Pray that God will set and keep the worshiping watchmen whom He is calling on the walls of Jerusalem twenty-four hours a day, that they will take no rest and give Him no rest until He makes Jerusalem a praise in the earth. The foundation of this worship watch is local believers living in Jerusalem, but we also encourage worship leaders, worshipers and teams of worshipers from the nations to join us in augmenting this watch.

I believe God will birth 24-hour worship in other places throughout the world!

# Chapter 10

# Overcoming the Watch of the Enemy

**overcome:** 1. to get the better of; conquer (*overcome* an enemy) (*overcome* temptation); 2. to make helpless or exhausted (*overcome* by gas); 3. to gain superiority - win (we shall *overcome*) (*Webster's New Encyclopedic Dictionary*, 1996).

## Overcomers Through the Lord Jesus Christ

If we are to be the Church triumphant, we must appropriate the power to overcome the "watch of the enemy." Revelation 12:10-12 speaks of the enemy as the accuser of the brethren day and night:

> **Then I heard a loud voice in heaven say: "Now have come the salvation and the power and the kingdom of our God, and the authority of his Christ. For the accuser of our brothers, who accuses them before our God day and night, has been hurled down.**
>
> **"They overcame him by the blood of the Lamb and by the word of their testimony; they did not love their lives so much as to shrink from death.**
>
> **"Therefore rejoice, you heavens and you who dwell in them! But woe to the earth and the sea, because the devil has gone down to you! He is filled with fury, because he knows that his time is short."**

*WE ARE IN A WAR!* We know that the Lord Jesus is victor, but when in a war we need to be sensitive to the direction of the Commander-in-Chief. We need to be watching the Father and listening to His voice. Thank God that He is watching over us.

We not only need to be sensitive to the directives of the Commander-in-Chief, our Lord Jesus, and our Father, but we also need to be aware of the devices of the enemy. These must be the two most important things when involved in a war. We have a 24-hour watch in Jerusalem. God is raising up 24-hour prayer all over the world and He's calling us to be His watchmen. But our enemy also has a 24-hour watch! He's trying to accuse us 24 hours a day!

We are overcomers through the Lord Jesus Christ. But we don't want to give Satan any room in our lives, so that he has no ground to accuse us. Satan has been thrown down to the earth, the heavens rejoice and all who dwell in the heavens. Where do we dwell? We are seated in heavenly places in Christ Jesus (Ephesians 2:6). Some are very excited because they're citizens of the nation of Israel. I think that's the most exciting place on earth to have one's citizenship, but I'm most excited that my citizenship is in heaven. That's much better than having citizenship in Israel!

> **He who dwells in the shelter of the Most High will rest in the shadow of the Almighty... A thousand may fall at your side, ten thousand at your right hand, but it [the attack of the enemy] will not come near you (Psalm 91:1,7).**

> **Be self-controlled and alert [on the watch]. Your enemy the devil prowls around like a roaring lion looking for someone to devour. Resist him, standing firm in the faith, because you know that your brothers throughout the world are undergoing the same kind of sufferings (1 Peter 5:8-9).**

Satan is going around trying to devour us, but we are overcomers because of the Lord Jesus Christ. We're told to be self-controlled. That could also mean to be controlled by the Holy Spirit. If our lives are controlled by the Holy Spirit, if we're on the watch and stand firm, we can overcome.

## The Full Armor of God

> **Finally, be strong in the Lord and in his mighty power. Put on the full armor of God so that you can take your stand against the devil's schemes. For our struggle is not against flesh and blood, but against the rulers, against the authorities, against the powers of this dark world**

**and against the spiritual forces of evil in the heavenly realms. Therefore put on the full armor of God, so that when the day of evil comes, you may be able to stand your ground, and after you have done everything, to stand.**

**Stand firm then, with the belt of truth buckled around your waist, with the breastplate of righteousness in place, and with your feet fitted with the readiness that comes from the gospel of peace. In addition to all this, take up the shield of faith, with which you can extinguish all the flaming arrows of the evil one. Take the helmet of salvation and the sword of the Spirit, which is the word of God.**

**And pray in the Spirit on all occasions with all kinds of prayers and requests. With this in mind, be alert [on the watch] and always keep on praying for all the saints (Ephesians 6:10-18).**

Not only are we to be self-controlled and on the watch and give Satan no room in our lives, but we are also to put on the whole armor of God.

If we're in warfare, we need to make sure that we have on the full armor of God every day. We need to have our head and our mind covered with the helmet of salvation, our loins girded around with the truth of the word of God, and need to be wearing the breastplate of righteousness. We are dressed in the righteousness of the Lord Jesus Christ. As the song says, "dressed in His righteousness alone, faultless to stand before the throne."

With our feet, wherever we walk, we should proclaim the gospel of peace in the Lord Jesus. We should take up the shield of faith to extinguish all the fiery darts of the enemy. There are more fiery darts flying around now than there have ever been in history. Revelation 12:12 says that the time of the enemy is running out, that he is more upset than ever before. So we need to make sure we always have on the shield of faith.

## Stand Firm!

I remember, on New Year's eve of 1990, worshiping the Lord and waiting on Him. He said the 90's would be the decade of more spiritual warfare than any decade in history. We need His covering!

It's already happening, and we still have a few years left in this decade. We should take the two-edged sword of the Spirit, which is the Word of God, to destroy the works of the devil that would come against us and His people in these days. We should destroy the works of the devil that would stop people from being born into the kingdom of God.

Why should we put on the whole armor of God? First of all, so that we will be able to stand against the wiles of the devil. Then, when the evil day comes, we will be able to stand our ground. Many throughout the world use the term "stand your ground," but it's not some secular cliche. It's taken from Ephesians 6:13, talking about standing your ground against the enemy! Next, we're reminded that after we've done everything, to stand. Then stand firm. Four times God calls us to stand! The days are coming when we're going to have to know how to stand. IF WE DON'T KNOW HOW TO STAND, WE WILL FALL.

May God teach us how to stand in these last days, because He wants us to be the triumphant Church. Ephesians 6 is the essence of standing. *Having done everything, continue to stand.*

**You, dear children, are from God and have overcome them, because** *the one who is in you is greater than the one who is in the world* **(1 John 4:4).**

The coming of the Lord may occur tomorrow; then again it may not happen for ten years or more. We don't know when the Lord is coming back; but we do know that between now and the end the warfare is going to increase. So we need to learn how to overcome the watch of the enemy.

Not long ago, on the Mount of Olives, we were spending much time in worship and prayer over issues involving the Arab and Jewish people, *Aliyah* (the return of the Jewish people to Israel) and other areas. It was as though we were spiritually under siege. For a number of days it was so strong that I was almost paralyzed, unable to work. When you're spiritually under siege, if you can't do anything else, you can still stand. *Stand your ground! Having done everything, stand! Stand firm!*

**You adulterous people, don't you know that friendship with the world is hatred toward God? Anyone who chooses**

to be a friend of the world becomes an enemy of God. Or do you think Scripture says without reason that the spirit he caused to live in us envies intensely? But he gives us more grace. That is why Scripture says: "God opposes the proud but gives grace to the humble." Submit yourselves, then, to God. Resist the devil, and he will flee from you (James 4:4-7).

If we're willing to stand long enough, the enemy is going to flee. When the enemy came to Jesus on a forty day fast, Jesus stood His ground! He used the sword of the Spirit against the enemy. After Jesus quoted the Scriptures on three different occasions, the enemy left Him, planning to come back at a more opportune time. If the enemy left the Lord Jesus to do something else, he'll leave us too. He sees the futility of coming against those who are willing to stand their ground. It's a spiritual principle: If we're willing to stand, after awhile the enemy will run. He'll go after someone he thinks isn't willing to stand.

## Enduring Hardship

We need to learn to endure hardship as good soldiers of Jesus Christ.

Endure hardship with us like a good soldier of Christ Jesus. No one serving as a soldier gets involved in civilian affairs—he wants to please his commanding officer. Similarly, if anyone competes as an athlete, he does not receive the victor's crown unless he competes according to the rules (2 Timothy 2:3-5).

Those who are born in Israel are called *sabras*. A *sabra* is actually a cactus; the outside is very hard and prickly, but the inside is very soft and sweet. They say that *sabras*, people who are born in Israel, are hard on the outside and soft and sweet on the inside. It's because there are many trials in the natural, living in Israel. It was much more difficult over the last forty years than it is now; but we need to be like *sabras*, as good soldiers of Jesus Christ, because the spiritual battles will ever increase between now and the coming of Messiah.

We need to learn to endure hardship. We need to get tough on the outside but not on the inside—hardened to the difficulties but not to the people. We need to remain tender towards the Lord and towards one another; but our skin needs to be toughened towards the enemy. What we're dealing with today, in terms of spiritual warfare, is just "boot camp" for what's coming in the years ahead.

I was sharing some of these things with our staff in Jerusalem and said, "If you think being under a little spiritual siege is difficult, what are you going to do when all the nations of the world come against Jerusalem?" We'd better get ready for the warfare that's coming. It's not just coming in Jerusalem, the eye of the storm (Isaiah 31:9 says that Israel is the fire and Jerusalem is the furnace—like living in a fiery furnace), it's coming all over the world.

While I was fasting recently, the Lord said He wanted us to stand with Him for Jerusalem. I know that's not going to be easy. I don't know what it will mean in the days ahead, but I hope to remain faithful by the grace of God. I know that my destiny and calling are in Jerusalem. But wherever we are, in Jerusalem or another location, we need to learn to endure hardship as good soldiers of Jesus Christ, because the warfare will become increasingly more intense between now and the time Jesus returns.

## The One Enthroned in Heaven Laughs

It was interesting the way the Lord broke our siege situation in Jerusalem, spiritually. We had been standing for days. One morning, as I was seeking the Lord, He told me to turn to Psalm 2. What really impressed me were verses 4 to 9:

> **The One enthroned in heaven laughs; the Lord scoffs at them. Then he rebukes them in his anger and terrifies them in his wrath, saying, "I have installed my King on Zion, my holy hill [Jerusalem]." I will proclaim the decree of the LORD: He said to me, "You are my Son; today I have become your Father. Ask of me, and I will make the nations your inheritance, the ends of the earth your possession. You will rule them with an iron scepter; you will dash them to pieces like pottery."**

The Lord is asking us to ask Him for the nations. That morning in our prayer meeting, I shared this Scripture with the brothers and sisters who were there, and God broke into our meeting. Some of the maturest intercessors broke out in holy laughter—and the enemy ran! We had the victory! There's a time to weep and a time to laugh. He who sits in the heavens laughs because all the nations are coming against Jerusalem, His purposes, and His people.

Why did He tell us to pray *"Thy kingdom come, Thy will be done, on earth as it is in heaven?"* If the Lord in heaven is laughing, there are times when He wants to release His laughter through us on the earth. God has many strategies for overcoming the watch of the enemy and I believe this is one of them in these last days.

## Winning the Battle for Our Minds by Watching the Lord and His Word

**For though we live in the world, we do not wage war as the world does. The weapons we fight with are not the weapons of the world. On the contrary, they have divine power to demolish strongholds. We demolish arguments and every pretension that sets itself up against the knowledge of God, and we take captive every thought to make it obedient to Christ (2 Corinthians 10:3-5).**

One of the main ways the enemy is trying to come against us is through our minds. God says that we should take *every thought* captive to the obedience of Christ.

Proverbs 23:7 (KJV), says that as a man **"thinketh in his heart, so is he."** *May God help us to meditate upon His Word.* If a person is spending more time watching television than he is watching God and His Word, he must be living in idolatry—because most of what's on television is the "watch of the enemy." There are some good things on TV, but not much on TV has to do with watching the Lord. If you want to overcome the watch of the enemy, make sure you are spending much more time watching the Lord and His Word than watching television.

> And the peace of God, which transcends all understanding, will guard your hearts and your minds in Christ Jesus (Philippians 4:7).

These are the things that we should meditate upon, that we should watch, fill our minds with:

> Finally, brothers, whatever is TRUE, whatever is NOBLE, whatever is RIGHT, whatever is PURE, whatever is LOVELY, whatever is ADMIRABLE—if anything is EXCELLENT or PRAISEWORTHY—think about such things (Philippians 4:8).

Dwell (abide) in these things. He who is most praiseworthy and honorable and lovely and true is the Person of the Lord Jesus, and the Word of the Lord. So we need to spend the majority of our time upon the meditation of the Lord and the Word of the Lord. Then our minds will be renewed.

> Do not conform any longer to the pattern of this world, but be transformed by the renewing of your mind. Then you will be able to test and approve what God's will is— his good, pleasing and perfect will (Romans 12:2).

> One thing I ask of the LORD, this is what I seek: that I may dwell in the house of the LORD all the days of my life, to gaze upon [to meditate on, to watch] the beauty of the LORD and to seek him in his temple (Psalm 27:4).

There is nothing more desirable to do than to meditate upon the beauty of the Lord and to watch the Lord in His temple. May the Lord help us to be watchmen of Him, meditating upon Him. As the Psalmist says, **"My meditation of him shall be sweet"** (Psalm 104:34 KJV).

## Watching the Schemes of the Enemy

> [Forgive]... in order that Satan might not outwit us. For we are not unaware of his schemes (2 Corinthians 2:11).

The enemy has many evil devices, evil schemes. I don't claim to know all of them, but I would like to mention just a few. First of all, in the context of this Scripture, it says that we should forgive one another. There's much power in forgiveness. The Lord Jesus said on the cross, **"Father, forgive them; for they know not what they do"** **(Luke 23:34 KJV).**

The Lord's Prayer says, **"Forgive us our debts, as we also have forgiven our debtors" (Matthew 6:12).** One of the tactics of overcoming the devices of the enemy is forgiving one another. If we forgive one another, that defuses problems in the body.

I have heard that *Youth With A Mission* (YWAM) has taken a team through the Middle East and Arab countries, re-walking the steps of the Crusaders, asking forgiveness for all the things the Crusaders did against the Muslims. That could loose something in the Holy Ghost that could bring a major revival. Repentance and forgiveness are weapons of overcoming the devices of the enemy.

Another of the enemy's schemes comes on the aftermath of a great victory. Some of the times that the enemy has come against me the hardest is after a great victory (like Elijah). I've seen spiritual leaders fall, as wounded soldiers, because they were vulnerable after a great victory. We've taken numerous prayer missions to different countries. There are always many people praying 24 hours a day for us during that time. But many times, at the conclusion of the prayer mission, the prayer cover drops because people think it's over. In reality, that may be the time when prayer covering is needed the most. Even coming off a fast, or going into a fast, can be a vulnerable time. That's when the enemy came to Jesus, when He was on a fast.

Another device of the enemy: a person's greatest strength can be his greatest weakness. In the natural that would seem ridiculous, but many times God calls people to an area where they have no natural ability at all. He wants His strength to be made perfect in their weakness. Sometimes people think they know everything about an area; they become proud and the enemy moves into that situation. **"Let him who thinks he stands take heed lest he fall" (1 Corinthians 10:12 NKJV).**

The enemy can also come against us through our brothers and sisters. This is unfortunate, to be wounded by our brothers and sisters. The Lord Jesus was wounded in the house of His friends. When Satan was speaking through Peter, Jesus rebuked Peter and said, **"Get behind me, Satan" (Matthew 16:23).**

Still another of the enemy's devices or strategies is to divide and conquer. He wants to divide fellowships and ministries and then conquer. As we are watching, as His watchmen, we will overcome the watch of the enemy through prayer and fasting. In some cases, God may want to remove from ministries those who are not really faithful people. All things will work together for good if we're standing and breaking the powers of the enemy that would try to divide and conquer, because God wants His true believers to be dwelling together in unity. United we stand, divided we fall.

Sometimes the enemy will appear to us as an **"angel of light"** (2 **Corinthians 11:14).** We need the gift of discerning of spirits in these last days more than we've ever needed it before! We're not going to be able to survive in the coming decade unless we increase in the discerning of spirits that has so graciously been given to us by the Holy Spirit.

Other strategies of the enemy include the lust of the flesh, the lust of the eyes and the pride of life.

**Do not love the world or anything in the world. If anyone loves the world, the love of the Father is not in him. For everything in the world—the cravings of sinful man, the lust of his eyes and the boasting of what he has and does—comes not from the Father but from the world. The world and its desires pass away, but the man who does the will of God lives forever (1 John 2:15-17).**

*May we not be ignorant of the enemy's devices regarding the lust of the flesh, the lust of the eyes, and the pride of life. May God deliver us from these things, as we keep our minds focused on the Lord Jesus and upon His Word and continue to rejoice in Him.*

## Overcome by the Blood of the Lamb and the Words of Our Testimony

Revelation 12:11 shows us there are two ways that we overcome the enemy. The first way is to overcome him by the blood of the Lamb. We need to have our bodies covered with the blood of the Lamb, our minds covered with the blood of the Lamb (Communion on a daily basis can be a way of focusing on and apprehending by faith the protection we have through the blood of Jesus). We need to have our minds, bodies, vehicles, tape machines, fax machines, and other doorposts of our houses covered with the blood of Jesus. We need to cover everything with the blood of Jesus because the warfare is getting more intense. One drop of the blood of Jesus is more powerful than all the weapons of the enemy, so we need to remember the blood of Jesus.

The second way we overcome is by the word of our testimony— sharing our testimony that Jesus shed His blood for us and that we have citizenship in the kingdom of God; that others might be born into the kingdom of God. Jesus shared His testimony with the enemy. He quoted the Scripture to him and overcame by the Word of God. He said, **"It is written..."** and quoted the Scriptures on numerous occasions. It's an example to us of how we should overcome the enemy, by the blood of the Lamb and by the word of our testimony.

## Watch and Pray

If the enemy is always watching, day and night, to accuse us, we need to be always on the watch. If we're going to discern the tactics of the enemy we need to be God's watchmen. That's why, on numerous occasions in the New Testament, the Lord emphasized watching over praying. He said,

> **"Watch and pray so that you will not fall into temptation"** (Matthew 26:41).

> **"Be always on the watch, and** *pray that you may be able to escape all that is about to happen*, **and that you may be able to stand before the Son of Man"** (Luke 21:36).

**"Escape"** could mean several different things. First of all, it means to be delivered from the enemy who would come against us, and to stand against him—to RUN from the evil that's in the world, and run into the arms of the Lord Jesus. Jesus prays in John 17:15 that we not be taken out of the world, but protected from the evil one until He comes. He wants us to be here as His light and His salt. But He wants to keep us from the evil one in the midst of this present evil age. He also wants us to be able to *"stand before the Son of Man."*

As we read in Ephesians 6, it says *"stand"* four times. The times may become extremely difficult in the end, but if we're willing to stand against the powers of the enemy and keep our eyes on the Person of the Lord Jesus, we'll be prepared for the coming of the Lord. We'll be able to stand at the coming of the Son of Man.

**And pray in the Spirit on all occasions with all kinds of prayers and requests. With this in mind, be alert [on the watch] and always keep on praying for all the saints (Ephesians 6:18,19).**

Our mind should be on the fact that we should be praying and interceding in all kinds of ways. We need to be praying for one another in these last days. We always need to be on the watch, praying for the people in spiritual leadership, for the poor, widows, orphans, needy, for everyone that God puts in our spirit and everyone that the Father puts on our heart to pray for. I believe that we're going to see, in increasing ways, the Lord raising up 24-hour prayer watches over all the earth. The Muslims pray five times a day and Islam has grown much faster than Christianity in the last fifty years.

It's time for those who believe the truth to be on the watch! *May God raise us up as watchmen in these days, and may God raise up corporate watches in this land in increasing ways, that the watch of the enemy will be overcome! May we arise with God on His watch (as His watchmen) and may the enemy and his watch be scattered.*

# Chapter 11

# Watch for the Hunters

"However, the days are coming," declares the LORD, "when men will no longer say, 'As surely as the LORD lives, who brought the Israelites up out of Egypt,' but they will say, 'As surely as the LORD lives, who brought the Israelites up out of the land of the north and out of all the countries where he had banished them.' For I will restore them to the land I gave their forefathers.

But now I will send for many fishermen," declares the LORD, "and they will catch them. After that I will send for many hunters, and they will hunt them down on every mountain and hill and from the crevices of the rocks" (Jeremiah 16:14-16).

## Watching with a Heart for Israel

The church I attended as a child in Pennsylvania had a theological belief in Israel. They had some head knowledge, but not fully the Lord's heart for Israel. It was a Bible Church without a full understanding of the working of the gifts and graces of the Holy Spirit for today, but I praise God for their commitment to the Bible, Israel and the nations.

At the age of twenty, I received the baptism in the Holy Spirit and then unfortunately became involved in replacement theology. I felt I had been robbed of the baptism in the Holy Spirit as a child, so assumed what I had been taught about God's promises for Israel was also in error. I now thought all the promises in the Bible were for the Church. For the next ten years my belief was that God was finished with Israel and that the Church had completely replaced Israel. Unfortunately, there are many nominal but also Spirit-filled Christians in the United States, Europe and worldwide also in the deception of replacement theology. We pray that God will lift the veil from their eyes. As the Jewish people need to have the veil lifted from their eyes, so do many people in the Church regarding Israel.

Upon visiting Israel in 1982, God lifted the veil from my eyes and showed me His heart and end-time purposes for the Jewish people and for the Nation of Israel. During that time I met with about ten people from different European nations. They were preparing for the exodus of the Jewish people out of Russia, although it hadn't yet begun. After this visit we began taking many groups to Israel. Twenty-five Messianic pastors from the United States participated, for many their first time in Israel. Each year we also held a national celebration for Israel's birthday; we had a 200-voice black choir singing Hebrew songs in Washington, DC.

## Prophetic Prayer Missions -Watching as Joshua and Caleb

In 1985 the Lord showed me that I was to take a prayer team of forty people to Egypt. Through this God birthed a new thing by the Holy Spirit. Having just arrived from the United States, we were in a hotel in Cairo, planning to worship for five minutes before going to bed. But the Holy Spirit fell upon us; people began prophesying, and worship continued for two hours! Muslims were touched all over the hotel and one opened his life and received the Lord Jesus Christ.

Through prophecy the Lord said, *"You're no longer going to be doing tours, you're going to be leading prophetic prayer missions."* He said, *"Like Joshua and Caleb, wherever you put your feet, possess it for the kingdom of God."* We were told to anoint our feet, go to the top of Mt. Sinai and blow a *shofar*, a ram's horn, in four directions, to the north, south, east and west, calling the Jewish people back to the land of Israel. (This was in the same place where Moses had the vision of coming out of Egypt.)

As we were leaving Egypt and entering Israel to celebrate the Feast of Tabernacles, the Lord spoke to me and said, *"You just relived the exodus out of Egypt. Next year you're going to Russia to help prepare the way for the exodus out of the land of the north."* I said, "God, we may end up in Siberia. I don't think I want to go to Russia—can't

I go with someone else?" And He said, *"No, I want you to take forty people into Moscow."*

## WATCHMEN AS FISHERS

So we went to Moscow in 1986, and the first thing the Lord directed was a Jericho March around the Kremlin. I said, "God, if they find out what we're doing, surely we'll be in Siberia." But I discovered it wasn't so difficult. Because the Communists didn't believe in God, they didn't care if we prayed! Our group did a Jericho March around the Kremlin, praying in the Spirit. We prayed for the release of the Jewish people, for the walls of Communism to come down, and for the gospel of Jesus Christ to penetrate Russia.

The Lord also had us take in thousands of Bibles. *Let My People Go* was translated into Russian. We took tens of thousands of copies and we shared the love of God with many Jewish people. The Lord had us go back every year for seven years, and each time we did another Jericho March around the Kremlin. Many people were praying worldwide. Only two hundred Jewish people had come out of Russia before 1986, but about a week after our trip that year, the Communists agreed to release twelve thousand people who came out later in 1986! God has subsequently released over eight hundred thousand Jewish people to Israel from the Land of the North. **The year before 1986 there had been only two hundred Jewish people released, since then over eight hundred thousand!**

In 1996, ten years later, I led another Jericho March around the Kremlin just before the elections. Pastors and others from Moscow joined us and God again intervened. The Communists were stopped at the gates again!

During *Pesach* (Passover) the Jewish people for thousands of years have remembered the exodus from Egypt. In Jeremiah 16 we see that the exodus from the North and the other nations will be much greater than the exodus from Egypt. The Jewish people will forget the exodus from Egypt, because the exodus from the North will be so much greater!

This will be very significant. God opened the Red Sea. Three million Jewish people came out of Egypt. None were left behind. The land of Israel was born. What could be more significant than that?

What we're beginning to see will culminate in something of greater significance, because two things will occur that did not happen in the first exodus. Before Jesus ascended, He said to the Jewish people in Jerusalem, *"You will not see me again until you say, 'Blessed is he who comes in the name of the Lord'"* (**Matthew 23:39**).

In Ezekiel 37, the Lord spoke of how He's going to gather His people from all over the nations back to Israel. He said He will join them together in the land, bone to bone, flesh to flesh. He will put flesh on them and will breathe on them by the Holy Ghost. They will rise up as an exceedingly great army.

A small number of Jewish people are turning to the Lord in the nations of the world, and more will come to Him in the future, but most will return as dry bones—people who are spiritually unawakened, not born again by the Spirit of God. Ninety-eight per cent of the Jews returning from Russia come back in unbelief. The same is true worldwide. So the Lord says: *"You will not see me again until you say 'Blessed is he who comes in the name of the Lord'"*—until the Jewish people receive their Messiah. This last exodus will manifest something not seen in the first exodus. First, the Jewish people back in the land of Israel will receive their Messiah. Secondly, when they do this, the clouds of heaven will not be able to hold the Lord Jesus! The Father will release Him from heaven! He will put His feet on the Mount of Olives!

## Gathering from the North, South, East, West

In Washington, DC in 1987 I was praying in our *House of Prayer* and received a vision of judgments coming on America. Bombs were exploding and I saw that the Islamic terrorists would be coming against America—possibly the Communists as well. Islamic terrorists' bombs are currently exploding in different parts of the world, including the United States. The Lord told me that it's time for the American Jewish people to return to Israel. He said to warn them, and to encourage them to come home.

The United States has been good to the over six million American Jews, but God did not say, "I choose New York, I choose Miami, I choose Los Angeles, I choose Paris." He said, *"I choose Jerusalem!"* Many Jewish people probably wish God had said, "I choose New York." I don't know why He didn't—it would have been much easier, because almost as many Jewish people live in New York as live in Israel.

God's ways are higher than our ways. He has a plan for the Middle East. It's no accident that God put the Jewish people in the middle of an Islamic world. He will make the entire region a blessing in the midst of the earth by revealing Himself to the Muslims and the Jews and reconciling them in Messiah.

I had thought that the Jews were free to leave the West and to go back to Israel, but that they were bound in Russia. In 1987, while in Russia, I asked the Lord, "Why haven't the Jews returned to Israel from the West? I understand why they haven't returned from Russia, because they're bound by Communism here." The Lord spoke to me and said, *"The Jews are more bound in the West then they are in Russia."* I found that hard to believe at first. Then He gave me the Scripture,

**For we do not wrestle against flesh and blood, but against principalities, against powers, against the rulers of the darkness of this age, against spiritual hosts of wickedness in the heavenly places (Ephesians 6:12 NKJV).**

This has proven to be true. Over eight hundred thousand Jews have come home from Russia since then; very few have returned from the West.

I appreciate visions, but what do the Scriptures say about the return of the Jewish people? The Bible is our sound and sure foundation. I thought perhaps there were between twenty and forty Scriptures about *Aliyah*, the return of the Jewish people. I asked my secretary to search the Scriptures for all the verses. She usually worked very fast, so I wondered why it took her so long. There are over seven hundred Scripture verses calling the Jewish people back to Israel! God must be serious! Why isn't He calling all the Italians to go back to Italy or all the people who have moved from the Spanish-speaking nations to return to their countries? Because He has a unique purpose and plan to work through the Jewish people in these last days.

The exodus that we're discussing is not just the exodus from Russia. Some people think that what God is doing today is bringing the Jewish people back from the land of the North, from Russia, but this is just the beginning. Jeremiah 16:15 continues:

> [man will say] "As surely as the LORD lives, who brought
> the Israelites up out of the land of the north and out of all
> the countries where he had banished them." For I will
> restore them to the land I gave their forefathers.

God says He's going to bring them home from the north, south,
east and west. As surely as He's bringing them from Russia today,
they'll also come from the south, east and west! God's word will not
return void. It will accomplish that which He's purposed. And God
has purposed to bring the Jewish people home from all the nations,
even the West.

> "Then they will know that I am the LORD their God, for
> though I sent them into exile among the nations, I will
> gather them to their own land, not leaving any behind. I
> will no longer hide my face from them, for I will pour out
> my Spirit on the house of Israel, declares the Sovereign
> LORD" (Ezekiel 39:28-29).

As with Egypt, they're all coming back, none will be left behind!
When all the Jews return from the United States, France and Great
Britain, it will be a bigger miracle than the Jews coming out of Egypt.
It will be a very big miracle! As surely as the Lord has shaken the
nations of the former Soviet Union, God will shake America, France
and Great Britain.

God is bringing His people from other nations. A few years ago,
on our prayer mission to Russia, we also went to what was formerly
Yugoslavia. We were in what is now five separate countries, divided
from different parts of Yugoslavia. The Lord had us warn the Jewish
people to leave Yugoslavia. We talked to the chief Rabbi and to many
Jewish people and encouraged them to come home. They said,
"Well, we're not going to go home; Communism just fell, we're going
to rebuild our culture in our land." Two months later all hell broke
loose, and they were trying to flee for their lives. We also prayed close
to the borders of Albania. A couple of weeks later all the Albanian
Jews boarded airplanes and came back to Israel in two days!

In 1991, Jay Rawlings went with me to Damascus. No one
thought the Jews would ever come out of Damascus. It looked like the
most difficult place in the world. We did a Jericho March around the
original borders of Israel, praying for God to pour out His Spirit on

the Muslims, to draw them into the kingdom of God and to reconcile them with the Jewish people in Messiah. Right after that, the peace process began and now almost all the Jews from Damascus and Syria have come out of Syria.

I recently met with the Chief Rabbi of Syria, Abraham Chamra, an exceptional leader who made *Aliyah* to Israel from Syria and who called all the Syrian Jews in New York and elsewhere to come home to Israel. May many other Rabbis follow his example.

God answers prayers! He's shaking South Africa. One reason He is shaking South Africa is to bring the Jews home. During the summer of 1992, I spoke to many Israelis living there. They say that their destiny is back in Israel. They are coming back. Other South African Jews who are not Israelis are returning to the land of Israel.

There was a severe famine in Ethiopia. God had caused the Ethiopian Jews to begin returning. I went there to pray. Tens of thousands came home in Operation Solomon. Fifty thousand more have been located. *Let My People Go* has recently been printed in Amharic for the Jews in Ethiopia. I went to Morocco to encourage the Jews to return. God is bringing them from all directions!

Prior to that, I took twelve intercessors to the East. The Lord sent us to Beijing to do a Jericho March around Tienanmen Square, and to believe God to intervene regarding Communism in the East. We also prayed for the release of the Jewish people from the East and for the gospel to continue permeating China. We went to Kaifaing, the center of the Chinese Jewish community. These Jewish people knew no one who had returned from China. Eleven people said they want to make *Aliyah* from China, so we're believing God for the funds. From there we went to Hong Kong. We met a 92-year-old man in the Synagogue. We prayed with him, and he said he wants to come back to Israel. God says He will bring the lame, the children, the old men with canes. He's bringing them all back to Israel from the four corners of the earth.

Then we went to Bombay, the largest Jewish community in Asia. Our tour guide was a Hindu who was engaged to a Jew! We were introduced to the Jewish community, including the Jews from Baghdad. They're beginning to return in increasing numbers from India. I was in Madras, where Thomas went from Jerusalem as a disciple of Jesus, and there's a whole family of Messianic believers there—grandparents, parents, children—who are all coming back to Israel.

Many people believe that the ten lost tribes of the House of Israel are hidden in Islam within Asia—in India, Pakistan and Afghanistan! I talked to many people in India who have met Muslim people from Kashmir and other parts of India and Pakistan who light candles every Friday night and affix *Mezzuzot* (a small cylinder containing the *Ten Commandments*, used by Jewish people) over their door posts!

God says He's going to bring His people home, not leaving any behind. In the last few years I've met many Americans who only recently learned they were Jewish. Because of the Holocaust, their parents didn't want to tell their children. God is uncovering people's identities because He's purposed to bring them back to the Land of Israel. His Word will not return void! It will accomplish that which He's purposed!

I believe that as surely as the Lord is uncovering the Jews in the West, He will begin to uncover the ten lost tribes in the East, even those hidden in Islam. We had a tremendous prayer meeting in India. We prayed that God would bring visions and dreams of the highway leading back to Jerusalem to the people from the ten lost tribes hidden in Islam; that they would exit Pakistan, India and Afghanistan and find their way back to Jerusalem.

In many places where the Jewish people live in the world today, there is turmoil happening. What is going on? I believe God is beginning to shake the nations.

> **At that time his voice shook the earth, but now he has promised, "Once more I will shake not only the earth but also the heavens." The words "once more" indicate the removing of what can be shaken—that is, created things—so that what cannot be shaken may remain. Therefore, since we are receiving a kingdom that cannot be shaken, let us be thankful, and so worship God acceptably with reverence and awe, for our "God is a consuming fire" (Hebrews 12:26-29).**

God says He's going to shake everything that can be shaken. *As surely as God has shaken the Soviet Union, He's going to shake the West.*

In the world economy today, many countries that were the poorest are starting to have economic increases. There is an economic revival in China, India, Argentina, Israel, and many eastern countries. Many very poor Latin American countries are also experiencing a big revival. God is pouring out His Spirit on them. Many of these countries have already been shaken to the core, and because the things in which they felt secure are gone, they have nothing but the Lord.

I've traveled in over eighty countries and believe that the greatest enemy to the gospel of Jesus Christ is neither Communism nor Islam. I believe it's materialism and secular humanism. That is what is quenching revival fires more than anything else.

Even in Saudi Arabia, Sudan, Algeria and Iraq an incredible revival is breaking out. Forty to fifty thousand have received the Lord in Saudi Arabia—foreigners as well as nationals. When foreigners go there, there is little to do. Many gadgets we have in the West are banned, so they become bored. They're receiving Jesus as their Messiah, spending time in the Scriptures and coming to know the Lord!

## Shaking Everything that Can Be Shaken

God says He's going to shake *everything* that can be shaken. I believe there are three basic reasons: First, so that the Bride will make herself ready. Do you still have some things that can be shaken from your life? May God shake everything from us that can be shaken, so that only His kingdom may remain within us. That's the first reason God is shaking everything, to prepare His Church for His coming.

Second, God is shaking the unbelievers out of the world and into the kingdom of God, that they would become desperate for God. It's God's mercy because He wants to shake us into His kingdom and shake the things of the world from us.

Third, God is going to shake all the Jewish people out of the nations and bring them back to the land of Israel. The seven hundred Scriptures shall be fulfilled! God said through Amos,

> **"I will bring back my exiled people Israel...I will plant Israel in their own land, never again to be uprooted from the land I have given them"** (Amos 9:14-15).

We're living in the time of the last exodus to Israel. They will never have to be uprooted again. Only those moving from Russia to the United States will have to be uprooted again. For those moving back to Israel, it's the last return.

## Discerning the Hunters

**This is what the Lord says to me: "Go, post a lookout and have him report what he sees. When he sees chariots with teams of horses, riders on donkeys or riders on camels, let him be alert, fully alert." And the lookout shouted, "Day after day, my Lord, I stand on the watchtower; every night I stay at my post. Look, here comes a man in a chariot with a team of horses. And he gives back the answer: 'Babylon has fallen, has fallen! All the images of its gods lie shattered on the ground!' O my people, crushed on the threshing floor, I tell you what I have heard from the LORD Almighty, from the God of Israel" (Isaiah 21:6-10).**

This passage in Isaiah is about our being watchmen, being on the alert day after day, standing on the watchtower. It talks about watching because Babylon is falling. All the images of its gods are lying shattered on the ground. I believe we live in the days when Babylon in the West is going to fall. God is going to bring economic shakings on the United States, France and Great Britain. It's already beginning to happen. The gods of our cultures will fall down, and this will free people to put their trust in the Lord. The strongholds that are holding them in the West must be broken. This will free the Jewish people to turn their eyes towards Jerusalem, sparking a massive *Aliyah* from the West, an exodus even greater than the exodus out of Egypt.

A report of an Islamic Fundamentalist meeting held in Paris told of "new assertiveness" by Muslims across Europe. Among their demands are Koranic schools and the loosening of immigration restrictions. France, which has the largest European Muslim population (over five million) is said to give little accommodation to their demands. Islamic organizations of France fear manipulation of young Muslims by extremists outside of the movement, that "they could become a time bomb that will explode in one day."

Great shakings could come to France and England and I believe that we live in a time when God is allowing Islamic Fundamentalism and economic shakings to shake His people loose from their apathy and complacency, that we would turn our hearts towards Him. We also see a great growth of Islam in the United States. In 1995, Louis Farrakhan and Islamic Fundamentalist leaders led a Million Man March on Washington DC, which even many black Christians joined. Eight years ago in Washington, Farrakhan stated that soon the heads of the Jewish people would be rolling down the aisles. After the 1995 March, Farrakhan said that he is going to establish the Nation of Islam on American soil. He then went to visit Khadafi in Libya, Saddam Hussein in Iraq and to Iran to raise money for that purpose. Meanwhile, terrorism is escalating in America.

As mentioned in Chapter 8, at the beginning of the second millennium A.D., hundreds of thousands of Ottoman Turks, the greatest army in that day, came against the castle of the Knights of St. John in Rhodes on three different occasions, but the Knights of St. John stood their ground. Only two thousand resisted hundreds of thousands of Islamic forces. Because of their stand for Europe and the Lord Jesus Christ, the Islamic plan to take Europe was thwarted. As we end the second millennium, again we need to be on the watch for the hunters.

Where is the resistance movement today? Where is the resistance movement in prayer that is stopping Islam? Where is the resistance movement that is sharing the Good News with the Muslims? I believe that we're living in the days of the hunters.

> **"But now I will send for many fishermen," declares the LORD, "and they will catch them. After that I will send for many hunters, and they will hunt them down on every mountain and hill and from the crevices of the rocks" (Jeremiah 16:16).**

God in His mercy sends the fishers to help His people return to Israel. The fishers are good people who are helping the Jewish people come back to Israel—people like Jabotinsky who was going through Europe warning them to return. Many of you are potential fishers, if you're not already being fishermen.

We can see the potential of economic crisis coming to Europe and America. The Jewish people have always been blamed for economic problems. There have even been trials in France where they've been blamed, such as the Dreyfus Case. We know economic shakings are coming. We know terrorism is on the rise. Now is the time of God's mercy, days of prevention when the Jewish people can go back in ease with all their finances.

One day I was praying and the Lord showed me trains and planes going back to Israel. The locomotive was coming out of Russia, but behind the locomotive were many cars on the train going back to Israel. Thank God this train is not going to Auschwitz, it's going to Jerusalem. I remember something I saw on the walls in Auschwitz when I was there several years ago. It said, "He who does not learn from the lessons of history is doomed to repeat them." Unfortunately about 90% of the Jewish people in Europe were killed in the Holocaust because they did not hear God's voice warning them to leave.

On these trains and planes there were also many Jewish people from other places... Ukraine, South Africa, Argentina, Canada, India, the United States; cities such as London, Budapest, Los Angeles, Miami, Philadelphia, Chicago, Boston, New York, Paris, Lyon and Marseilles. The trains and planes are moving through the nations. The Lord is saying, "People, get ready, there's a train and a plane a-coming picking up passengers from coast to coast, country to country, bringing them back to their homeland in Israel."

## Fishers to Pray, to Warn, to Encourage

As God's fishers in these last days, there are three things we can do before the hunters come—the hunters are the anti-Semitic people, such as neo-Nazis, Islamic Fundamentalists, etc.

First of all, we can pray. The Lord says that He will bring people to His holy mountain and give them joy in His house of prayer. He says that He will make His house a house of prayer for all nations (Isaiah 56:7). He then declares that He will gather the exiles of Israel that have not yet been gathered (v.8). We need to pray for the Jewish people in all nations to be gathered back to Israel.

"I will surely gather all of you, O Jacob; I will surely bring together the remnant of Israel. I will bring them together like sheep in a pen, like a flock in its pasture; the place will throng with people. One who breaks open the way will go up before them; they will break through the gate and go out. Their king will pass through before them, the LORD at their head" (Micah 2:12-13).

"Do not be afraid, for I am with you; I will bring your children from the east and gather you from the west. I will say to the north, "Give them up!" and to the south, "Do not hold them back." Bring my sons from afar and my daughters from the ends of the earth—everyone who is called by my name, whom I created for my glory, whom I formed and made" (Isaiah 43:5-7).

Secondly, as fishers, we need to warn the Jewish people. The book I wrote about *Aliyah* is now in twenty languages. I believe it's becoming a prophetic word in these days, for Europe and the Americas as well. Some people believe that the fishermen need some bait, and tens of thousands of people have given this book to their Jewish neighbors. Many of you work and live with Jewish people. God wants you to intercede to break the stronghold of materialism and to warn and encourage them to come back to their homeland.

"Behold, I will send for many fishers" (Jeremiah 16:16 KJV). I believe this is a *rhema* word for today. The Lord is now sending many fishers throughout the world.

Thirdly, the Lord says that we should help the Jewish people return to Israel, financially or in whatever way we can. Isaiah 49:22 says that God will beckon to the Gentiles, and they will carry them back to Israel on their shoulders and in their arms. In the first century, the Jewish people took the gospel to the Gentiles in the four corners of the earth. Now God is saying to the Christian Gentiles, "Watch for the hunters, and help the Jewish people come back to Jerusalem and to their Messiah in these last days."

*May God bless you and use you as His watchmen, as His fishers, as His intercessors, to help His people to be delivered from the hunters and to come back to their homeland and to their Messiah. May the Jewish people watch for the hunters and flee: Don't wait for the hunters—make Aliyah to Israel in God's time of mercy and grace before the difficult days come. God bless you.*

I urge anyone who is willing to make yourself available to be God's watchman for Israel, to be God's intercessor for Israel, to be God's fisher; to say: "I'm willing to do whatever God wants me to do, and I make myself available to You, Lord, King of the Jews."

*Father, we lift up each person to You. Father, we believe You for Your increased anointing of intercession upon our brothers and sisters, and for the release of the Jewish people to their land and to their Lord. We believe You to give them, true watchmen for the hunters, the boldness and the courage to speak to the Jewish people as You direct them, to encourage them to make Aliyah to Israel and to their God! We also believe You, Lord God, to enable them to help financially and whatever other way, in helping the Jewish people to come back from the nations. Thank You that You will bless those who bless Your Jewish people, according to Your Word, "I will bless those who bless you" (Genesis 12:3). In Jesus' name. Amen*

# Chapter 12

# Watching the Fig Tree and All the Trees

## Prophetic Prayer Focuses for World Redemption

As Jesus taught His disciples about the signs of the end of the age,

> **He told them this parable: "Look at [watch] the fig tree and all the trees. When they sprout leaves, you can see for yourselves and know that summer is near. Even so, when you see these things happening, you know that the kingdom of God is near" (Luke 21:29-31).**

The fig tree symbolizes Israel. We can see this throughout the Old Testament. The Lord is saying that when the fig tree (Israel) and all the other trees (all nations) blossom, when they start sprouting leaves, we know that the coming of the Lord is near.

In 1967 three things began happening that were signs of the end times. For the first time in thousands of years, Jerusalem came under a Jewish government, as Luke 21:24 says would happen: **"Jerusalem will be trampled on by the Gentiles until the times of the Gentiles are fulfilled."** Just like the wall in Berlin later came down, so did the wall in Jerusalem. This happened during the Six Day War, and the Jewish people went to the Western Wall of the Temple. As they were weeping, God began to pour out the Holy Spirit and reveal Messiah to them.

At that time there were only one hundred or so indigenous Messianic believers in Israel and a few thousand in the world. Today there are approximately three hundred thousand Messianic believers in Israel and the world—some say more. The fig tree is blossoming. It is like a small wave beginning to build which will climax in the veil being completely lifted from the eyes of Israel as they come to their Messiah, mourning for the one they have pierced (Zechariah 12:10).

In 1967, as the times of the Gentiles began to be fulfilled and the Jewish people began to receive Messiah, it was only a beginning. Actually more Gentiles have received Messiah since 1967 than in all history since the time of Jesus' birth. As the wave of the Gentiles reaches a crescendo, the fullness of the Gentiles will come into the olive tree, and then the natural branches will be fully grafted back into their own olive tree. According to Luke 21:32, this generation (since 1967) will not pass until this is fulfilled. I'm not sure if it is a 40-year generation or a 70-year generation, but I believe He is coming in this generation!

> **"And this gospel of the kingdom will be preached in the whole world as a testimony to all nations, and then the end will come" (Matthew 24:14).**

We know that Jesus is coming back, the end is coming when the gospel of the kingdom is preached to all the nations of the world. We see this is beginning to happen rapidly. There are hardly any nations to whom the gospel has not been preached. The gospel is now going into Albania, Mongolia, Cuba, Libya, Pakistan, Afghanistan, Kazakhstan, Kyrgyzstan, Tajikstan, Turkmenistan, Uzbekistan, Maldives, Comoro Islands, all the Arab Nations, and even Israel. The curtains have now been pulled back from all the nations.

But *ethnos*, the Greek word for "nations," doesn't mean just the larger nations of the world. It also means people groups, language/culture groups. There are still approximately ten thousand such groups where a local church is not planted. The end will come when there's a witness of the gospel established in each "nation" of the world—not only the larger nations, but also the smaller nations, the *ethnos*, the language/culture groups of the world. In places around the world such as China, India, and many of the Muslim nations, there are still numerous people groups who don't have a church established among them.

But there is a plan, and people are working towards this happening, possibly by the year 2001 or soon after. So we need to be

God's watchmen, praying, interceding, believing God and working to see this accomplished—that the Great Commission will soon be completely fulfilled. When this is accomplished, the end will come. It's not the end of eternity; it's the end of this age. Then Jesus is coming back to put His feet on the Mount of Olives, and we're going to live in a new heaven and a new earth!

Matthew 24:14 refers primarily to the Gentile nations. Regarding Israel:

> **I do not want you to be ignorant of this mystery, brothers, so that you may not be conceited: Israel has experienced a hardening in part until the full number of the Gentiles has come in. And so all Israel will be saved, as it is written: "The deliverer will come from Zion; he will turn godlessness away from Jacob. And this is my covenant with them when I take away their sins"** (Romans 11:25-27).

At the time of the fullness of the Gentiles, God is going to lift the veil completely from the eyes of the Jewish people. It's already beginning, but it won't be completely lifted until the fullness of the Gentiles comes into the kingdom.

In 1992, in the Jerusalem House of Prayer for All Nations, the Lord revealed that He wanted us to pray for five geographical areas of the world, starting with the center and extending outward. Those areas are Jerusalem, Israel, the Arab-Jewish Middle East, the remaining 10/40 Window nations, and all the rest of the nations. Then, in January of 1996, He revealed three other areas—ourselves, those closest to us, and our community leaders—making a total of eight, representing new beginnings. Jesus is coming soon, and we will enter a new millennium.

## 1. Watching Ourselves

Romans 14:12 says each man will have to give an account before God for his own life. So our first responsibility is to watch over our own life—to make sure that we are abiding in the vine, and His Word is abiding in us. We need to be certain that we have oil in our lamps, and are ready for His coming, secure in Him as a part of the blossoming of the fig tree or the other trees, as a Jew or Gentile.

Jesus warned in Matthew 26:41: **"Watch and pray so that you will not fall into temptation."** May God first help us to be faithful watchmen, in watching Him and His Word and in watching over our own lives, as well as being faithful watchmen to whatever degree He calls us to beyond ourselves.

## 2. Watching Others Closest to Us

In our case, this is *Messianic Community of Reconciliation*. In your case, it may be your family, your community or house fellow-ship, an expression of God's Church in your city, or all three.

Our first responsibility beyond ourselves is to watch over those for whom God has given us direct responsibility. This may be our family, husband, wife, children or home fellowship group. Like Jesus with the three or twelve disciples—that was His family. The Bible says God sets the solitary in families (Psalm 68:6). It is not healthy to be an isolated Christian. It is interesting that only twelve molecules can be joined to one atom at a time. I believe it is no accident that Jesus had twelve disciples in His closest community. He was following God's natural laws.

In Jerusalem we average twelve full-time Community Members in *Messianic Community of Reconciliation*. Those involved with us full time over the last ten years have been Jewish, Arab, Chinese, Indian, French, African, German, Japanese, Dutch, Papua New Guinean, Australian, Spanish, Russian, Canadian and American, as well as others from most all the major cultures and languages of the world!

We live together in community. With us, literally "the world is a community" in Jesus! As in the Messianic Congregation in Jerusalem in the first century (Acts 2:42), we worship and pray together daily (an average of two hours corporately, as well as individually at least one or two hours a day), break bread (Communion) each day, fellowship and have regular times of teaching. We also share the love of God in our city and work together as a servant community of *Jerusalem House of Prayer for All Nations*.

This Community is home. We are seeking first His kingdom. Every person and every culture must be submitted first to His kingdom and culture for us to be living in unity and spiritual awakening. We live on the Mount of Olives where Jesus prayed the Lord's Prayer:

> **"Our Father who art in heaven,...Thy kingdom come, Thy will be done on earth as it is in heaven" (Matthew 6:9-10 NASB).**

I feel as if we are praying the Lord's Prayer, representing all the major regions of the world as a type of first fruit of Isaiah 56:4-8.

God speaks to us many times through each other as co-watchmen together in the community! We need one another and are dependent upon each other to function in this community, even as a physical body, and are blessed with great diversity of gifts from many cultures and nations.

As one can imagine, there are many challenges between different personalities, cultures and languages as God is preparing us on earth to be together in heaven. Isaiah 31:9 says Israel is the fire and Jerusalem is the furnace, so living in community in Jerusalem is like living in the fiery furnace! But Jesus is our Chief Shepherd. He and the pastors of our Community are watching over us spiritually, and the blessings are greater than the challenges.

*As we are co-watchmen with the Lord over those He calls us to as a community, may all our needs be met, and may we be continually protected, blessed and sheltered as a community. May we have the grace to watch and pray and serve together in the Lord's purpose, to see the full blossoming of the trees of the nations and of the fig tree, Israel, in preparation for His coming back to the Mount of Olives.*

## 3. Watching Community Leaders

> **"... that all of them may be one, Father, just as you are in me and I am in you. May they also be in us so that the world may believe that you have sent me" (John 17:21).**

Mount of Olives spiritual leaders (watchmen) meet to pray and share together! At this writing, this is the end of my tenth year living on the Mount of Olives. Last year I met some of my neighbors for the first time, and was surprised to find that one of my closest neighbors is a born again Greek Orthodox Priest. He had an open vision in Greece at the age of seven, calling him to come to the Mount of Olives to pray for the return of the glory of God and Jesus to this mountain!

My other neighbor is a born again Catholic, the only non-cloistered member of the nearby Carmelite community who are committed to meditation on the Holy Scriptures day and night and who love Jesus very much.

For the past year, five leaders on the Mount of Olives—the Greek Orthodox Priest, the Catholic Carmelite, a leader of the Protestant Lutheran Sisters of Mary, a Dutch Reformed leader and myself, all born again believers—have been meeting to pray together for two hours every other month. This has been very special, as the Mount of Olives is the very place Jesus went after He prayed the high priestly prayer just before He died, was raised from the dead and ascended into heaven, *"that all of them may be one"* (John 17:21). Now at this very place born again believers who live here on the Mount of Olives, representing the different historic and present streams of the Church, are praying to the Father to make us one, for all born again believers worldwide. This was born out of persecution and early morning prayer.

For nine years I would awaken to the Muslim prayers at 4:00 A.M. In October 1995, for one week, I could not go back to sleep. I thought of binding the enemy, but then God spoke to me, "This is not the enemy, this is Me." He said, "I want you to rise and lead the community in 4:00-6:00 A.M. prayer on Fridays and Sundays for the blessing of Abraham in the Messiah to come to both of the natural sons of Abraham, the Jews and the Arabs. He said He wanted us to begin the day worshiping Him and placing Him in the Highest Place as the Great High Priest, and to celebrate the resurrection. We began this and have been doing so ever since!

A few days later I met my closest neighbor, the Greek Priest, for the first time, as well as the Carmelite leader. God called the five of us to meet to pray. Just before this, the mother of the Priest was martyred at their house, and our houses were being broken into. In many ways I believe God birthed this fellowship of spiritual leaders (watching) on the Mount of Olives out of persecution and beginning early morning prayer as we began to put Jesus first in the Highest Place at the beginning of the day.

Pray that God will help us to be watchmen, for protection over our communities and each others' communities, and for the salvation of those living on this mountain. May we continually live the high priestly prayer that the Father will make us one (all true believers on earth) that the world may know He has sent His Son (John 17:21), preparing the way for the fullness of the Gentiles to come in and for the salvation of Israel.

## 4. Watching for Jerusalem

> **I have posted watchmen on your walls, O Jerusalem; they will never be silent day or night. You who call on the LORD, give yourselves no rest, and give him no rest till he establishes Jerusalem and makes her the praise of the earth (Isaiah 62:6-7).**

Jerusalem is literally in the center of the world; it's like the "navel" of the earth. We all know that the gospel began in Jerusalem, and Jewish believers went all around the world with the gospel. Now we see that the places the Good News has reached the least in the world are Jerusalem, Israel and the Arab countries. It's as though we're coming full circle. Now we're seeing a critical need to pray especially for this region that has been reached least with the Good News.

Today missiologists call this region, centered in Jerusalem, the *10/40 Window*, which includes North Africa, the Middle East, India, China, the whole distance to Japan and many countries in between. The Lord showed us that because we live in Jerusalem and it's the very center of the *10/40 Window*, we should spend much time praying for Jerusalem.

All Christians in the world are commanded to **"Pray for the peace of Jerusalem: May those who love you be secure (prosper)"** **(Psalm 122:6 NIV/KJV).** We are also called to intercede for the city in which we live: **"Also, seek the peace and prosperity of the city [for in its peace you will find peace] to which I have carried you into exile" (Jeremiah 29:7)**, we who live in Jerusalem have to pray double. But you, wherever you are, are commanded to pray for the city of Jerusalem as well as for your own city.

In Jerusalem today there are about six congregations of Arab believers and twelve congregations of Messianic believers. We need to pray that God will bring them together in increasing ways. There's been a small beginning, but I believe God wants to join them together in a much fuller and very intimate way, to pray and fellowship together.

I also pray that God will lift the veil of replacement theology from many of the Arab believers who are blinded to God's purposes for Israel. I believe that Jewish and Arab believers flowing together are the strongest foundation for the unity of the body of Messiah in Jerusalem. Pray especially for the coming together of the pastors, because they will lead the flock into unity. Every three months we meet together, as Jewish and Arab and international leaders, for prayer and fellowship.

We also need to pray for revival among the believers in Jerusalem, that they would spend more time in prayer and fasting, believing God for the fullness of the revival that He's purposed for our City. Many people visit during the conferences, holidays and other times of the year, but living in Jerusalem is much different than coming for a big event. The warfare in Jerusalem and the Middle East is probably more intense than in any other place in the world, due to the end-time battles, in the natural and spiritual, that are focused on this city, culminating in the coming of Messiah.

Pray also for both religious orthodox Jewish people and secular Jewish people, that they trust in God and their Bible and know their Messiah. There is so much division among them. Many of the secular are atheists or agnostics and politically liberal, while the religious are more politically conservative and more based in the Old Testament—and only Messiah can unite them.

## 5. Watching for Israel

The Lord showed us that we need to pray for Israel. All the nations of the world are going to come against Israel and against Jerusalem. It's the land of the Bible, where Messiah is coming back. Much prayer is needed for Israel.

A book was written about twenty years ago called *The Fig Tree Blossoms*[1], based on Luke 21:29-31. It speaks of 1967, when Jerusalem became a united city under Jewish rule for the first time in thousands of years. Not only did something happen in the natural, but spiritually the fig tree began blossoming. There were only three or four Messianic congregations in Israel at that time. Now there are about fifty congregations in addition to all the Orthodox congregations! We know the fig tree is beginning to blossom; we know that Messiah is coming back soon.

Messianic congregations are being raised up in every major town all over the country from Kiryat Shmona in the north all the way down to Eilat in the south. There are congregations in Haifa, Netanya, Nahariah, Ashdod, Tel Aviv, Jerusalem, Tiberias, Be'er Sheva, and in many other towns all over the land, in many places where there were none since the first century. God is raising up congregations all over the land of Israel! The fig tree is beginning to blossom in Israel, in the natural and in the spiritual. God is restoring His people to Himself. He's grafting the natural branches back into the olive tree. Hallelujah! God is working!

At the same time, many Arabs are receiving the Lord in different parts of the country. In a number of places the Arab congregations who have church buildings have opened the doors of their churches to the new Messianic congregations being birthed. They're saying, "We want you to use our building on Saturday. We meet on Sunday, but the Jewish believers meet on Saturdays." Now new congregations

---

1.   Paul Liberman, *The Fig Tree Blossoms*, Fountain Pr., 1976.

are starting in the West Bank, and three radio stations are opening to reach the Arabs with the Good News. We don't hear about these things on CNN or on BBC. All we hear is the bad news, but the Good News is permeating the land of Israel! God is reconciling the Jewish and Arab believers to Himself in Israel. We need to continue to pray that this will grow, and that the Good News of Messiah will permeate the land of Israel.

Within the past decades, more believers are coming to Israel from other nations. Many have come from Russia; many are beginning to come from the United States; many have come from France, from South Africa, from all over the world. It's time for the ark to come back to Jerusalem! Remember what happened in the time of David: He brought back the ark. What was the ark? It was the presence of God.

Where is the presence of God today? Among the Jewish people, it's in the Jewish people who trust in their God, the *Ruach HaKodesh* (Holy Spirit) and Messiah are the ones who have received the Holy Spirit. I believe it's time for the ark to come back to Jerusalem again. God wants to bring His presence back to Jerusalem—by pouring out His Spirit upon the people who are there and drawing them into the kingdom and also by bringing the believing Jews back to the land. Hallelujah!

## 6. Watching and Praying for the Arab-Jewish Middle East

The sixth area where God is working is referred to in Isaiah 19:23-25:

*In that day there will be a highway from Egypt to Assyria. The Assyrians will go to Egypt and the Egyptians to Assyria. The Egyptians and Assyrians will worship together. In that day Israel will be the third, along with Egypt and Assyria, a blessing on the earth. The LORD Almighty will bless them, saying, "Blessed be Egypt my people, Assyria my handiwork, and Israel my inheritance" (Isaiah 19:23-25).*

**He has set his foundation on the holy mountain; the LORD loves the gates of Zion more than all the dwellings**

of Jacob. Glorious things are said of you, O city of God: "I will record Rahab and Babylon among those who acknowledge me—Philistia too, and Tyre, along with Cush—and will say, 'This one was born in Zion.'" Indeed, of Zion it will be said, "This one and that one were born in her, and the Most High himself will establish her." The LORD will write in the register of the peoples: "This one was born in Zion." As they make music they will sing, "All my fountains are in you" (Psalm 87).

Therefore, remember that formerly you who are Gentiles by birth and called "uncircumcised" by those who call themselves "the circumcision" (that done in the body by the hands of men)—remember that at that time you were separate from Christ, excluded from citizenship in Israel and foreigners to the covenants of the promise, without hope and without God in the world. But now in Christ Jesus you who once were far away have been brought near through the blood of Christ.

For he himself is our peace, who has made the two one and has destroyed the barrier, the dividing wall of hostility, by abolishing in his flesh the law with its commandments and regulations. His purpose was to create in himself one new man out of the two, thus making peace, and in this one body to reconcile both of them to God through the cross, by which he put to death their hostility. He came and preached peace to you who were far away and peace to those who were near. For through him we both have access to the Father by one Spirit (Ephesians 2:11-18).

For many centuries, many millennia, one couldn't say that the Middle East has been a blessing in the midst of the earth. But the Lord says that this region is going to become a blessing in the midst of the earth. It's going to take a miracle in the midst of many shakings! God is beginning to do something in the Middle East. He is beginning to shake and tear down many things that are opposed to His purposes so that the highway of Isaiah 19 can be built.

In January of 1993, we coordinated a meeting in Cairo, Egypt where thirty pastors from Israel came together with fifty pastors from Egypt. It was a great miracle, because the last place the Jewish people wanted to go was back to Egypt! God is doing something by the Holy Spirit. I simply wrote a letter to the pastors in Israel and approximately 75 to 80% of those to whom I wrote sensed God's leading to go along to Egypt. Almost half the pastors in Israel went to Egypt! We spent three days praying for each other—the Egyptian pastors for the Israeli pastors and vice versa. We had a worship team called the Egyptian-Israeli Worship Team. Three Messianic pastors and two Arab leaders were on the worship team, and God's presence fell very strongly as we sang Arabic and Hebrew songs together and prayed for revival in both countries.

It's interesting to note that it says that this highway is going to begin in Egypt. It even says **"blessed be Egypt my people."** In most places in Scripture when "my people" are mentioned, it's referring to the Jewish people. That can also have a spiritual application to the Church, but here it says, **"Egypt my people."** That's very unusual. When you think of Egypt, perhaps you think of Pharaoh and all the Egyptians being drowned in the Red Sea! You don't think of **"Egypt my people."** But God is going to bring a big revival in Egypt and they'll become the people of God. They'll receive the Lord. He says there will be a highway from Egypt to Israel to Assyria. This includes Iraq and Syria. It also includes Lebanon and Jordan. You can see God is shaking all these nations on both ends of the highway.

One end of the highway is in Cairo, Egypt, where a major earthquake took place in October of 1992. More than 540 were killed, 6,500 injured and about 8,300 buildings damaged. God is shaking the whole highway. Even in Israel there are many shakings. God is allowing this shaking because He wants to bring many people into His kingdom. He wants to reconcile the Jews and Arabs together in Him. On the other end of the highway is Baghdad, Iraq. There has been much shaking with the war and bombings. But there's a big revival coming even there. Many Iraqis are receiving salvation as a result of the situation.

In June of 1993, we coordinated our first meeting in Cyprus, where twenty-six pastors came together from ten different Middle Eastern nations. Pastors came from all the countries surrounding Israel, including Saudi Arabia—from nine Arab countries and from Israel. The Israeli representatives were both Arab and Jewish leaders. This is the first time something like this has happened. There were six Jewish pastors and twenty Arab pastors, and a tremendous unity formed among us as we were together. Pastors were from Israel and Lebanon, Syria, Iraq, Kuwait, Jordan, Egypt, Saudi Arabia, Bahrain, Oman, almost all the countries from the Asian-Arab nations. We spent four days together sharing, praying and interceding together. The congregations are growing in all these countries!

Including the Cairo meeting, we have met nine times as Jewish and Arab leaders representing all the Arab nations and Israel. Of the next eight meetings, six were in Cyprus and two were part of *All Nations Convocation Jerusalem*. We can see that God has birthed the first fruit of Isaiah 19:23-25!

During one meeting, the Holy Spirit was focusing on unity between the body of believers in Egypt and Israel; another time on Syria and Israel; twice on Jordan and Israel (with an earthquake happening in Jordan and Israel just a few hours after one of these two meetings); another time on the western part of the *10/40 Window* from Morocco to Iraq; and once on unity of the whole body of believers from different streams of the Church from different nations in the Middle East. The last time we met in Cyprus, the focus was on Lebanon and Israel. A year in advance, we planned to meet one day ahead with brothers from Lebanon and Israel. As we met (it just happened to be during the difficult time between Lebanon and Israel, *Operation Grapes of Wrath*) God did a special thing in bringing reconciliation between the spiritual leaders of these nations!

I was in Baghdad in 1995, where there is a congregation of almost one thousand believers. There is a growing movement of prayer and many people are coming into the kingdom since the Gulf War, which has brought an openness to the gospel in the country.

Also, many Bibles have come into the country, and now they even print Bibles there.

I was greatly blessed on a recent trip to Kuwait, where God is moving in a special way. Over twenty thousand believers meet in one compound, thirty-five congregations from seventy nations speaking twenty-two languages. They have also begun a *House of Prayer for All Nations* and a *24-hour Prayer Watch*. Many Arabs are turning to Jesus!

God is also working in Saudi Arabia. It is estimated that there may be close to fifty thousand believers in that country. Many from other nations came to know God while working in Saudi Arabia. I have talked with many people from the United States who received the Lord in Saudi Arabia. One factor leading to revival there is that there's not much to do and people get bored—so they get to know God! It's the best place to go to know God! I never would have dreamed it, but that's what is happening. And these people are becoming intercessors for Saudi Arabia, praying for God to pour out His Holy Spirit. Many are coming to know the Lord. In fact, Jesus has been sovereignly appearing at the Black Stone in Mecca and revealing Himself to people there. I believe we're going to see a great revival in that country; that God is going to intervene and the name of the Lord will be lifted up.

The Christian Missionary Alliance Church in Syria, which had only five congregations about ten years ago, now has close to twenty! The Good News is spreading throughout Syria. In Lebanon the churches are growing. It's a real media center, where the Good News is going out all over the Middle East through radio and television. In Egypt there are congregations that have over one thousand believers. In Morocco, Algeria, Lebanon, Sudan and Jordan, congregations are growing. In all these nations, the Church is born and growing very well. So we can see the Good News is spreading all over the Middle East.

We need to pray for the government leaders in the Middle East because some of them are open to the Good News, at least in limited ways. While most of them are not strongly supportive of Israel, and some not supportive of Israel at all, most are against Islamic

Fundamentalists. Sometimes we think these leaders are not the best, but they could be a lot worse. The fact that they're standing against Islamic Fundamentalism and that some are allowing the Good News to be shared is a miracle. So we need to lift up these leaders before the Lord.

You may recall the situation when the Shah of Iran was in power. He was thought to be very bad and the United States used its pressure to have him removed. But after him came Khomeini, who activated Islamic Fundamentalism. So we need to be grateful that the Arab leaders in the Middle East are basically standing against Islamic Fundamentalism in Saudi Arabia, Iraq, Syria, and all over the Middle East. Mubarek is standing very strongly against it in Egypt. As Muslim leaders, they're actually more open to the Good News than they are to Islamic Fundamentalism. So we need to pray that God would cause them to continue to stand strong, that the Good News would go forward and triumph.

A pastor friend of mine in Czechoslovakia went to heaven and God brought him back to life. When he was in heaven he saw in the spirit that Communism was going to be overthrown in Russia, and how it was going to happen. He saw the demonic forces moving out of Russia and going into the Middle East. It's interesting that since the fall of Communism in Russia there's been an increasing escalation of terrorism and Islamic Fundamentalism in the Middle East. The principle makes sense, because the evil forces have to be embodied in something; if Communism fell, those spirits would indeed be looking elsewhere. But if God be for us, who can be against us? He has triumphed over all evil forces through the cross of Christ. Although we are as sheep sent to the slaughter, in all these things we are more than conquerors through Christ who loves us! (Romans 8:31-39)

## 7. Watching - Praying for the Rest of the 10/40 Window

**From the west [Morocco], men will fear the name of the LORD, and from the rising of the sun [Japan], they will revere his glory. For he will come like a pent-up flood that**

**the breath of the LORD drives along. "The Redeemer will come to Zion, to those in Jacob who repent of their sins," declares the LORD (Isaiah 59:19-20).**

The seventh area that we'll consider is the rest of the *10/40 Window*. As we look at a map of the center of the world, we can see Morocco, across Northern Africa to Israel, the Middle East, through the Arab-Muslim Middle East, India, China, and over to Japan. In this area live 1.1 billion Muslims, 1 billion Hindus, and 600 million Buddhists, totaling 2.7 billion people—over half of the world's population. This region is the least evangelized part of the whole world, anywhere from zero to a maximum of 10% evangelized, while all the rest of the world is over 10% at least nominal Christian, if not born again. Some nations are almost 50% born again. Right in the center of this region is Israel, from where the Good News went to the four corners of the earth in the first century. I believe that the Lord also wants us to focus on this area, the rest of the *10/40 Window*.

In September of 1993, we had a week in *Jerusalem House of Prayer for All Nations* where we prayed for all these nations. There are almost sixty nations in this *10/40 Window*. We spent one-half to one and one-half hours praying for each one. Representatives from many *10/40 Window* nations came to Jerusalem to join with us in prayer. Others living in Jerusalem who originated from those nations also joined with us as we focused our prayer on the three main religions of this region.

During the summer of 1993, we led a Watchman Prayer Mission of thirteen intercessors to China where we did a Jericho March around Tienanmen Square, praying for God to intervene among the Buddhists. We were also in Bombay and marched around the largest temple in Bombay, believing God to intervene regarding Hinduism. Earlier we had gone to the Arab World Center and prayed for God to intervene in bringing the Arabs to know Him. So we're believing, as are many people around the world, that God is going to bring a big revival across this entire region.

During the first week of October 1993, teams of intercessors from the United States, Europe and different parts of the world were sent into the *10/40 Window*. They spent a number of days in intercession in all these countries. So while there have been proportionately very few believers in many of these countries, there is a major prayer focus, believing God for the fulfillment of the Great Commission in this least evangelized part of the world. And God is working! In September 1995, we held a second *10/40 Window Convocation* in *Jerusalem House of Prayer for All Nations*, and again we prayed over all *10/40 Window* nations. Many breakthroughs took place and the following month teams were sent into all those nations.

We know there are many problems in some of those countries, such as the problems that have taken place in Somalia, an Arab nation for which much prayer is needed. While the Christian world was fighting the hardest for the Muslims in Iraq, many Christians in Somalia were being killed and the Christian world was doing little, if anything, about it. The same thing happened in Syria a number of years ago, and the Christian world did not respond. I believe we need to learn to defend our own people at least as much as we're defending the Muslims! We need to stand in the gap in intercession, and the Christian nations should be doing whatever they can to defend the rights of Christians in other parts of the world.

One nation on which we really need to focus our prayers in these days is Sudan. It's the only Arab nation out of eighteen countries in the whole Arab world that is strongly Islamic Fundamentalist. Located on the border, their strategy is to take Egypt. They're sending many Islamic Fundamentalists into Egypt. Their strategy is to take the whole Arab world and to kill the Christians. In Sudan many Christians have been killed, and it was reported that twenty thousand Christian children were taken from their parents.

We need to believe that God will intervene in whatever way in the Sudan, through military means, through intercession, and that Islamic Fundamentalists will receive the Lord and become peace-loving, and that the Good News will triumph over this nation. Many years ago, before the missionaries were ordered out, there was an organization called the Sudan Interior Mission, and many other missionary organizations that God had used in tremendous ways in the Sudan. I believe we really need to focus our prayer on Sudan in these days, that revival will continue to grow and spread.

Pray also for the Turko-Persian region where over two hundred million people live, mostly Muslim, and only about twenty-five thousand born again indigenous believers. The indigenous church was almost totally liquidated in this region hundreds of years ago. But today it has been reborn in every nation—and is growing. Hallelujah!

There was also a war in Afghanistan, said to be as bad if not worse than in Yugoslavia. There was very little media coverage because the press couldn't get in. Some people believe there could be up to a million Jews from the ten lost tribes hidden in Islam in Afghanistan. I believe the war torn nation of Afghanistan is also an important nation for which we should pray. Continue to pray for the many problems now between Muslims and Christians in Bosnia, which was part of Yugoslavia. Pray for the Good News to penetrate that area.

In northern India there have been tremendous wars between the Muslims and the Hindus. In Kashmir it's been going on for quite awhile, continually getting worse. There are hidden Jews in that area, people who light candles on *Shabbat*, but who are hidden in Islam. We need to focus prayer on these areas that we may not hear so much about. Pray for their salvation.

It's very important that we're watching not just the areas that the news media is telling us about, but the areas that the Holy Spirit is bringing to our remembrance for prayer. The news media isn't following the Holy Spirit as much as following whatever is politically advantageous, what makes good news. There are many hidden things we need to be praying for that only the Holy Spirit will bring to our remembrance. We look forward to when the Good News of the Lord through the Holy Spirit will cover the *10/40 Window* as the waters cover the sea.

## 8. Watching - Praying for All the Rest of the Nations

**"These I will bring to my holy mountain and give them joy in my house of prayer. Their burnt offerings and**

sacrifices will be accepted on my altar; for *my house will be called a house of prayer for all nations.*" **The Sovereign LORD declares—he who gathers the exiles of Israel: "I will gather still others to them besides those already gathered" (Isaiah 56:7-8).**

The last area for which we must pray is all the rest of the nations of the world. In Isaiah 56:7-8 the Lord says, **"My house will be called a house of prayer for all nations,"** so God wants us to pray for all nations. In our *House of Prayer* we pray for all the nations of the world.

All nations really need prayer. One country that has been in total disarray, where there has been much bloodshed, is the French-speaking nation of Zaire. We had difficulty even communicating with them because of the situation. It was one of the most beautiful countries in Africa, with many resources, but has been totally devastated by its leadership. A 24-hour Prayer Watch has begun there, and the Lord has recently answered our prayers. Their leader for about thirty years has been replaced, a new government formed, and the nation renamed Congo Kinshasa. We need to continue to pray that God's full destiny for this nation will be realized. Neighboring nations of Rwanda and Burundi also need God's intervention from heaven.

Liberia is also at war, and there's much prayer needed. We also need to continue to pray for South Africa, and a breakthrough for Ireland between the Catholics and Protestants, that God's purposes will be worked out. The Lord wants us to be a house of prayer for all nations, and we need to allow the Holy Spirit to direct us in our prayers, especially for the most important prayer focuses: *unity and spiritual authority in the Church* and the *salvation of souls*, the fulfillment of the Great Commission! This is what Jesus shed His blood for. Pray that the fullness of the Gentiles will come into the kingdom of God and Israel will receive Messiah and that the natural branches and wild olive branches will be one in Messiah.

In September 1994, *All Nations Convocation Jerusalem* was organized, and leaders participated in Jerusalem from one hundred forty nations. We saw many breakthroughs as we prayed together for

Israel, the Arab-Jewish Middle East and all nations! This was organized by *Jerusalem House of Prayer for All Nations.* Regional Coordinators worked with us from the twenty regions of the world. There was a special gift of unity among us.

On *Yom Kippur,* at the end of the *Convocation* a Jewish leader from Jerusalem and Arabs from Jordan led Jewish and Arab leaders from throughout the Middle East in a prayer affirming the covenant between them in Messiah. They then reached out together and blessed the 140 nations represented as a prophetic act of what is said will happen in Isaiah 19:23-25. The next morning I woke up in the hotel at 4:00 A.M. and was sitting in my chair when *an earthquake occurred* centered in Jerusalem and Amman, Jordan. It reminded me of Revelation 8:3-5 where it says an angel lifted the prayers of the saints up before God and an earthquake occurred on the earth.

The second *All Nations Convocation Jerusalem* was held in the City of the Great King (Jerusalem) from September 13-26, 1996. Praying pastors and prayer leaders (including the leading pastors in many nations) gathered from 188 nations to worship and present their nations' prayer needs to the King of Kings in His city, during the ten Days of Awe. (On the Jewish calendar this is from *Rosh HaShana*, the Feast of Trumpets—the Jewish New Year—until *Yom Kippur*, the Biblical Day of Atonement.) Many believe this is the time of the 2000th anniversary of His birth and the 3000th anniversary of the reign of His forefather, King David, in Jerusalem (Isaiah 9:7).

God did a corporate work of grafting the Church from the nations (Gentiles) into the Olive Tree (the Jewish people), and grafting the Natural Branches back spiritually into their own Olive Tree (Romans 11:11-24). This included fasting on Friday for the blessing upon the Arabs, and on *Yom Kippur* for the *Aliyah* and blessing of the Jewish people, that they would all come to know God.

We were very encouraged by the continual gift of unity God gave the twenty-four of us from the twenty regions of the world as we served together as Regional Coordinators for the *Convocation.*

The seven most-needed prayer requests were presented for each nation, and then we prayed over each nation as the National

Delegate held his/her nation's flag. There were tremendous breakthroughs as one person after another repented for their nation's sins toward God and other nations. As we prayed through the world, we continued to ask forgiveness, extend forgiveness, and bless one another with much crying and remorse. We began with the Americas and Western Europe and ending on *Yom Kippur* with Gentile and Jewish believers spontaneously weeping and travailing in prayer for Zion to bring forth her children. This took place at Kibbutz Ramat Rachel where Rachel wept for her children. On the other hand, there was a great sense of joy as we worshiped the King of Jerusalem, led by some of the best Hebrew, Arabic, French and Spanish worship leaders in the world.

Leaders of 24-hour watches from different regions of the world shared. We are now in relationship with 24-hour watches in almost one hundred nations. We are believing that before the end of this century there will be 24-hour watches in every nation of the world to pray for the peace of Jerusalem, Israel and the Middle East to prepare the way for the fulfillment of Isaiah 62:6, 7 & 10. This is in addition to continual 24-hour worship and prayer in *Jerusalem House of Prayer for All Nations*. Also, for twenty-four days (from before *Rosh HaShana* until after *Sukkot*, i.e., the Feast of Tabernacles) we coordinated continual 24-hour worship on Mount Zion—probably the first time this has happened on Mount Zion in Jerusalem since the Temple times. On October 1, 1997, God birthed a 24-hour worship watch on the gates of Jerusalem. See the report of *Jerusalem Watch of the King* in Chapter 9 for further information on this watch.

We had a special luncheon for Christian government leaders, including the Queen of Lesotho, chiefs of two different sections of South Africa, the head of the Supreme Court of French Polynesia, government ministers of the Solomon Islands and Palau, and the wife of a candidate for the presidential elections in Nicaragua. Leaders of dozens of nations testified that their nations have now opened diplomatic relations with Israel in answer to prayers from the first *Convocation*.

Also, in over eighty locations around the world there were *Simultaneous Convocations* where large or small groups of watchmen joined with us in simultaneous prayer throughout the ten days of the *Convocation*. As we said many times, *the nations will never be the same!*

As we did a special prayer walk from *Jerusalem House of Prayer for All Nations* on the Mount of Olives (from where Jesus entered Jerusalem on a donkey) we carried palm branches and had a white donkey leading. Jesus will come back on a white horse soon! We stopped at the crest of the Mount of Olives (where Jesus said the veil was over the eyes of the Jewish people and that the Gospel was opened to the Gentiles). There everyone prayed in his own language for the fullness of the Gentiles from the nations to come into the kingdom, and then two Messianic pastors prayed for the Holy Spirit to be poured out upon Israel.

Twenty-four pastors led the National Delegates from all the nations on different prayer tours through all the cities and villages of Israel, for God's peace plan to prevail through the Prince of Peace. Man's peace plan will ultimately fail, but God's peace plan will be successful because Messiah is the Prince of Peace (Isaiah 9:6-7)!

In Jeremiah 1:10, the prophet was told to **"uproot and tear down, to destroy and overthrow, to build and to plant."** The veil will have to be removed from the eyes of the Arab and Jewish people before God's peace plan will prevail (Isaiah 28:14-17). All of man's ways to peace will ultimately fail. In addition to all the Jewish cities, we also prayed through the Arab cities of Gaza, Nablus, Hebron, Ramallah, Jenin, etc., for God's purposes to be fulfilled with a great outpouring of the Holy Spirit, to bring many Arabs to know the Lord. As Jesus said, **"You will not finish going through the cities and villages of Israel, before the Son of Man comes!" (Matthew 10:23)** Congregations are being born in many cities and villages!

As a Gideon's army of over three hundred (close to four hundred delegates from the nations), we prayed overlooking Bet Shean and Afula in northern Israel where Gideon's army defeated the Midianites. We also prayed from Mt. Meron, the northern place where God had birthed the vision of the Prayer Tour. From Mt. Hermon, we prayed that the dew (anointing of the Holy Spirit) would fall on all the cities and villages of Israel (as pastors were leading in prayer tours over all these places)—even to the skirts of the garments, to Eilat (Psalm 133). We asked that these pastors from 188 nations represented would mobilize prayer and support from their nations for Israel!

In the first century, the Messianic Jewish leaders took the Gospel from Jerusalem to the ends of the earth. God was also speaking about restoration at *All Nations Convocation Jerusalem*. We believe as the nations are mobilized to pray for the nations and Israel that soon the fullness of the Gentiles will come in and the salvation of Israel will come back to and out of Zion. Only a few years ago there were dozens of nations with no indigenous believers. Today there are indigenous believers in all the nations of the world! At this *Convocation* we saw Christian leaders bringing the fire back to Jerusalem from all the ends of the earth: Canada, Greenland, French Polynesia, Argentina, Australia, New Zealand, Solomon Islands and representatives from all the 188 nations. We are coming full circle in history.

To our knowledge this is the most nations ever gathered in Jerusalem for any event in history. We give all the glory, honor and praise to the Great King of Jerusalem who gathered us together unto Himself. He has called us to further fulfill and advance His end-time purposes in preparing the way for His soon coming, so that He can take up His throne in Jerusalem and reign as King of the Jews and all nations.

*May God help us individually and corporately to be faithful watchmen in watching the fig tree (Israel) and all the trees (the Nations).*

# Chapter 13

# Watching for Other Signs of the End Times

In addition to "watching the fig tree and all the trees," covered in the previous chapter, we are given ten signs of the end times that we need to be watching.

In Luke 21, Jesus is speaking to His disciples about the signs of the end of the age. The first twenty-four verses, in one sense, are directed more towards the believers before 1967; the remaining verses, towards the believers in our generation. It's all applicable, because the Word of God is applicable to everyone, but much of what is mentioned in the first twenty-four verses happened in the first century. Then, verse twenty-four is transitional: **"Jerusalem will be trampled on by the Gentiles, until the times of the Gentiles are fulfilled."**

Jesus goes on and talks about the last days. Some people say that the last days began with the time of Jesus, but I believe Jesus may be speaking here of the last generation starting in 1967.

After Jesus told His disciples that the time would come when the stones of the temple would be thrown down, they asked Him, **"Teacher... when will these things happen? And what will be the sign that they are about to take place?"** (Luke 21:7) Jesus responded, telling them to watch for the following signs:

## 1. Watch that You Are Not Deceived

**"Watch out that you are not deceived. For many will come in my name, claiming, 'I am he,' and, 'The time is near.' Do not follow them"** (Luke 21:8).

The first sign that we need to watch for in the end times is that we are not deceived. Some people say that we don't have to worry about being deceived. I've heard some Bible teachers make statements like, "Even if Satan himself prayed for you, you wouldn't have to worry about being deceived." But I believe we really need to be alert to deception in the last days. Jesus Himself warns, "Watch out that you are not deceived."

Jesus repeats this in Matthew 7:15, saying,

> **"Watch out for false prophets. They come to you in sheep's clothing, but inwardly they are ferocious wolves. By their fruit you will recognize them."**

We know that in these days there are many false prophets—many "larger" and "smaller" false prophets. Since Jesus' time, Buddha, Confucius and Mohammed have arisen. There have been people such as Rev. Moon, David Koresh, and the leader of the recent Heaven's Gate Movement/mass suicide. Many Jewish people proclaimed Rabbi Menachem Schneerson to be the Messiah. After his death, many of his followers believed that he would be raised from the dead. They were reading Isaiah 53, saying that it was about Rabbi Schneerson. In one sense, this prepared their hearts to be open to the coming of a Messiah. Obviously he was not the fulfillment of the Messianic prophesies. We can see many other false prophets, false Messiahs, rising up in these days.

In Zechariah 13:5, it says that there will be many false prophets in the last days, and people will say, **"I am not a prophet. I am a farmer."** Although God is working through the prophetic ministry in these days, we need to recognize that in the former days He spoke through the prophets, but in the last days He will speak through His Son. We need to hold fast to the Head, to the Lord Jesus, because He is the primary Prophet, Priest and King.

We should not be led by every prophetic word that's being spoken, but we need judge it according to the Scriptures. The spirit of the prophet needs to be subject to the prophet. We need to be on the alert, remembering the first warning that Jesus Himself gave, **"Watch out that you are not deceived."** We need to be watchmen, making sure that whatever people are saying is based upon the Word of God, and that we're holding fast to Jesus Himself. God wants us to draw closer to Jesus and to be very much in His Word. It says in Matthew 24:11-12, that many false prophets will appear and deceive many people, and that because of the increase of wickedness, the love of most will grow cold. Many people will be deceived in the last days and will fall away from the faith.

We know that we're living in the days when the anti-Christ will arise very soon. Some people believe the church will be raptured out before the anti-Christ comes on the scene. Other people believe we will live through the great tribulation, or through at least part of the tribulation. People have different ideas. But we know that the spirit of anti- Christ has always been with us. We also know that deception will increase tremendously in the last days. In fact, if the time of the anti-Christ were not cut short, even the elect would be deceived (Matthew 24:22-24). But, praise God, the days will be shortened. We know that the last days are going to be very difficult.

How do we keep from being deceived in the last days? I believe there are four ways to make sure that we're walking with God, and to help keep us from deception:

## 1) Passion for Jesus

The first thing is to make sure that our love for Jesus is not growing cold. As we read in Matthew 24:12, because of the increase of wickedness, the love of most will grow cold. The Lord Jesus wants the fire of our love for Him to be kindled, that we live with a passion for Him. And if we're passionately in love with Jesus, our love will not be cold. Instead, our love will be red hot like fire.

But to stay passionately in love with Jesus we must spend quality time in intimate communion with Him through the Holy Spirit. In the midst of our busy lives we must jealously guard this time with Him, even as our Lord jealously desires our fellowship, faithfulness and love.

> **You adulterous people, don't you know that friendship with the world is hatred toward God? Anyone who chooses to be a friend of the world becomes an enemy of God. Or do you think Scripture says without reason that the spirit he caused to live in us envies intensely? (James 4:4-5)**

The essence of wickedness that causes our love to grow cold is idolatry and/or putting anything or anyone before the Lord. If we are passionately in love with Jesus, who is the Truth, we will not be deceived. He is the Truth and deception is a lie. *May we hold fast to the Head, and love Jesus with all of our heart, soul, mind and strength.*

## 2) Passion for the Word of God

A second passion that we should have is a passion for the Word of God, the Bible. His word is truth. If we are in love with His word, we are in love not only with the person of Jesus who is the truth, but with the word of God which is the truth. It says in John 17:17 that we are sanctified by the truth of the word of God. His word is truth!

**Why do the nations conspire and the peoples plot in vain? The kings of the earth take their stand and the rulers gather together against the LORD and against his Anointed One. "Let us break their chains," they say, "and throw off their fetters" (Psalm 1:1-3).**

## 3) Love for the Holy Spirit, the Spirit of Truth

**"But when he, the Spirit of truth comes, he will guide you into all truth" (John 16:13).**

The Lord wants us to love the Holy Spirit. If we're confessing our sins and asking the Lord to fill us with the Holy Spirit afresh every day, we will have a passionate love not only for Jesus and for the Word of God, but a love for the Holy Spirit, who is the Spirit of truth.

## 4) Love for One Another and Obeying Your Leaders

**And let us consider how we may spur one another on toward love and good deeds. Let us not give up meeting together, as some are in the habit of doing, but let us encourage one another—and all the more as you see the Day approaching (Hebrews 10:24-25).**

**Obey your leaders and submit to their authority. They keep watch over you as men who must give an account. Obey them so that their work will be a joy, not a burden, for that would be of no advantage to you (Hebrews 13:17).**

Another way to avoid being deceived is to be in fellowship with one another, encouraging one another and building up each other with the love of God. We are the body of Jesus. He shed His blood that we should be one. Many times people go off by themselves, they reject pastoral leadership, teaching and counsel, the enemy starts lying to them and there's no pastor with whom they're in fellowship to help correct, encourage, or strengthen them. Then they go into deception.

We've seen people come to the Mount of Olives saying that they were Elijah and the two witnesses. Many people fall into deception by not being in fellowship with the body of believers. It's important that believers are part of a local fellowship, community or congregation, and that we are in fellowship with one another.

*"Watch out that you are not deceived,"* Jesus warned. What is deception? Lies, or believing a lie. Satan is the author of lies; he is the father of lies; his whole kingdom is based upon lies. But if we are passionately in love with Jesus who is the truth, passionately in love with Word of God which is the truth, passionately in love with the Holy Spirit who is the Spirit of truth, and in a loving relationship with one another and our pastor, I believe that the Lord will help to keep us from deception. Hallelujah!

## 2. Watch for Wars and Rumors of Wars

**"When you hear of wars and revolutions, do not be frightened. These things must happen first, but the end will not come right away... Nation will rise against nation, and kingdom against kingdom" (Luke 21:9-10).**

Another sign of the end times is many wars and rumors of wars, nation rising against nation. It's incredible, but there have been only 292 years of peace in the last 6,000 years. In the last 55 centuries, there have been 14,531 wars. Three and a half billion people have been killed in these wars. There have been 1656 arms races since 650 B.C. Of these arms races, all except sixteen ended in war, while sixteen ended in economic collapse of the countries involved.[1]

---

1. Gwen Shaw, teaching, *Signs of the End Times*, 1993.

There has not been one day in the last 250 years when there hasn't been a war going on. In fact, there has been an average of twelve wars being fought every day.[1] Incredible! There have been wars and rumors of wars; we can see this is one of the signs of the end times.

We have seen nation rising against nation. A few years ago the former Yugoslavia was one nation; now it is five nations. Eritrea was once part of Ethiopia; now Ethiopia is divided into two nations. Areas of South Africa have divided into separate nations. Canada recently defeated an attempted separation by the Province of Quebec. Around the world there is a move toward ethnic groups wanting to become nations. Nation is rising against nation.

God has purposed to bring people to His throne from every tribe, tongue, people and nation, from each *ethnos,* which is a language/cultural people group. And there are still thousands of these groups where people have not been born again. Many such groups are in India, in China, in Papua New Guinea, but God is going to bring people into the kingdom from every one of these larger as well as smaller "nations." Although the enemy has been focusing on dividing nations, God is focusing on bringing people from every tribe, tongue, people and nation into the kingdom of God. Hallelujah!

## 3. Watching for Earthquakes

**"There will be great earthquakes... in various places, and fearful events..."** (Luke 21:11).

Major earthquakes have been recorded as follows: the 14th century, 157; the 15th century, 174; the 16th century, 253; the 17th century, 278; the 18th century, 640; the 19th century, 2119. As of the third quarter of 1992, nearly 900,000 earthquakes had been recorded in the 20th century. This averages to one earthquake every hour![2] We can see that earthquakes are increasing.

1.  Director of Stockholm International Peace Research Institute, quoted by Gwen Shaw, *Signs of the End Times,* 1993.
2.  Barry Segal Ministries, Inc., "Earthquakes Can Tell Time," *Dispatch From Jerusalem* 17, no. 3 (1992).

The most destructive known earthquake on record was in Shansi, China in 1556, when 830,000 people were killed.[1] There have been earthquakes throughout the world, not only in China but also in Iran, Latin America, the Philippines. Even in the Middle East there have been many earthquakes.

I have experienced only two earthquakes and both were in the Middle East. On the afternoon of *Yom Kippur*, the closing day of *All Nations Convocation* of 1994, a leader from Jerusalem and a leader from Jordan led us in affirming the covenant of the Lord Jesus between the Messianic and Arab believers in the Middle East and blessing all the nations in prayer based on Isaiah 19:23-25.

I had been extremely tired, but the Lord woke me very early the following morning and suddenly the whole building started shaking! Later in the day I learned that the center of the earthquake was in Jerusalem and Jordan. I believe the earthquake was something (supernatural) from heaven. The prayers of the leaders from Jerusalem and Jordan the previous evening and the earthquake the next morning reminded me of Revelation 8:4-5, which describes the prayers of the saints being lifted up to heaven and then God shaking the earth.

Then, early one morning in 1995, the chandelier suddenly started shaking in my home on the Mount of Olives. People talk about "the big one" expected in California, but I thought of Jesus coming to the Mount of Olives. Instead, the earthquake was centered in the Gulf of Eilat, damaging many buildings and hotels in that area.

We don't know when "the really big one" is coming, but we do know that,

> **On that day His [Jesus'] feet will stand on the Mount of Olives, east of Jerusalem, and the Mount of Olives will be split in two from east to west, forming a great valley, with half of the mountain moving north and half moving south (Zechariah 14:4).**

---

1. National Earthquake Information Center. *"Significant Earthquakes of the World, 1992"* compiled by Waverly J. Person. Earthquake Data Base System of the U.S. Geological Survey. Golden, Colorado.

I believe that Jesus' feet upon the Mount of Olives is what will cause the earthquake. Alleluia! It will be an awesome thing when it takes place.

In 1992, there was a major earthquake in Egypt where none had occurred in the past. At least 541 people were killed, more than 6,500 injured, and about 8,300 buildings damaged or destroyed in the Cairo area. Shaking was felt in much of Egypt from Alexandria to Aswan, and in Israel from Eilat to Tel Aviv and Jerusalem.[1] Even many church buildings were damaged or destroyed in Egypt.

In Iran, many earthquakes have taken place. It says in Revelation Chapters 16 - 19 that the cities of the nations are going to collapse. Incredible shakings are going to come. We can see from the acceleration of earthquakes that this has been happening over the centuries. Fasten your seat belt! God is going to shake everything that can be shaken. The cities of the nations will collapse and Babylon is going to fall, in the political sense. I believe this is tied to the United Nations and the cities of the world. Babylon is a worldwide system politically. There is also a spiritual Babylon (Revelation 17), which I believe may have a connection with Rome and any other religious systems that comprise the New World Order.

I believe that we will see great shakings take place in a religious as well as a political sense in the nations of the world during the coming decade(s) before Jesus comes back. I believe great shakings will take place in the Roman Catholic Church and throughout the Protestant churches—within the charismatic movement as well as in the evangelical churches. Everything will be shaken that can be shaken. But the kingdom of God, which cannot be shaken, will remain. God will shake everything in our lives that can be shaken. But whatever part is of His eternal kingdom, Jesus within our lives, will not be shaken, because His kingdom cannot be shaken.

## 4. Watching for Famine and Pestilence

"There will be... famine and pestilence in various places..." (Luke 21:11).

---

1. Ibid.

Millions and millions of people in the world have literally starved to death in the last number of decades. More than a million people starved to death in Ethiopia. Famine has also hit Somalia, Mozambique, Chad, Liberia, Sudan, India, and China. We have seen incredible famines. There have been prophecies that there will be famine in the United States of America and other Western countries. We can see the signs of the times. Certainly there are and will be famines in many places.

Luke 21:11 also mentions pestilence. Webster defines *pestilence* as "a contagious or infectious epidemic disease that spreads quickly and has devastating results."[1] This accurately describes AIDS. No one knows exactly how many people in the world have AIDS, but recent estimates show that over three million people have already died of AIDS. Uganda, Zaire and Thailand are among the high risk nations of the world.

If AIDS continues at the present rate, the World Health Organization estimates that 40 million people will be infected worldwide by the year 2000.[2] The leading cause of death among men between the ages of 25 and 44, in some of the cities of the world today, is AIDS—more than heart attacks, more than cancer, more than any other cause. In the United States, AIDS is a major problem. Even in Israel today, people are dying of AIDS.

## 5. *Watching Signs in the Heavens*

**"There will be... great signs from heaven" (Luke 21:11).**

**"There will be signs in the sun, moon and stars" (Luke 21:25).**

A fifth sign of the end times is great signs in the heavens. When God made the lights in the heavens, the sun, the moon and the stars, He said,

**"Let there be lights in the expanse of the sky to separate the day from the night, and let them serve as signs to mark seasons and days and years" (Genesis 1:14).**

---

1. Webster's New Encyclopedic Dictionary, 1996 ed., s.v. "pestilence."
2. Harrison's Textbook of Internal Medicine, 1994 ed.

They were to be signs in the heavens. When the wise men came to Jerusalem looking for Jesus, they were following the star. God was working through the heavens; they were following the star and the star led them to Jerusalem (Matthew 2:1-12).

Beginning the evening of April 3, 1996, a total lunar eclipse occurred during the Feast of Passover, *Pesach*. This was the first of three lunar eclipses to occur during a single Biblical year. Of further interest is the fact that all three were on the only Biblical festivals which occurred during the full moon. The second total eclipse began on the evening of September 26, 1996, which was the Eve of the Feast of Tabernacles, *Erev Hag HaSuccoth*. The third eclipse (90%) was on March 23/24, 1997, *Shushan Purim*. All three were visible from Jerusalem.[1]

Of special interest, the second of these eclipses occurred on the last evening/early morning of the final day of *All Nations Convocation Jerusalem '96!* Another astronomical event, visible only from Jerusalem, occurred on the second day of *Rosh HaShana* at the beginning of the *Convocation*. On September 15, 1996, *Yom Teruah*, a unique alignment of several constellations spoke to some as representative of Revelation 12:1-2. Described by Greg Killian as "interesting speculation...not gospel truth...this particular positioning [of constellations] has never occurred before, and will never occur again, due to the precession of the equinoxes."[2]

Even as God was working in the heavens when the stars led the wise men to see Jesus, he is still working in the heavens today. God set signs in the heavens from creation and He knows the beginning from the end. In the beginning He knew what was going to happen in these years and I believe He stages all things for these signs to be released, even for the time of His coming. We don't know exactly when He is coming back, but we live in prophetic days. God says in His Word that there will be signs in the heavens in the end times. They are truly beginning to be seen.

1. Greg Killian, *Lunar Eclipse* updated July 24, 1996, [article on-line]; available from gkilli@aol.com; Internet; accessed 7 August 1996.

2. Killian, *"Revelation 12:1-2"* [article on-line]; available from http://members.aol.com/ghilli/home/bethulah.jpg; Internet accessed August 7, 1996.

Witnesses have testified that in Nepal many people received Jesus because they saw Him appear in the heavens. Gwen Shaw said that Jesus was appearing in the sky of Somalia, and Muslims were receiving Him. It is interesting that in the South Pacific the stars are lined up in such a way that they form a cross. Called the *Southern Cross*, it is as a perpetual sign in the heavens. The South Pacific is called the South Land of the Holy Spirit. I don't believe it was an accident that God positioned the stars in the South Pacific as a cross. Praise God!

## 6. Watching for Persecution and Martyrdom

**"But before all this [the end of the age], they will lay hands on you and persecute you" (Luke 21:12).**

It is not the most popular thing to talk about, but Luke 21:16 says, **"You will be betrayed even by parents, brothers, relatives and friends and they will put some of you to death."**

In the first century, eleven of the twelve apostles were martyred, and we know that in the last days there will also be martyrs. There have already been many people martyred. In Sudan, tens of thousands have been martyred for their faith in the last few years. Millions have been martyred for their faith in Jesus Christ in Saudi Arabia, China, Russia, all around the world.

One of my friends from Sunday school in Pennsylvania (U.S.) was serving as a missionary in Columbia, South America, working as a Bible translator. He was martyred about twenty years ago. Earlier this year, the greatest evangelist in the history of Bolivia was martyred. He had led more people to the Lord than anyone in Bolivia's history. He was in Columbia, preaching against drugs and the corruption of drug dealers. The drug dealers were getting saved and he was killed.

**When he opened the fifth seal, I saw under the altar the souls of those who had been slain because of the word of God and the testimony they had maintained. They called out in a loud voice, "How long, Sovereign Lord, holy and true, until you judge the inhabitants of the earth and avenge our blood?"**

**Then each of them was given a white robe, and they were told to wait a little longer, until the number of their fellow servants and brothers who were to be killed as they had been was completed (Revelation 6:9-11).**

We don't hear people preaching from this very often, but it is a sign of the end times.

Scripture speaks of the full number of the Gentiles coming into the kingdom of God and the full number of Jewish people coming to their Messiah (Romans 11:25-26). There is something in the purpose of God that the full number of martyrs for the faith must be completed. It says that those who are martyred for their faith will be part of the first resurrection.

Yet there is a fear of death among many Christians. Muslims are blowing themselves up with suicide bombs, believing they are going to paradise when actually they are going to hell. But among Christians there are many paralyzed by the fear of death. We should be the boldest people in the world because we know the truth. We should be beyond the fear of death because **"to live is Christ and to die is gain" (Philippians 1:21). "[Nothing] will be able to separate us from the love of God that is in Christ Jesus our Lord" (Romans 8:39).**

The question was, **"Who shall separate us from the love of Christ? Shall trouble or hardship or persecution or famine or nakedness or danger or sword? As it is written: 'For your sake we face death all day long; we are considered as sheep to be slaughtered'" (Romans 8:35-36).**

Many people quote the Scripture, **"we are more than conquerors through him [Christ] who loved us."** We all like that verse, but in context it follows, **"No, in all these things [trouble, hardship, persecution, famine, nakedness, danger, sword] we are more than conquerors through Christ who loved us" (Romans 8:37).**

Living alone on the Mount of Olives when we began the ministry, I remembered the words of Jesus—that when people tried to come against Him, He said, **"My time has not yet come" (John 7:6).**

I believe that we are protected by the Lord and nothing can touch us until our time has come, whether it is next year or twenty-five years from now or when we're one hundred years old. For me, *to live is Christ and to die is gain*. If we are walking in the Holy Spirit, we are under God's protection until our time has come.

## 7. Watching for Betrayal and Hatred

**"You will be betrayed even by parents, brothers, relatives and friends, and they will put some of you to death. All men will hate you because of me" (Luke 21:16-17).**

Another sign of the end times is betrayal and hatred of one another. We can see this happening, especially as we see Muslims and Jewish people coming to salvation. There is incredible hatred and betrayal from their families. Many times Arab Christians don't trust Muslim converts coming into their fellowship because they are afraid they may be informers who will betray or hate them. A similar situation exists among Messianic believers. A new believer may not be trusted, fearing he may be an informer.

As more Muslims and Jews are coming to faith from different backgrounds, the fear of betrayal and hatred can be taking place in many, many ways. We really need God's discernment and His help to trust one another and to believe the best when we see people coming to Messiah from those backgrounds. We need to be loyal to the Lord, but also to one another, because the enemy's tactic is to divide and conquer.

Not only is God continually watching over His creation, the watch of the Lord, but Satan, the accuser of the brethren, **"accuses them before our God day and night" (Revelation 12:10).**

Satan is working to try to bring a spirit of accusation throughout the body, to bring betrayal and division. His tactic is to divide and scatter, while God's tactic is to unify and gather unto Himself. We need to stand against the spirit of betrayal; it is one of the major signs of the end times. But praise God, if we are loving Him, loving His Word, loving the Holy Spirit, and loving one another, we can stand against this spirit of betrayal.

*As we are on the watch of the Lord, watching the Lord and He is watching us, we can stand against the watch of the enemy, in Jesus' name.*

## 8. Watching for the Times of the Gentiles to Be Fulfilled

**"They will fall by the sword and will be taken as prisoners to all the nations. Jerusalem will be trampled on by the Gentiles until the times of the Gentiles are fulfilled" (Luke 21:24).**

This Scripture was partially fulfilled in 1967. Prior to that time, the Mount of Olives, the area of the Garden Tomb, the Upper room, the Temple Mount and the Western Wall were all part of Jordan, not Israel. There was a wall dividing Jerusalem, as a wall divided Berlin. But praise God, the wall came down in the Six-day War in 1967, and Jerusalem was reunited.

Then the Jewish people could go to the Western Wall. They started weeping and touching the wall of the Temple. It was at that time that the "fig tree" started blossoming. The Jewish people also started receiving their Messiah. You could say that Jerusalem was no longer trampled on by the Gentiles, because for the first time in thousand of years it became a united city under Jewish rule. Today we can see that Jerusalem is the united capital of Israel!

We can see that this was a turning point because, in Luke 21:29-30, Jesus continued with a parable of the fig tree (Israel) and all the trees (the nations), that **"when they sprout leaves... the kingdom of God is near."** He then said, **"this generation will certainly not pass away until all these things have happened" (Luke 21:32).**

I believe that we live in the last generation, the generation when Jesus is coming back. We don't know how long this generation will be, forty years or seventy years, but God began something in 1967, and the fig tree and also the trees of the nations started blossoming spiritually in increasing ways.

More Jews have come to Messiah since 1967 than in all previous years put together. Then there were only a few thousand Messianic believers throughout the world, but now there are hundreds of thousands of Messianic believers in Israel and in the nations of the world. So praise God, one of the signs is that Jerusalem is no longer being trampled on by the Gentiles, but that it came under Jewish rule in 1967, and the fig tree started blossoming—so we know that summer is near.

## 9. Watching the Roaring and Tossing of the Sea

**"On the earth, nations will be in anguish and perplexity at the roaring and tossing of the sea" (Luke 21:25).**

In the United States of America, in the last few years, there have been incredible hurricanes and floods, a sign of the end times. The seas will be roaring and tossing more and more as we see the day of Jesus' return approaching.

During the summer of 1993, in the Midwestern United States, two months of heavy rain caused the Mississippi River and its tributaries to flood in ten states, causing almost 50 deaths and an estimated $12 billion in damage to property and agriculture. Almost 70,000 people were left homeless.

Some of the costliest natural disasters in U.S. history and their total cost (including uninsured losses) were: 1989 - Hurricane Hugo, $5.9 billion; 1992- Hurricane Andrew, $30 billion; and 1993- Midwest flooding, $12 billion.[1]

In the Antarctic there is an ice sheet melting. If this does not change, enough water will be released for the Pacific Ocean to rise eighteen feet, inundating America's coastal cities, Europe and the entire world.[2] There will be an incredible roaring and tossing of the seas. Many cities of the world will be flooded and suffer much devastation.

## 10. Watching for Terror and Apprehension

**"Men will faint from terror, apprehensive of what is coming on the world, for the heavenly bodies will be shaken" (Luke 21:26).**

Verse 26 speaks of the tenth sign of the end times: *"Men will faint from terror, apprehensive of what is coming on the world."* There has been an increase in terrorism in the world and its rate of

1.    1995 *Information Please Almanac*, p. 405
2.    *Christian World Report*, March 1993; quoted by Gwen Shaw teaching, *Signs of the End Times*, 1993.

growth is incredible. During 1996, one bus after another was blown up by terrorists in Israel. About thirty Jewish people were killed on buses. More were killed by the bombing of a mall in Tel Aviv. In Lebanon hundreds of Americans were killed by bombs some years ago. Israeli soldiers have been killed in Lebanon. Terrorism is happening in inconceivable ways in Saudi Arabia—many Americans were recently killed. Terrorism has been increasing in Ireland, Sri Lanka, France and many other nations.

A TWA jet blew up after leaving New York City when I was leaving for New York (cause unknown)![1] America has been shocked by bombings of the World Trade Center in New York City, the Federal Building in Oklahoma City, and the discovery of plans and materials for potential bombing of the New York subway system. At the '96 Olympics in Atlanta, a woman was killed and one hundred eleven people wounded by a homemade pipe bomb.[2] This increase of terrorism is a sign of the end times. Men will faint because of fear of terror.

President Clinton called a Terrorism Conference in Egypt to try to stop terrorism, and subsequently called a second one. There have been numerous Terrorism Conferences in different parts of the world in the attempt to stop terrorism. Everywhere we turn, the signs of the end times are here—we are living in the end times.

Luke 21:11 says there will be fearful events and great signs from heaven. Although Luke 21, especially from verse 24 onward, can be applied to all people, it is written specifically to believers in our generation. We may soon see greater signs of terror coming from the heavens, as mentioned at the end of Luke 21:26, **"for the heavenly bodies will be shaken."**

Recent examples of possible terror from the heavens:

1) Shoemaker-Levy comet that bombarded Jupiter with 21 fragments several years ago.
2) Hale-Bopp with its closest approach to Earth on Purim-March 23/24, 1997 (same date as third lunar eclipse). According to Greg Killian, some sources are calling this "Wormwood," but "if this comet is to be like the Biblical Wormwood it will

1. *Time Magazine*, 5 August 1996; "The Search for Sabotage", p. 26.
2. Ibid, "Terror's Venue", p. 21.

need to break up and have only a piece hit the Earth. If the whole comet hit the Earth it would be unlikely for any life to survive." The last time that comet Hale-Bopp visited the inner solar system was about 3600 years ago, when Israel was about to leave Egypt to go the promised land under the leadership of Moses.

We are living in the last days. As the song goes

*Signs of the times are everywhere.*
*And there's a brand new feeling in the air;*
*Keep your eyes upon the eastern sky,*
*Lift up your head, redemption draweth nigh.*[1]

Jesus is coming soon!

---

1.   Gordon Jensen, "*Redemption Draweth Nigh,*" Benson Music.

# Chapter 14

# Watching for the Coming of Messiah

## Jesus Is Coming Soon

I live, pray, fellowship and work with an average of twelve other full-time watchmen in *Messianic Community of Reconciliation* on the Mount of Olives in Jerusalem, where Jesus ascended into heaven and where He is coming back very soon. This is probably the most focused place on earth to watch for His coming, as it will be the place His feet will touch. Part of our calling in the midst of this Arab-Muslim community is to prepare a glorious place for His feet (Isaiah 60:13). We hope any of you from the nations whom God would be calling to join our community, or to lead or join a team to participate in Jerusalem Watchman's Week, will respond to that call.

For the majority of you who read this book, who probably will not come to Jerusalem until after Jesus comes, we pray that this book and especially this last chapter will be helpful in enabling you to become an overcoming watchman prepared for His soon coming. The blessed hope is for the saints who attain to and apprehend the promises in the seven beatitudes of the *Book of Revelation*, looking [watching] for the blessed hope and glorious appearing of our Lord and Savior Jesus Christ.

> On that day his feet will stand on the Mount of Olives, east of Jerusalem (Zechariah 14:4).

> Now there is in store for me the crown of righteousness, which the Lord, the righteous Judge, will award to me on that day—and not only to me, but also to all who have longed [watched] for his appearing (2 Timothy 4:8).

> Look [watch], he is coming with the clouds, and every eye will see him, even those who pierced him; and all the

**peoples of the earth will mourn because of him. So shall it be! Amen. "I am the Alpha and the Omega," says the Lord God, "who is, and who was, and who is to come, the Almighty" (Revelation 1:7,8).**

We live in the last days of the Last Day, in the days of the dawning of the bright Morning Star mentioned in Revelation 22:16. Watching for the coming of the Messiah is the most mentioned aspect of the twenty aspects of watching presented in chapters 5 and 6 of this book. Truly He is coming soon, at which time the world will be totally transformed, as Jesus will reign as King of the Jews and of all nations from Jerusalem. So I believe it is the most appropriate way to end this book.

Two thousand years ago, Jesus said He is coming soon. We continue to watch two thousand years later than when He personally said He was coming soon. Now we most probably live in the generation of His coming. He may come for you any day and hour, any minute. If we are watchmen we will not be caught unprepared, but will always be watching, waiting and longing for His appearing.

I am writing this last chapter in a little guest house on a hillside just above the Sea of Galilee overlooking the Mount of Beatitudes where Jesus gave the beatitudes to His disciples. Our community just spent some time together there, meditating on the beatitudes. Here Jesus called His disciples away from the multitudes to teach them His ways to blessedness (Matthew 5:1-12), which are a total reverse of the ways of the world! Again today, Jesus is calling His disciples (the true watchmen) to Himself out of the multitudes to teach them His seven ways to blessedness from the *Book of Revelation,* to prepare us for His soon coming.

The Book of Revelation is the Book of Completion. This is confirmed by the many times the number *seven*, the number of completion is mentioned in this book. It mentions *seven* beatitudes, *seven* spirits of God, *seven* golden lampstands (the seven churches), *seven* stars (the angels of the seven churches), *seven* ways or keys to be overcomers, over *seven* blessings of overcoming, over *seven* times the Spirit says, **"He who has ears to hear let him hear what the Spirit is saying,"** *seven* seals, *seven* trumpets, *seven* plagues and bowls filled with the wrath of God. Ten times the number of fullness (*seven* things or more) are mentioned that apply to the fulfillment of God's purposes in the last days to prepare us, as His watchmen, to be His glorious Church, Bride, Wife and Temple throughout all eternity.

The Book of Revelation is a revelation of Jesus Christ. The days between now and when Jesus returns will be very difficult, probably the most difficult in the history of the world. Seven beatitudes listed in this book show us that if we are watching Jesus, abiding in Him and obeying His word in these ways, we are called blessed and we are preparing as overcomers for His coming.

## The First Beatitude: Those Who Take God's Word to Heart

**Blessed is the one who reads the words of this prophecy, and blessed are those who hear it and take to heart what is written in it, because the time is near (Revelation 1:3).**

According to John, the time was near two thousand years ago. It is now at the door. Watchmen are exhorted to read the written Word of God and to watch the Word, the Living Word Jesus. We are declared blessed if we read His Word because the Holy Spirit will draw us into closer intimacy with Jesus. We are also declared blessed if we hear the word. In the *Book of Revelation* the Holy Spirit says through John to the seven churches, **"He who has an ear, let him hear what the Spirit says to the churches."** This admonition is found about twenty times throughout Scripture.

If we, as God's watchmen, hear what the Spirit says to the seven churches (Revelation 2 & 3) we can be delivered from this present evil age. All the things that were deceiving the seven churches are similar to the things deceiving the churches today. We are to be conformed into the likeness of the bridegroom, prepared for Him as His bride (Romans 5:25-27). Also in these last days, if we have ears to hear, we will be hearing the seven trumpets of Revelation blowing (Revelation 8-11), being prepared ourselves and preparing others to watch and totally trust in Jesus.

**"Faith comes by hearing and hearing by the word of God" (Romans 10:17).** Truly blessed watchmen are those who not only hear the word, but take it to heart.

Jesus says *seven* times to the *seven* churches, **"He who has an ear, let him hear what the Spirit says to the churches."** Then He gives *seven* keys or ways to become overcomers and *seven* blessings for those who not only hear, but hear in a real way and truly take the word to heart and become overcomers, as He overcame and sat down with His Father on His throne.

## The Seven Keys to Overcoming and Seven Blessings of Overcoming for Watchmen Who Take the Word to Heart

### Seven Keys or Ways to Become an Overcomer

1.  You have forsaken your first love. Remember the height from which you have fallen! Repent and do the things you did at first (Rev. 2:4,5)
2.  Be faithful, even to the point of death (Rev. 2:10).
3.  Remain true to my name (Rev. 2:13).
4.  Only hold on to what you have until I come (Rev. 2:25, 3:11).
5.  Wake up! Strengthen what remains and is about to die (Rev. 3:2).
6.  Endure patiently (Rev. 3:10).
7.  Buy from me gold refined in the fire (Rev. 3:18, 19).

### Seven Blessings of Overcoming

1.  To him who overcomes, I will give the right to eat from the tree of life which is in the paradise of God (Rev. 2:7).
2.  He who overcomes will not be hurt at all by the second death (Rev. 2:11).
3.  To him who overcomes, I will give some of the hidden manna. I will also give him a white stone with a new name written on it, known only to him who receives it. (Rev. 2:17).
4.  To him who overcomes and does my will to the end, I will give authority over the nations. I will also give him the Morning Star (Rev. 2:26,28).
5.  He who overcomes will be dressed in white. I will never blot out his name from the book of life, but will acknowledge his name before my Father (Rev. 3:5).
6.  He who overcomes I will make a pillar in the temple of my God. Never again will he leave it. I will write on him the name of my God and the name of the city of my God, the new Jerus-

alem, which is coming down out of heaven from my God (Rev. 3:12).

7.  To him who overcomes, I will give the right to sit with me on my throne (Rev. 3:21).

Just as in Matthew 13:13-23, the one who has eyes to see and ears to hear the word and truly takes it to heart will be the overcomer, the true watchman. **"I have hidden your word in my heart that I might not sin against you" (Psalm 119:11).**

The best way to prepare to be an overcomer in the future is to be an overcomer each day, daily denying ourselves, taking up our cross and following Jesus as His disciple. Dietrich Bonhoeffer, who wrote *The Cost of Discipleship,* said that when Christ calls a man, He bids him to come and die. Bonhoeffer later died as a martyr himself. Many of Jesus' disciples were called to be martyrs in the first century and I'm sure the same will be true in the last days. We are also to do the good works Jesus calls us to do, as **"faith by itself, if it is not accompanied by action, is dead" (James 2:17).**

In Revelation 4:1 John says,

**And the voice I had first heard speaking to me like a trumpet said, "Come up here, and I will show you what must take place after this."**

He saw a throne in heaven with someone sitting on it, twenty-four other thrones with twenty-four elders dressed in white, and the seven lamps (churches) blazing with the seven Spirits of God. Four living creatures around the throne day and night never stop saying,

**"Holy, holy, holy is the Lord God Almighty, who was, and is and is to come" (Revelation 4:8).**

This watch in heaven has been continuing for thousands of years!

**Then I saw in the right hand of him who sat on the throne a scroll with writing on both sides and sealed with seven seals. And I saw a mighty angel proclaiming in a loud voice, "Who is worthy to break the seals and open the scroll?" (Revelation 5:1,2)**

> Then one of the elders said to me, "Do not weep! See, the Lion of the tribe of Judah, the Root of David, has triumphed. He is able to open the scroll and its seven seals" (Revelation 5:5).

In Revelation 5:1-5 the Lion of Judah is worthy to open the seven seals and then we watch with the Apostle John the opening of the first seal:

> I looked [watched] and before me was a white horse! Its rider [Jesus] held a bow and he was given a crown, and he rode out as a conqueror bent on conquest (Revelation 6:1,2).

## The Second Beatitude: Those Who Die in the Lord

> "Blessed are the dead who die in the Lord from now on." "Yes," says the Spirit, "they will rest from their labor, for their deeds will follow them" (Revelation 14:13).

We are to be watchmen for Jesus, who is coming very soon for His bride. Every second, many people on earth die and meet Jesus as Savior or Judge, so none of us know when He will come for us. We must always be on the watch and pray, as none of us, His watchmen, know the day we will meet our awesome God, the Chief Watchman.

Revelation 14 says most will worship the beast and his image. There will be no rest for them day or night. This calls for patient endurance on the part of the saints who obey God's commandments and remain faithful to Jesus. It is wisdom for His watchmen that we are sealed in Him, that we be prepared to meet our God every day, as we don't know the day or hour that He will come for us. It is appointed unto man once to die and after that the judgment. *Blessed are the dead who die in the Lord.*

As we see the other seals opened (Revelation 6-8), we see the judgment of God released in the earth. The fifth seal being opened reveals under the altar the souls of those who were slain because of the word of God and the testimony they maintained. Each is given a white robe and told to wait a little longer until the full number of the fellow servants and brothers who were to be killed, as they were, is completed. To die as a martyr for Jesus is a high and holy calling.

The sixth seal is opened, revealing the sealing of the 144,000 from all the tribes of Israel, is followed by a great multitude. These servants of God are possibly a picture of all the redeemed community, Israel and the Church. The seventh seal is opened and then the prayers of the saints ascend before God from the golden altar. Then the angel takes the censer filled with fire from the altar and hurls it to the earth. Afterward, the seven trumpets begin to be sounded, releasing the greater judgments of God on the earth.

## The Third Beatitude: Those Who are Clothed in Jesus the Messiah

**"Behold, I come like a thief! Blessed is he who stays awake [on the watch] and keeps his clothes with him, so that he may not go naked and be shamefully exposed" (Revelation 16:15).**

This scripture is one of three times Jesus Himself speaks in these seven beatitudes. He is speaking as the seven bowls of God's wrath are being poured out on the earth and the nations are being gathered for Armageddon. Then follows the revelation of the great prostitute church, Babylon, riding the back of the beast.

Revelation 17:16 says the political beast will hate the prostitute church and will bring her to ruin and leave her naked, eat her flesh and burn her with fire! In the midst of this very difficult time, probably the most difficult of any time (if it were not shortened even the elect would be deceived), Jesus speaks out. He says we are blessed if we stay awake (on the watch) and are clothed with the Lord Jesus (put on Lord Jesus Christ), having the white robes of righteousness, being dressed in His righteousness alone, and wearing the whole armor of God (Ephesians 6, Psalm 45).

**Rather, clothe yourselves with the Lord Jesus Christ, and do not think about how to gratify the desires of the sinful nature (Romans 13:14).**

> **Therefore, as God's chosen people, holy and dearly loved, clothe yourselves with compassion, kindness, humility, gentleness and patience (Colossians 3:12).**

He is calling us to Himself to make sure we are dressed in our bridal garments, betrothed as His bride to Himself at the very time the false prostitute church is being found naked and exposed. Babylon is falling and being destroyed and the Revelation 18 nations will be destroyed at Armageddon. This time is at hand. Jesus spoke these words specifically for us in the midst of this final perverse generation.

> *Blessed are you if you are on the watch and have your clothes with you so you may not be found naked and be shamefully exposed. He who has eyes to see let him see and has ears to hear let him hear and take it to heart.*

## The Fourth Beatitude: Those Invited to the Wedding of the Lamb

> **Then the angel said to me, "Write: 'Blessed are those who are invited to the wedding supper of the Lamb!'" And he added, "These are the true words of God" (Revelation 19:9).**

The Lord Jesus, our Warrior King and Bridegroom has been waiting for a long time for His wedding to His Bride. I believe when He turned the water into wine two thousand years ago, His first miracle at a wedding in Cana of Galilee, He was already thinking of His wedding. If you are single and need some patience, ask Jesus. He has been waiting two thousand years for His wedding. He has a lot of patience and He can give you a double portion! If you are single or married, get prepared for (don't miss) the big one (wedding) that will last for all eternity!

Some people believe we are waiting for Jesus to get ready for the wedding. He has been ready and waiting with great patience for the fruit of the earth to come forth! The wedding will take place as soon as the bride makes herself ready. As Revelation 19 says, this will happen at the time He condemns the great prostitute who corrupted the earth by her adulteries. True and just are His judgments! The time of the wedding will be a time of rejoicing and gladness and giving glory to Him! For the bride has made herself ready!

Jesus Himself, the Word of God, the Holy Spirit and Fire, trials and persecutions are all part of the things God uses to prepare (refine) us to be the bride of His Son. We become ready by yielding to God and His dealing in all ways and making sure that we have oil in our lamps by confessing our sins every day, and being filled afresh each day by the Holy Spirit. We must make sure that we are watching, wise virgins with oil in our lamps, not sleeping and drowsy foolish virgins with no oil.

When at midnight the cry rings out, *Here's the bridegroom, come out to meet Him,* who are those who are blessed and who are invited to the wedding supper of the Lamb? The virgins who have oil in their lamps, those who will be ready when He comes will go in with Him to the wedding banquet and the door will be shut. Later the others will also come. **"'Sir! Sir!' they will say, *'Open the door for us!'* But He will reply, *'I tell* you the truth, I don't know you'"** (Matthew **25:1-13**).

Fine linen, bright and clean, will be given the bride to wear, representing the righteous acts of the saints (Revelation 19:8). But, intimacy with Jesus is the most important factor in these last days. Doing good works for Jesus is not a replacement for intimacy with Him. Therefore keep watch regarding your intimacy with Jesus, and allow Him to do His good works through you, because you do not know the day or the hour of the wedding!

## The Fifth Beatitude: Those Who Are Overcomers and Consequently a Part of the First Resurrection

**Blessed and holy are those who have part in the first resurrection. The second death has no power over them, but they will be priests of God and of Christ and will reign with him for a thousand years (Revelation 20:6).**

Here again, in the fifth beatitude, it seems that there is a special blessing for the martyrs:

> I saw thrones on which were seated those who had been
> given authority to judge. And I saw the souls of those who
> had been beheaded because of their testimony for Jesus
> and because of the word of God. They had not worshiped
> the beast or his image and had not received his mark on
> their foreheads or their hands. They came to life and
> reigned with Christ a thousand years (Revelation 20:4).

This scripture is not clearly understood and agreed upon by all theologians and I certainly don't claim to have total understanding. Many believe the one thousand years is referring to a literal millennium that we are about to enter in the coming years or decades. Other Christians see it in numerous different ways! When or how it will take place may not be exactly clear, but one thing is clear—there will be a first resurrection and those who are not part of it will not come to life until these thousand years are ended.

It also appears that the overcomers and martyrs are the ones who will sit on the thrones and be given authority to judge and will be those who partake in the first resurrection—those who die to self and totally yield to God, even if it leads to death. Actually, if we are a Christian we have already died, been buried and risen from the dead in Jesus Christ (Galatians 2:20). While the Church has tended to try to stop martyrdom at any cost, the Lord of the Church seems to see it as a special blessing and privilege.

Muslim fanatics going to hell as martyrs sometimes seem to have more boldness and fearlessness than those of us in the Church who will inherit thrones in heaven! Martyrdom will increase between now and when Jesus returns. May God help us to be overcomers, as mentioned seven times in Revelation 2 and 3, even if it means martyrdom.

> "They overcame him by the blood of the Lamb and by
> the word of their testimony; they did not love their lives
> so much as to shrink from death" (Revelation 12:11).

## The Sixth Beatitude: Those Who Keep the Word

Jesus Himself is speaking for the second time in this beatitude. He says,

"Behold, I am coming soon! Blessed is he who keeps the words of the prophecy in this book" (Revelation 22:7).

"If you obey my commands, you will remain in my love, just as I have obeyed my Father's commands and remain in his love" (John 15:10).

No longer will there be any curse. The throne of God and of the Lamb will be in the city, and his servants will serve him. They will see his face, and his name will be on their foreheads (Revelation 22:3,4).

"These words are trustworthy and true. The Lord, the God of the spirits of the prophets, sent his angel to show his servants the things that must soon take place" (Revelation 22:6).

"Do not seal up the words of the prophecy of this book, because the time is near. Let him who does wrong continue to do wrong; let him who is vile continue to be vile; let him who does right continue to do right; and let him who is holy continue to be holy. Behold, I am coming soon! My reward is with me, and I will give to everyone according to what he has done" (Revelation 22:10-12).

Let His words in the Book of Revelation be like a fire and hammer to prepare us as faithful watchmen for His coming. If we keep the words of the prophecy of this book we are blessed.

I warn everyone who hears the words of the prophecy of this book: If anyone adds anything to them, God will add to him the plagues described in this book. And if anyone takes words away from this book of prophecy, God will take away from him his share in the tree of life and in the holy city, which are described in this book (Revelation 22:18,19).

"Is not my word like fire," declares the LORD, "and like a hammer that breaks a rock in pieces?" (Jeremiah 23:29)

## The Seventh Beatitude: Those with Washed Robes

> "Blessed are those [watchmen] who wash their robes, that they [as watchmen] may have the right to the tree of life and [that they] may go through the gates into the city [and be with Him in the New Jerusalem as His bride]" (Revelation 22:14).

If we are wise watchmen prepared for and watching for the coming of Messiah we will always keep our robes washed. We need daily repentance, forgiveness and cleansing, and we need to keep short accounts with God. St. Francis said, "What a man is before God, that he is and no more." If our robes are not washed we are nothing before God!

Always try to be a bride without spot or wrinkle (our sins are forgiven if we confess our sins). He is just and faithful to forgive us our sins and to cleanse all unrighteousness. Spiritually we need to always have our robes washed in the blood of the Lamb, and be dressed in robes of His righteousness alone, faultless to stand before His throne.

Another way of saying the same thing: we are only faultless through the blood of Jesus so we can be partakers of Jesus, of the Tree of Life—of His divine nature and because our robes are washed, we can also go through the gates into the city. The Holy City, the New Jerusalem, contains elements of Jerusalem, the Temple and the Garden of Eden. The second Adam, Jesus the Messiah, wants to take us back to the Garden of Eden, to the Tree of Life, through the gates of the New Jerusalem to Himself, the Lamb, who is the Temple.

> I did not see a temple in the city, because the Lord God Almighty and the Lamb are its temple. The city does not need the sun or the moon to shine on it, for the glory of God gives it light, and the Lamb is its lamp. The nations will walk by its light, and the kings of the earth will bring their splendor into it. On no day will its gates ever be shut, for there will be no night there.
>
> The glory and honor of the nations will be brought into it. Nothing impure will ever enter it, nor will anyone who

**does what is shameful or deceitful, but only those whose names are written in the Lamb's book of life (Revelation 21:22-27).**

Nothing impure will ever be able to enter the gates of the city, only those whose robes are washed in the blood of the Lamb. If we are God's watchmen we will hear the Spirit and the bride say *"Come."* Only if we have intimacy and fellowship with the Holy Spirit and are filled afresh each day will we have faithful ears to hear the Spirit say *"Come."* And only those who hear the Spirit say *"Come"* will hear the bride say *"Come"* and be invited to the wedding by the bridegroom!

All of us who hear and are thirsty will come and drink of the free gift of the river of the water of life. The river of life is clear as crystal flowing from the throne of God and of the Lamb, down the middle of the great street of the city! The tree of life is on each side of the river yielding its fruit every month, the leaves of the tree are for the healing of the nations (Revelation 22:1,2).

Let us keep watching and be prepared as His bride for the coming of our Messiah-King-Bridegroom whose last words in the Bible—*the Book of Revelation*—written almost two thousand years ago, are **"Yes, I am coming soon!"** *May we say, by keeping watch and being adequately prepared,* **"Amen. Come, Lord Jesus."** *May* **"the grace of the Lord Jesus be with [all] God's people,"** *helping us to be prepared and prepare the way for Messiah.* **Amen (Revelation 22:20-21).**

# Appendix

PART I:      Additional Models of 24-Hour Watches

PART II:     How to Start a 24-Hour Watch

PART III:    Scripture References

PART IV:     Jerusalem House of Prayer for All Nations - Watchmen Participation Options

PART V:      Other Materials Available to Help Watchmen and Watches

## APPENDIX - PART I

## ADDITIONAL MODELS OF 24-HOUR WATCHES AND WATCH GROUPS

Greater understanding of the different watch models may be found through testimonies of existing 24-hour watches and watch groups throughout the world (Chapter 9 and the additional watch reports that follow). If you desire further information from any of these watches, please feel free to contact us in Jerusalem for their addresses (see order form at end of appendix). The following Watches are arranged in the order of their being established (1983-1996).

| | |
|---|---|
| *1. 24-Hour Prayer Watch,*<br>*U.S. Center for World Mission*<br>Pasadena, California | *Prayer Tower*<br>**Madras, India** |
| *3. 24-Hour Prayer Watch*<br>**San Pedro Sula, Honduras** | *4. The Local Church Praying*<br>**Burkino Faso, West Africa** |
| *Helsinki Prayer Watch*<br>**Helsinki, Finland** | *6. Bethel*<br>**Sri Lanka** |
| *7. Prayer for Ireland,*<br>*Christian Renewal Centre*<br>**Belfast Ireland** | *8. 24-Hour Prayer Watch*<br>**Hansarang, Korea** |
| *9. Prayer Watch—Zambia*<br>**Zambia** | *10. Shu Kwang Christ Church*<br>**Jiling, China** |

| | |
|---|---|
| *11. Watch of the Lord—Fiji*<br>**Fiji** | *12. South Pacific Prayer Movement*<br>**Solomon Islands** |
| *13. 24-Hour Prayer Watch*<br>**Paramaribo, Suriname** | *14. Brussels Prayer Watch*<br>**Belgium** |
| *15. 168-Hour Prayer Net*<br>**Hungary** | *16. The Tower of Prayer,*<br>*The New Anointing Church*<br>**Mexico City** |
| *17. House of Prayer for All*<br>*Nations—Papua, New Guinea*<br>**Papua, New Guinea** | |

## 24-HOUR PRAYER WATCH
## U.S. CENTER FOR WORLD MISSION
## PASADENA, CALIFORNIA

During the summer of 1983, when a big push was being made to encourage a million people to have a part in paying for our campus by contributing $15 apiece, it was recognized that this was not only a financial need but a need for more prayer as well—if the remaining unreached people groups around the world were to be reached with the Gospel and have a viable church in their midst. It was during this time that our 24-hour prayer room/watch was started.

At one time of special need, three people were assigned for each four-hour period, but most of the time it has been individuals. Occasionally, one other or a group will join that person. Shifts begin at 2, 6, and 10, both A.M. and P.M. Each person on staff, plus others who want to take part, is assigned two or three shifts each month.

A huge map of the world (about 6' x 10') adorns one wall. Later a new one was put up because the world had changed so much in the last several years. We stand in front of this map and pray for individual missionaries or nationals we know in the various countries, or get acquainted with some of the new countries.

Other aids to prayer are available at the desk, such as Oswald Chambers' *My Utmost for His Highest*, plus several translations of the Bible, although most people bring their own. Since the emphasis of the USCWM is on the unreached people groups of the world, another important guide to prayer is the *Global Prayer Digest*, the daily devotional guide which tells about some unreached group we should pray for, along with a story about that group or a missionary biography, plus something from the Word emphasizing missions.

There is also a small bulletin board where ongoing needs of staff are listed: chronic illnesses, expectant mothers, needs for additional staff, etc.

The present location of our prayer room is a large room on the top (third) floor of our Center building (Hudson Taylor Hall) which is conducive to prayer, away from most of the activity going on during the day. When the new map was put up, the room was also painted, a rug added, and some shelves put up with dolls of many nations displayed... another reminder of the many people groups without Christ.

We have a journal on the desk where some merely sign their name during their shift, while others write comments on the Scripture they've been reading or other thoughts they wish to share with the community about a need they see, encouragement, etc. Each one of these logs tells much about the spiritual life of the campus. Another notebook is used for specific prayer requests. These may be related to some staff or agency person, or needs of our various churches.

In addition, many people phone us with requests for prayer, not only locally, but often from a distance. It seems that some consider our prayer room to be a "hot line," which it is not, and we occasionally need to encourage the caller to seek professional help. However, we often pray on the phone for the need presented. A column is provided on the right-hand side of the page for the answers, or for additional information about the need.

Because someone is always in this room, all phone calls for the campus are sent to this phone during off-office hours. Sometimes this may be considered a disturbance to prayer, but it has often been the means of blessing to the caller and/or to the prayer watch person in one way or another. We are praying for the unreached around the world.

**Evelyn Varney**

**PRAYER TOWER**
**MADRAS, INDIA**

### Jesus Calls Ministry

On 26 September 1977, while Bro. Dhinakaran waited in fasting and prayer, the Lord Jesus appeared to him and directed him to train evangelists desirous of preaching the Word of God with signs and miracles. In obedience to the Lord's command, the *Jesus Calls*

*Institute of Power Ministry* was set up on 12 July 1980. Those offering themselves for this ministry are trained by Bro. Dhinakaran in an intensive course lasting fifteen days. It is those who have sat in the presence of God for this training and emerged as committed evangelists, filled with the power of the Holy Spirit and His gifts, who minister as Prayer Warriors. From time to time they are being given orientation in ministering to those languishing in sorrow and seeking assistance at the *Jesus Calls* office itself by Bro. Dhinakaran.

### The Prayer Tower Commissioned

On August 12, 1983, the *Prayer Tower* was prayerfully commissioned by the former C.S.I. Bishop of Madras, Rt. Rev. Dr. Sundar Clarke, with the good wishes of the Vicar General of the San Thome Cathedral of the Catholic Church—the late Father A.J. Adaikalam—and the President of the Indian Evangelical Church, Rt. Rev. Dr. Ezra Sargunam.

On top of the *Prayer Tower* is a neon light; and the text it flashes, "PRAYER BRINGS VICTORY," seems to proclaim that victory is assured for the prayers raised from here. Since August 1983, from all over the world, with no distinction of caste, creed or race, millions of prayer requests have come to the *Prayer Tower*.

Victims of diseases, those involved in accidents, the unemployed, failures in business pushed into debts—these are some who contact the *Prayer Tower* at times of crises. Then there are those who have problems at home and in the family who ask for prayers at the *Prayer Tower*. Some want to be prayed for God's blessings on their birthdays, wedding anniversary days or before going to an examination. Invariably, they experience miracles in answer to our earnest prayers for them; and tens of thousands have informed the *Prayer Tower* of the timely help they received.

### Individual Prayers by Prayer Warriors

All over the world those experiencing severe problems are desirous of meeting Bro. Dhinakaran in person to pour out their hearts to him and seek his prayers to lighten their burdens. But, as Bro. Dhinakaran has to be engaged in various activities of the ministry, has to spend hours in fasting and prayer and also minister in various outstations, it is humanly impossible for him to meet all such persons and pray for them. That is why we have appointed Prayer Warriors trained by Bro. Dhinakaran who courteously receive all those who come to *Jesus Calls Prayer Tower*. They ascertain their problems and speak to them words of comfort. They screen certain specially designed video cassettes of Bro. Dhinakaran, which help people realize God's presence and receive His comfort.

The Prayer Warriors then take them to a quiet room, anoint them with prayer oil and pray in tears, imploring the Lord to perform the miracles they need. Immediately, they are released from the grip of the devil. Filled with the peace of God and cured of their diseases, they go home rejoicing with God's abundant blessings. Audio and video cassettes, besides several publications of *Jesus Calls,* are available for further help in the spiritual growth by many who have discovered the love and compassion of Christ by a visit to the *Prayer Tower*. Every day many hundreds of men and women from all over the world visit the *Prayer Tower*. For those who desire individual prayer, the *Jesus Calls* office functions on all days from 9 A.M. to 8 P.M.

Twice every day Bro. Dhinakaran and Bro. Paul Dhinakaran pray for the Young Partners enrolled in the *Jesus Calls Young Partners Plan*. We have made special arrangements in the *Prayer Tower* for prayers being offered for them around the clock. Even as a Book of Remembrance is kept in the presence of God (Malachi 3:16), several volumes—with a page for each young partner, a photograph, full particulars and special needs—are kept in the *Prayer Tower*, for the Young Partners to be remembered all the time in the presence of God.

Every day hundreds of people all over the world telephone the *Prayer Tower*—which functions round the clock—and pour out their needs. The Prayer Warrior at this end then asks, "Is there any help I can render?" and with the utmost concern elicits further details about the emergency which prompted the call. The prayer request is then registered and the Prayer Warrior prays movingly, with a great deal of concern, adding a few words of comfort and assurance of God's intervention.

Because the Lord's eyes are ever open and His ears ever attentive to the prayers offered here, He performs the miracles needed from time to time. The prayer requests each day are then sent to Bro, Dhinakaran for his private prayers. A letter of comfort is then dispatched along with a free booklet.

### The Sacrifice of Prayer Warriors

Prayer Warriors are all holding high offices in various secular walks of life. Yet, out of their love of God and concern for grief-stricken fellow men, they labor day and night in this prayer ministry. They are engaged in their secular jobs during the day from morning till evening. Then they keep awake the whole night at the *Prayer Tower* and pray with much burden for all those who contact them for instant prayer help. In the morning again they go to their places of work. It is such sacrifice they make which brings miracles in the lives of those who lean so heavily on this prayer ministry.

**D.G.S. Dhinakaran**

### 24-HOUR PRAYER WATCH
### SAN PEDRO SULA, HONDURAS

Cloward and Reina Bennett are the Directors of the 24-hour prayer watch in Honduras. This work started in 1986. They had ministered in Honduras for many years. The Lord spoke to them and told them that they should go to North America. They were not sure why they were going, like Abraham, whom God called out of his nation and told to go to a land of which he was not sure.

While in North America, they felt in their spirits that things were not well in their country. It seemed as if their country would be the next to fall into the hands of the Communists, who were next door in Nicaragua. Unlike Abraham, who was not to return to his country, they were told by God to return to their country and to their people. The verse that the Lord spoke to them was this:

**"As long as it is day, we must do the work of him who sent me. Night is coming, when no man can work" (John 9:4).**

They felt that night was about to fall upon their country from the threat of Communism and the internal revolution that was about to take place. They felt this was not a physical battle but a spiritual one, and that the Church was called to fight that battle. They prayed and felt that God gave them the strategy: that if His people would pray, there would be *a new dawn instead of a sudden night*, as the word in John stated. The Lord was requiring a people who would pray.

When they returned, what they had seen in the spirit was exactly what was happening in the natural. God intensified the need for them to pray. They felt that drug dealers, prostitutes, etc. operate on a 24-hour basis, but the church prays for only one-half to one hour a week, so God was requiring them to find a place where they could pray 24 hours a day. They located a place, spoke to different churches and announced on the radio that a new ministry was starting, but it didn't seem to catch the attention of many.

The Lord told them to make a large map of Honduras and to put a light bulb in the center of every state. These bulbs would go on and off constantly, as a reminder for people to pray, or the country would be in danger. In the center of this large map they were to put a large bulb that would not go out. This was to represent the light of the glory of the Lord shining on the country. As long as the people prayed, God's light on their country would not go out.

God's purpose for this ministry was to bring to light all the hidden secrets of the enemy so that they would be destroyed before they could be implemented. The enemy's first assignment was a woman witch doctor sent to a meeting to destroy either Cloward or his wife. After five hours of prayer, the witch doctor received salvation. Through this woman, God showed them what to pray for. She shared all the secret ways of what was happening through witch doctors, and how ministries were being destroyed through their activity.

The Bennets found out all the secret maneuvers in the city. In Honduras, each city is under a curse, so the former witch doctor was able to reveal specifically the things they should be praying for. The people started coming. Some would spend a full day or night praying, others would come for several days to fast and pray.

The election in Honduras was to be held in November of 1989. The people from this 24-hour prayer group felt impressed from the Lord to have an all night prayer vigil and a three-day fast, as the Lord wanted to reveal something. They felt great urgency and obeyed the Lord. Unknown to the group at this time, a secret Communist commander from Nicaragua had been sent to Honduras. His plan was to kill the two main presidential candidates, putting blame on the army. This would cause a revolution within the country and give Nicaragua favor in Honduras, a well-devised plan that was sure to succeed.

While the commander was in his hotel room, a great sense of fear came over him and he delivered himself over to the army. He revealed the secret plan, and how Nicaragua was going to use this plan as a stepping stone to take over the nation of Honduras. There was tremendous joy as the people saw how the Lord brought to light and destroyed the works of the enemy yet once again!

God has provided a radio ministry to encourage the people to pray more; the ministers from every church have opened up their doors. This ministry now functions as a body, where people are constantly coming in and going out, to pray or to be prayed for. They function as a body without a border, and they pray much for unity of the nation. They have seen tremendous answers to prayer.

Another specific answer to prayer was a Jericho march in June of 1989, before the election. The Lord wanted prayer for the man who was to be in power. The vision was shared with all the pastors, who agreed to go ahead with the march on October 23-29, ending with the national day of prayer. This was shared in the prayer meetings and on the radio. One month prior to the election approximately four hundred people met at 5A.M. and, without a sound, commenced the Jericho march. The next day's march, the numbers increased and everyone was sensing a closeness to the Lord. By October 25 and 26, people were wondering what was happening. By the last day, twenty thousand people were involved and an aerial view was taken of the whole march.

This entire time people were praying that the strongholds, not only in their nation, but in other nations, would be thrown down. Coincidentally (but probably not), the walls of Berlin fell at this time. The first answer to prayer was a physical evidence; the walls that divided the rich and the poor were thrown down; the walls of separation between churches and pastors fell. Also as a result of this, all witch activity ceased, their radio programs closed and most of the witches left the country. Since this march, the Lord has given us much favor in the nation. The word quickly spread and revival started in the country. People from every state have come to pray. Many churches have started prayer meetings and welcomed instruction about prayer.

By the power of God, a new dawn, instead of a sudden night, has come to Honduras!

**Cloward Bennett**

## THE LOCAL CHURCH PRAYING
## BURKINA FASO, WEST AFRICA

On the 9th of December 1987, the *Centre International Interdenominationnel d'Evangelisation Burkina Faso* was founded. Its main purposes are: 1) To proclaim the Gospel of Jesus Christ in Burkina Faso and in foreign countries; 2) To participate in the social development of the country by setting up primary and secondary schools, technical training centers, people's dispensary, etc. During these last nine years (1987-1996), the Lord was gracious to us by making this work prosperous. Our part in this growth was to present our requests to God by prayer and petition, with thanksgiving.

### The Esther Group

The Esther Group was born by a revelation from God Himself. He spoke to a small group of women from our church to wake up, as Esther did, to save the souls of our country, Burkina Faso, and all over the world. This attitude requires dying to one's self and a willingness to obey, as Esther did, so that the compassion of the Lord falls down upon his people. At the beginning, this Esther Group was made up of ten sisters submissive to the conditions of the Lord, which are obedience, compassion, sanctification, love for neighbor, and the vision of the work. When all these conditions were met, our God, who is faithful, fulfilled His promises.

Initially, every Saturday from 2 P.M. to 3 P.M. we had an intercession meeting and a monthly day of fasting. If a sin was among us, the Holy Spirit revealed it, and without shame we would confess, ask forgiveness from the Lord, and the Blood of Christ would cover it. The Lord answered our requests in these ways: we saw the church growing, husbands becoming believers, wives giving their lives to the Lord, servants of God rising up, barren being blessed, etc. Today the role of the Esther Group is primarily intercession, so that the churches gain in quality and in quantity before the Lord.

### The Ministry of Intercession

Because of the quick growth of the work, intercession is an essential part among us. A Ministry of Intercession has been set up with sections (departments) and section leaders for specific subjects of prayer such as: leaders and their families, evangelization, our nation, and the life of the Church. The scheduling of the intercession includes the local church praying, groups that pray together starting at 6 A.M. and continuing until 6 P.M., a prayer watch where more people come from 6 P.M. until 10 P.M., and other small groups that pray through the night, after which the morning prayer begins again. There are also special prayer weeks together and fasting by the local church.

Results of prayer from 1989 to 1993 had a beneficial effect on the ministry life and on the Evangelization Center through church planting in other towns, team evangelization, the setting up of social works (prisons, youth, hospital) and travels in French-speaking countries. At present, after a time of laxity, intercessory life started again in favor of the growth of the Church of Christ, workers in the field, servants of God on the battle field, the unreached (*10/40 Window*), and Israel. We rely on God's grace for the new phase of the ministry, stressing evangelization, mission, intercession and edification of the people of God. We give the glory to our Lord Jesus Christ.

In Ouagadougou, which is the capital city, there are more than eight congregations in the central church each Sunday. We collect the names of those who will be involved in the prayer watch that week, and each congregation works out its own program, its own schedule. We see that there is a love in the church now that people are interceding much more for others. In the provinces we have started more than 30 churches, and are encouraging them to pray and intercede. They are not yet able to carry it on 24 hours a day, but we have faith it will begin to happen there.

## The Hand of the Lord

Located in West Africa, we see the Muslims who surround us becoming softer toward the Gospel. As in most Muslim countries, after people come to the Lord, they're often treated very badly by their family and others. But with the 24-hour prayer chain, we now see that the Muslims who are being converted are actually reaching out to their families and converting them. We see this is happening through prayer. The prayer has really become the center of the church, the thing that is really indispensable.

If people are sick, without the money to go to the doctor, the people know to bring them to the Evangelistic Center in the church. And they are healed. We see people bringing others continually. To us it is not a place of evangelism, but it's first of a place of prayer, praying that God will intervene in their lives. After a few months they start coming regularly themselves, saying, "I'm coming to join you and I want to pray with you."

Most of the people who are leading a prayer group (chain) are people who were healed themselves at one time through prayer. There are women who have been there often concerning problems with their children. The people pray for them and then they see within a few months that God has answered. I can tell you that it's really a blessing from God when you come to this point of being able to live out a 24-hour prayer chain. There are times we don't know what to say, but God knows, and suddenly we just see that we should pray for a certain country—and we start praying for it.

In these last days we must raise ourselves up to prayer. We must stop murmuring and gossiping and just talking—there's no time to waste like that. And when you don't take a lot of time praying, then you end up taking a lot of time for other things and have problems in the church. You don't have peace in your heart. There's not love, and people say, "I will change churches, there's no love here." We have to put ourselves before the Throne of God. *May God bless you!*

**Pastor Mamadou Karambiri, Pastor Pierre-Damien Yelemou**

### HELSINKI PRAYER WATCH
### FINLAND

The Helsinki Prayer Watch was started in the spring of 1990. Tom Hess visited us in May of that year. He came from Herrnhut, East Germany, studying the birth phases of 24-Hour Prayer Watches. He told us that the Holy Spirit was birthing such watches in different cities of the world. He encouraged us to organize a Prayer Watch in Helsinki and in Finland.

So we published a large article on the subject in our paper. This article was a continuation of an article on Biblical hours of prayer published earlier. We started to enlist people for praying around the clock unceasingly 24 hours a day. Each prayer watcher occupied one or two hours a week. We collected names by means of coupons in connection with the article in the paper or from interdenominational meetings.

This 24-Hour Prayer Chain is still functioning today. Only very few have canceled over these years. We publish a list of prayer requests, and give encouragement in every paper. The paper covers our activities in Ex-Soviet, in Israel and Finland. We pray for the exodus of the Jewish people, that they will know their God, for each of the Tshernobyl (Chernobyl) children camps, for problems in Israel, and for the *Jerusalem House of Prayer* which Tom Hess oversees. A prayer time is given to every watcher individually, and is registered in our computer. Though each one focuses on the same list of items, there remains much scope for the Holy Spirit in prayer.

Less than five hundred people are involved in the Prayer Watch. Most of them are from Helsinki (larger area), but a lot are from other parts of Finland. Most week-hours have more than one watcher. We do not know each one personally, as many belong to different denominations.

Stephen Lightle encouraged Finnish Christians to seek God together for revival and a Jewish Exodus through Finland. Our main focus of prayer is that the Jews will know their God, and their exodus from the Ex-Soviet. We have different projects connected with these goals. Some of the answers and breakthroughs we have received are:

Breakdown of Soviet Communism;
Independence of the Baltic countries;
Appointment of Toimi Kankaanniemi (a Pentecostal believer) as Exodus and Development Cooperation Minister;
Exodus of Soviet Jews through Finland;
Establishment of camps in Finland, since 1990, for children from the Tshernobyl area (Byelorussia and Ukraine);
In 1995 and 1996, two hundred Jewish children in summer camps in Finland;
Bible School connected with camps;
Missions to the Baltics, Russia, Byelorussia, and the Ukraine. Forty tons of Bibles, Hebrew study materials, literature, medical aide delivered to many people in the Ex-Soviet. Many Jewish people expressed their desire to receive Messiah;
One family is supported in Israel.

Our hope and vision for the future is to be able to respond to crisis and challenges more quickly, and therefore more flexibility must be developed. We must have a checkpoint to detect possible passive Prayer Watchers. Our aim is still to increase the number of Watchers to one thousand in the future. The teaching of "Watching and Praying" is important for preparing us to be ready when Jesus comes.

**Rauno Nuoraho**

BETHEL
SRI LANKA

It is indeed strange but true, for truth is always strange, even stranger than fiction. When God called me out of being an advocate of the Supreme Court of Sri Lanka to be an advocate of the Lord Jesus Christ in that very same land, along with my wife and our little daughter, to serve Him in His full time service, it was indeed not an easy decision. For our daughter was only six years then, and He wanted us to live by faith, closing every earthly bank account and trusting only the Bank of Heaven—for as the Scripture says,

### "When the Son of Man comes again will he find faith?" (Luke 18:8)

When the Lord called my wife and me as a family on the 17th of September 1981 He wanted us on the day of our decision, as the word prophetically came to us, to plant seven churches right around the island of Sri Lanka from the North to the South and the East to the West. We had just started one, and it seemed to us then a most ludicrous proposition with one hardly being underway. Why He wanted seven churches and not six, even as the same was confirmed by another praying saint of God that very same day in 1981, we then could not comprehend or understand, for then we saw through the glass darkly.

Now, as we look back today on that revelation fifteen years ago on why seven churches, we understand more comprehensively. His ways are not our ways, and we thank God a million times over that we took that way of truth. As years slowly passed the truth of His word began to reveal why seven churches. If one goes to the beginning in Genesis 2:3, one finds that God blessed the seventh day. It doesn't say that He blessed the first day, the second, the third, the fourth, the fifth or the sixth but only the seventh day. Seven in the Bible represents the number of perfection or completion. The message in the Book of Revelation (the *omega* in the Bible, even as Genesis is the *alpha*) is addressed to the seven angels in the seven churches. There are seven candlesticks, seven stars, seven trumpets, seven vials, seven seals, seven mountains all not there by accident but by Divine purpose.

Today we have by His grace planted these seven churches in the places God Himself nominated, five of them being on the borders of the North, South, East and West. Seven churches of Bethel in Nugegoda, which we call our Jerusalem even as it is our headquarters and strangely has an upper room as the first church in Jerusalem met in an upper room on that great day of the Holy Spirit's first outpouring.

After we had completed the seven churches, the Holy Spirit, who moves so beautifully in that upper room in our "Jerusalem" in Nugegoda, prophetically spoke to us and called us "the church of the candlestick," even as we had planted seven churches. Then, strangely, the Lord in a more than marvelous way brought seven people from our church in Bethel Sri Lanka to *Jerusalem House of Prayer for All Nations* on the Mount of Olives in 1994. The *menorah* or the Jewish candlestick we then saw and understood in a new light which we had never seen before.

When we returned home to Sri Lanka that year, we took seven Jewish candlesticks with us back to Sri Lanka, not as an idol or icon, but with the revelation that even as the *menorah* is to the Jew and Israel a great light of seven, so are the seven churches in Sri Lanka to the island of Sri Lanka as a whole. Now we comprehend Romans 11 more fully than before, and thank God a hundred million times over that we have been grafted into the olive tree. The Lord wanted each of the seven churches from each of their center shafts to put out six branches each, so that soon and very soon we will have forty nine churches covering the whole of our beautiful island.

If that was not sufficient, the Holy Spirit, in the Sancta Sanctorum of our upper room at Nugegoda, our Jerusalem, reminded us that when Jesus came into the world the first time He did not come for shepherds who watch their flock by day, but shepherds who watch their flock by night. Each of our seven churches of Bethel, throughout our island, pray from 11-12 at midnight, binding all the powers of darkness that arise even as the thief cometh by night, and covering each of our individual believers in our respective seven churches.

In our headquarters at Nugegoda, from about 1993 September, a 24-hour prayer watch has been kept from the upper room in our little Jerusalem. Jesus did not say "pray and watch" but "watch and pray." We therefore now monitor every happening, beginning with Jerusalem in Israel and then pray, for God has not by accident put Jerusalem right in the center of the world map. The reason why God wanted this kept is because, like watchmen on a watchtower, we could warn of the advance of the enemy before they came to the gates. For when we are in the mountains of prayer we can always see what's going on in the valley, like Gideon from the mountain viewed the Midianites in the valley and their doings. More than on many occasions has God warned us of things in the ministry before they happened and so, too, concerning our land. More things are wrought by prayer than this world dreams of.

Surely the wind is blowing again. As in the day of Pentecost, the wind is blowing again. The other six churches of Bethel are also stirring to keep the 24-hour prayer. Every Friday we gather most of our believers to pray from 10:00 at night to 5:00 the next morning. It is not strange, then, that two years later, in 1996, God brought seven from Bethel once again to *Jerusalem House of Prayer* on the Mount of Olives.

**John Kitto**

### PRAYER FOR IRELAND
### CHRISTIAN RENEWAL CENTRE
### BELFAST, IRELAND

*Prayer for Ireland* was formed at the time of the IRA cease-fire in the autumn of 1994. It has several components:

• A 24-hour prayer chain was established. This is calling people to pray specifically for the unity of the Body (John 17); Renewal of the Church by the Holy Spirit; Healing of the Nation (2 Chronicles 7:14), which affects morals/ethics, family, education, etc.; and for Israel and the *10/40 Window;*

• Two monthly Prayer Focuses on issues related to the points above;

• Organization of prayer days and conferences;

• "Healing of the Nation Prayer Schools";

• Development of interchurch prayer groups around the country in all of the towns. These groups are meeting in a spirit of unity within a divided society and church, praying for their local communities, leaders—both spiritual and secular, for local issues present and historic, and for national issues. A number of these are already functioning effectively.

• We are also seeking to develop links with other prayer groups/ministries around the country.

General issues for prayer:

• Church leaders—many need a clear vision for the unity of the Body of Christ in Ireland. They also need to lead their congregations away from sectarianism. The church is full of sectarianism and division. This requires spiritual boldness in the midst of much intimidation, even when from within the church. Traditionalism and Free Masonry (within the Protestant churches) have a very binding influence on the spirituality of many congregations.

• Our secular leaders also need to develop a politics that is anti-sectarian in nature. This will take a miracle. The "Statelet" of Northern Ireland has a blatantly sectarian Covenant built into its foundation. This was endorsed by the three major Protestant church leaders of the time (1922). Many signed it in their own blood, vowing to establish and protect (even with guns) a Protestant State for Protestant People against Rome and Popery. On the Irish Nationalist side, similar appeals to blood sacrifice have been made throughout history—the goddess Eire requiring the blood of her young men to perpetuate her youth.

• We need to see a Spirit-borne move of repentance. I am at present part of a small working party seeking to address this issue.

• With the recent upsurge in violence—intimidation, fear, dominance and control are very frequently used words on both sides of our divided community. There are groups working within and across the divide to promote these feelings to maintain their own influence and control.

**Harry Smith**

### 24-HOUR PRAYER WATCH
### HANSARANG IN KOREA

In 1994, Barnabas Kim, professor at Hansarang Bible School in Seoul, attended *All Nations Convocation Jerusalem* and there heard about 24-hour prayer watches in other nations. This was quite a challenge, considering that Korea is noted for its enthusiasm in prayer. He felt that Korea, as a nation of prayer, should have been the first country to start this prayer watch. Also, because Hansarang is believed to have been called to be a supporter of Israel, especially of Messianic Believers, and to be a vessel to help promote the ministry of World Mission in Korean Churches, he had a burden to start this prayer watch at Hansarang in Korea.

Barnabas brought the book, *Let My People Go* by Tom Hess from Israel and gave it to Mikyung Kim[1], a mighty prayer warrior, to read. After reading, she was consumed with the desire to start a prayer watch. In late October 1994, she and three other sisters laid the foundation for this prayer watch. Average attendance at the regular prayer meeting is about ten, and the number of those who have pledged to take part in this 24-hour prayer watch is around fifty.

There were some great results gained from this prayer watch. Many personally received fresh anointings and revelations, and experienced prosperity and peace both in their finances and in their spiritual lives as the Scripture promised to bestow blessings upon those who pray for the peace of Jerusalem. For some who were struggling hard to set aside a time for prayer, this proved to be a good opportunity.

Since beginning the prayer watch we have seen some changes in the direction of our prayer. In the beginning, the prayer focus was on world mission, especially the *10/40 Window* region and Mikyung—the leader of this prayer watch—tried to exclude other prayers involving Korean society or Hansarang Ministry and its Bible School. Our aim was to see the whole world turn to God and worship Him. However, after awhile the Lord led her to realize that, in order for this to happen, prayer for Hansarang Bible School is needed as well since this is a place for sending out missionaries. We are not quite aware of the results of our prayer for other nations, but we have seen some good results in prayer for our Bible School. As one example, just a few weeks ago, our school faced a critical moment concerning our moving to another place, and the prayer support of this group helped overcome many difficulties. We believe God will greatly use our prayers more and more.

Presently, many students who joined the prayer watch are on short-term mission trips to other nations, so the majority of people who attend the 24-hour watch are staff. We are hoping to propagate this work and recruit more members to join.

Our vision for this prayer watch is to raise up mighty prayer warriors for each nation. I believe one truly mighty prayer warrior of God can take the responsibility for the souls of one nation. Currently, people are in the process of being trained in prayer. Also, a plan is underway to start an intercessor's school because we believe that

---

1. *Messianic Community of Reconciliation* at *Jerusalem House of Prayer for All Nations* was blessed to have Mikyung serving with them for three months during 1995.

prayer is the source of energy which causes this school to proceed and which changes world history. May God raise up His warriors in these last days!

**Barnabas Kim**

## PRAYER WATCH
## ZAMBIA

*Prayer Watch- Zambia* was launched in November 1994, following coordinator Venassie Mibenge's participation in the first *All Nations Convocation Jerusalem*. The Watch has received tremendous response from zealous intercessors. It is spreading like real wildfire. The President of our nation is also involved; he is a watchman, too! So is the Vice President. The President wrote us in full support of the 24-Hour Prayer Watch.

The ministry is not affiliated with any church, but has many prayer watchmen from different towns becoming involved. Every watchman is free to pray for fifteen minutes or more every day, and some decided to go for one hour every day.

Prayer Reminders (prayer requests) are distributed regularly to the watchmen, with a different prayer focus for each day of the week. Each prayer focus then has many suggested subtopics. Examples of prayer focuses are:

Sunday: The Government and the Ruling Party: Opposition Parties and their Leaders

Monday: Zambia; Israel

Tuesday: The Church and Leaders from all Christian Denominations; Married People and their Families; Single People

Wednesday: Health, Education, Firemen; Bribery, Corruption, Office Abuse; Pornography

Thursday: City, Town and Rural Councils; Journalism; Evangelism/Mission Work

Friday: Industries, Companies; Banks and other Financial Institutions; Transport

Saturday: 24-Hour Prayer Watch- Zambia; Finances; House of Prayer

We give thanksgiving to God for the answered prayer requests. Some of the most dangerous criminals in the country were shot dead during the first month of the Prayer Watch, especially on the Copperbelt. Let us pray for the criminals either to be saved through Jesus Christ or be eliminated by the Police from the innocent society.

A few months later, large volumes of pornographic materials were intercepted by Police as they were being smuggled into the country from South Africa by rail. More culprits have been brought to book. Praise God!

Huge masses of dangerous drugs being pushed into Zambia have been seized. Our God is not deaf nor His arm too short to save. The Lord really hears the Watchmen!

After what seemed like the beginning of a drought, the Lord heard our cry and blessed us with rains throughout the country. We believe the Lord has answered our prayers and we are going to have a bumper harvest.

*Pray for the outpouring of the Holy Ghost to be evident upon Zambia!*

### Rev. Venassie Mibenge

## SHU KWANG CHRIST CHURCH
## JILING, CHINA

Jesus said, **"Ask and it will be given to you; seek and you will find; knock and the door will be opened to you"** (Matthew 7:7-8). This is God's promise. Our church, *Shu Kwang* (Dawn) *Christ Church*, in Jiling Province, China, holds firmly to the cord of prayer and the building up of the prayer network. We have experienced the richness of God's provision.

In 1992, a group of ten Christians started to pray every morning and to have an overnight watch twice a month. Then, since November of 1994, the 24-hour prayer watch was established. From that time the church started to grow rapidly. There were three hundred members packed in an 87-square-metre small church. We were forced to have three services for worship. We needed to extend the building, which would be costly. Such great expense was beyond our capacity. However, we went to God, according to Psalm 81:10, and asked Him in faith, with mouth wide open, because it says in the Bible,

**"Is anything too hard for the Lord?"** (Genesis 18:14)

**"There is nothing too hard for Thee"** (Jeremiah 32:17).

244

Yung-nan Sun, the administrator and teacher at our church, led the church members to have a 40-day fast. As Joshua led the Israelites in a march around the city of Jericho, Yung-nan Sun led us in a march around our church once a day until God answered our prayer. During that 40-day fast, we continued in corporate prayer from 12 to 1 P.M. every day, wherever each believer was located.

Miraculously, God answered our prayer with immeasurable blessing, which was more than all we could ask or imagine (Ephesians 3:20). Now we have a big prayer sanctuary, 1647 square meters, that can hold one thousand people, a van for evangelism, and a 418-square-metre education building. Praise God for His mighty work! In the education building, we are able to train the believer. By the "gospel van," we are bringing forth praise and good news to awaken the sleeping soul.

*Let us pray together, so that worship and praise may fill the world. All the glory to the Father, who is in heaven!*

**Rev. and Mrs. Chao Yung Chien**

### SOUTH PACIFIC WATCH OF THE LORD—FIJI

After two months of prayer and fasting, *Watch of the Lord - Fiji* was launched at an ICEJ service on 16th December 1994. The Lord took control right from the beginning. The ICEJ Chairman wanted a report about the 1994 *All Nations Convocation Jerusalem*, which I attended as a delegate from Fiji. Praise the Lord, this was the Lord's way. Through ICEJ we were able to start the Watch as we had all the watchmen we needed. Our initial schedule for the Watch was as follows:

**Day of Watch:**

Commenced midnight Wednesday and ended midnight Thursday. Our first Watch was on 26th January 1995. Thursday was also a day of fasting for ICEJ, so this was a source of spiritual strength to both ministries.

**Allocated Time:**

20 minutes per watchman, or in some cases, per pair.

**Number of Watchmen:**

We started with 73 watchmen, but into our second month found that the Lord had recruited another 27 watchmen.

Thursday seemed to come so slowly for some watchmen, as they excitedly looked forward to their allotted time with the Lord. Some excited watchmen prayed two 20-minute periods or even an hour. Some hardly got to sleep as they waited for their time to go on duty, which meant bedtime was about 3:00 A.M. or even 4:00 A.M., but they woke up to another new day refreshed spiritually. Some even confused the days, so that they were praying both Wednesday and Thursday.

For the first two months, our prayers were for national leaders; for political, church, provincial and household leaders (fathers of every family in the nation); for schools, principals, teachers and students. A letterhead (page border) was designed, which is a chain signifying the 24-hour Watch. At the top of the chain is a circle surrounding the map of the Fiji Islands, with pointers signifying the clock. The words of the circle are *Watch of the Lord - Fiji Needs God.*

Fiji has been greatly blessed and has gone through major changes in the past two years, both in the Government and in the Church. We currently have been going through a series of revivals. Evangelists and prayer warriors from other nations, including our neighboring islands, have visited our shores, accomplished their mission, and departed again. It's amazing how God has lined them up one after another! And the response from our own people has been overwhelming. I believe that God is answering our (*Watch of the Lord*) prayers, as REVIVAL has been one of our Prayer Points for the last couple of months.

Our Prayer Group (Watchmen) has almost tripled within one year and we now number about 200, praise God. They include pastors, nurses, secretaries, clerks, housewives, teachers, soldiers, policemen, and students both from primary and secondary levels. It may be of interest that our youngest watchman is only nine years old. Fiji is a multi- racial country, so our watchmen consist of Chinese, Indians, Tongans, Japanese, Europeans and, of course, Fijians.

Initially, I sent out a Newsletter once a month, but I couldn't cope with that when the watchmen increased, so I have reduced it to one every two months. The feedback continues to be encouraging. Through all this I'm just worshiping and glorifying the Lord for His inspiration, and humbly wait as He leads us in His paths.

**Frances Tuicakau**

## SOUTH PACIFIC PRAYER MOVEMENT
## SOLOMON ISLANDS

The Prayer Movement in the Solomon Islands started with a burden for missions in the South Pacific. Those who helped organize the movement saw that churches needed to become involved in world missions. The group was small and therefore felt they needed to move together in the South Pacific Islands. With that thought, they decided to have a prayer movement. One week annually they brought people together from the South Pacific Islands to pray—nothing else.

Missions Commission is the missionary arm of the *Evangelical Fellowship of the South Pacific* (EFSP). This Commission was formed in Suva, Fiji in December 1989. At the second meeting of EFSP leaders, in Brisbane in August 1990, significant decisions were made towards the further development of EFSP and its Missions Commission. One of these decisions was the initiation of the Prayer Assembly. Encouraged by further insights gained by a number of South Pacific leaders who attended the Asia Mission Congress, 1990, held in Seoul, Korea, and also in 1991, it was decided to hold the first Prayer Assembly in Honiara, Solomon Islands in July 1991.

In this first Prayer Assembly about 200 people participated, with over 40 coming from outside the Solomon Islands: from Fiji, New Zealand, Vanuatu, Australia, Papua New Guinea and Canada. This assembly was a real success and little fires were sparked off in various parts in the region.

The second Prayer Assembly was also held in Honiara, in 1992. About 200 delegates came. Over 100 of these came from outside the Solomon Islands: from Australia, Papua New Guinea, Vanuatu, Kiribati, New Zealand, the United Sates and Finland. One of the most significant principles grasped was from the life of Nehemiah and his prayer. Identifying with the sins of his nation and his forefathers, Nehemiah repented and confessed them, pleading with God for mercy and forgiveness, and then sought God for revival blessing upon his land. The Lord laid similar burdens on representatives of various groups, churches, and nations. The time of intercession was really deep and moving. Papua New Guinea hosted the third Prayer Assembly in June 1993. Subsequent Prayer Assembly Conferences were 1994 in Brisbane, Australia, 1995 in New Zealand and 1996 in Fiji.

The Prayer Assembly movement is gaining momentum. People are linking up because of their desire to pray. This started as a weekly thing. Groups come and spend two or three days in prayer. The idea is to form 24-hour prayer watches, not just a few days a week. Those who come from distant places come for a week. The people who come here, come only to pray. They found out that if people do other things on the side, the unity is broken and the effectiveness of prayer is lost. About twenty to forty people are in each group, and there are many groups throughout the South Pacific.

The prayer focus centers upon:

Evangelism across the South Pacific Islands and around the world; that local churches catch the vision of having prayer groups and then be able to come together to pray.

Prayer for spiritual vitality within the churches in the region and an unclouded vision for world missions.

Prayer for the mobilization of a united missionary movement from the "Uttermost Part of the Earth."

Prayer for the national leaders of the nations in the region and the world, that our nations might be a living testimony and witness to the goodness of God Almighty.

There have been many answers to prayer. Some of the more significant ones are in regards to elections. One election was predicted to be a "bloody," but the groups rallied together and prayed—and it was one of the most peaceful. Also, throughout the summer games, there was much potential for uprisings, but the games were peaceful after much prayer.

The desire for the future is that in each country the people would go back to their churches and begin to build up a prayer movement within their region, then have it developed into 24-hour prayer groups. The hope is for each area or district to have their own prayer group, and then to have a national group for each country. Others hope for a prayer mountain where people could go to pray all night.

Prayer requests are being sought from around the world as fuel for the prayer groups. Although the prayer needs could not be passed nationally due to telephone communication limitations, they could be handled locally or within several groups.

**Rev. Michael Maeliau**

## 24-HOUR PRAYER WATCH
## PARAMARIBO, SURINAME

Things have been developing spiritually in Suriname in a splendid way, directly after *All Nations Convocation Jerusalem '94.*

• November '94: a breakthrough in the Hindu community. Many Hindu men came to the Lord, sharing with wives and children, neighbors and friends what they have found in our Lord Jesus Christ.

• January '95: the launching of a 24-Hour Prayer Watch. Intercessors from all Christian denominations participating. This is still going on.

• May 25 '95 (Ascension Day): First broadcasting from Suriname's first Christian radio station, *Radio Shalom.* In the meantime, three more Christian broadcasting units came into existence, two with a station.

• Women and youth have been holding days of prayer and fasting for the country, which was experiencing great difficulties. Immediately after, we saw great changes in the currency and the economic situation. A spirit of prayer and fasting is developing more and more in the country, and many are expecting an awakening.

• November 3 '95: Proclamation of the *Sibibusi Movement of Healing and Unity,* a movement where leaders and people of all Christian denominations are participating—the Bishop of the Roman Catholic Church next to the Bishop of the Moravian Church, and the Superintendent of the Pentecostal Churches and Moravian Church, as well as Baptist pastors, are members of the Advisory Committee. This never happened before, and is something completely new. At the moment, 70% of Suriname's population knows about this Movement and are behind its goals of healing and unity.

• The 1996 election surprised all groups. At the moment, talks are being held to establish the new Government and the new President. We think that in a week or so we will know if it will be the same one or another. The name of the Chief Justice was mentioned: a born again spirit filled lady who had been my weekly prayer partner for about four years.

• In June '96 we started a special prayer group, *Friends of Israel.* It is still small, but we believe that it will grow, especially with those who have been visiting Israel.

- Recently, it was front-page news that Suriname and Israel have made bilateral strings and the nonresident ambassador (residence Caracas) was here, visiting our government. It was a good thing to see all this also on television. He mentioned the good contact that Suriname, as a former colony of Holland, has always had with Israel. Three synagogues, two of them still in use, prove this.

**Paul Doth**

## BRUSSELS PRAYER WATCH
## BELGIUM

The Brussels Prayer Watch grew out of the relationships established as several pastors began praying together a few years ago. This led to city-wide prayer gatherings organized by these churches, led by Rick and Patti Ridings. By the grace of God, we began to see answers to these corporate prayers in the headlines of the Brussels newspapers (especially those prayers for God to expose sexual exploitation, political corruption and Freemasonry).

In 1994, we began to have an increasing conviction that God desired us to establish a 24-hour prayer chain in Brussels. This was confirmed at *All Nations Convocation Jerusalem* in 1994, when Rick heard the many reports of how God was raising up such prayer watches throughout the world. He felt that God would have the *Brussels Prayer Watch* be primarily an outgrowth of the growing relationship between these churches. This was presented to them, and it was decided that specific churches would sign up to cover as much of one day as possible.

Evangelical churches in Belgium are generally quite small (*Operation World* gives the percentage of evangelical Christians in Belgium as less than the percentage in India or Egypt), so it was agreed that two or three churches could take responsibility for one day per week, as needed. This was launched in May 1995.

Each two months, a newsletter is published, giving a subject of prayer for each week. Intercessors are encouraged to send in subjects they are receiving to be placed in the newsletter. As of autumn of 1996, about four days are taken and almost filled. We are in the process of contacting other churches, as we now have seen a city-wide pastors' prayer group launched, which brings together many additional pastors.

*Please pray with us that there will soon be a complete chain of 24-hour prayer in Brussels.*

**Rick Ridings**

## 168-HOUR PRAYER NET
## HUNGARY

### Background

In 1987, led by the Holy Spirit with the help of international intercessors and prophetic leaders (Steven Lightle, Johannes Facius), Hungarian pastors and leaders from different denominations gathered together to pray for unity and reconciliation. We were all touched by the Spirit of repentance. We asked each other for forgiveness and expressed our love and intention to continue this healing process. We decided to hold an interdenominational prayer day quarterly in Budapest. Roman Catholic, Lutheran, Reformed, Baptist and Free Churches were regularly present, each of them open for the work of the Holy Spirit.

We usually start the meetings with worship. After the teaching we give testimonies and share our views about the most important political and spiritual events on national and international levels. The emphasis is always on prayer. We form small groups, and following an introduction we pray:

a) for personal renewal and repentance;
b) for political leaders and progressive changes in the life of our nation;
c) for family and church issues;
d) for international tensions, Israel.

### Fruit

We experienced a new love and openness to cooperation among Christians. The Communistic era is finished. God fulfilled a prophetic vision: "The red stars will fall." It happened exactly so. Hungary opened the border for the East German tourists (1989) and the iron curtain had broken. It was a tremendous blessing that the changes were happening without bloodshed.

The Russian Red Army left our country. God led us to reach a brotherly hand to the surrounding nations. We were part of the conference for reconciliation in Prague '94. The nations of the former Austro-Hungarian Monarchy came together for asking and receiving forgiveness. Christian leaders prayed for the healing of historical wounds and for an end to the ethnic war in the former Yugoslavia.

### Sharing Prayer Net

Later God laid on our heart the desire to organize a continuous prayer net to protect our nation and to help churches and individuals to grow in faith and love. The first *All Nations Convocation Jerusalem* was held in 1994 in Israel. Inspired by the reports of different delegates, we started the Hungarian 24-Hour Prayer Watch in October 1995. It is called *168 Hour Prayer Net*. The described "Quarterly Prayer Day" and the *Prayer Net* are working side by side together and have the same leadership. Our first leader is Lajos Racz, a Reformed pastor, but the whole movement is supported by an interdenominational Pastor Group (Budapest) and the Reformed Pastor Meeting (pastors from different parts of Hungary).

All intercessors have the possibility to share prayer requests, questions, reflections concerning the events of the world and our nation, spiritual life and proclaiming the Gospel. The Prayer Net has a correspondence service, and publishes a prayer letter four times each year. We have intercessors from many congregations as Reformed, Baptist, Methodist, Free Church, Pentecostal and Faith Church (together 10 Churches, with 250 members). Because of prayer, the country was protected from high floods and obscene advertising in 1996.

### Vision

We want to realize our special responsibility in Mid-Eastern Europe. We believe we are in this area in a doorkeeper position in both a political and a spiritual sense. It is possible to reach many other former East-Block countries with the Gospel from Hungary. Probably Hungary will remain a transit way for the Jews from Russia to Israel. We hope that the Lord will grant greater unity in the Church. We have dedicated ourselves to serve the Lord by His power. That is why we want to keep on praying. God bless you, Shalom.

**Istvan Tatai**

## THE TOWER OF PRAYER
## THE NEW ANOINTING CHURCH
## MEXICO CITY

After eight years in God's service, the Lord called us to what has been the most important vision in our ministries. In 1989 God spoke to us to stand in the gap for Mexico, and to start the sequence of strategic spiritual warfares that are leading Mexico into the greatest revivals of all its history. The call was not only to pray, but to give our lives totally as soldiers in His hands; to give Him everything we were—even unto death.

The vision started with giving seminars on spiritual warfare throughout the country, and even into other nations of Latin America, and raising up warriors and intercessors to build a prayer network in Mexico and in the Continent.

In 1993 the Lord gave us a vision on how the strongholds of evil were built and interconnected all over the country, and how these fortresses were linked to the main thrones of Satan around the world. The revelation came abundantly over the starting team of watchmen, and the order came to go to these thrones and to destroy them in the name of Jesus; to deliver the people from the veils of captivity in order to see a harvest of millions of souls.

Great are the testimonies of His glory, but too small is the space to share them all. In 1994 the Lord allowed us to establish prayer teams in thirty of the thirty-two states in Mexico. God was pouring over the nation a mantle of prayer, of intercession, and a prophetic anointing to confront the forces of Satan.

In the same year we received the order to destroy the powers of witchcraft in the most satanic city in Mexico, called "Catemaco," a place where Satan himself came to make covenants with politicians and artists from all over the continent. The Lord moved the thirty teams and gave us around one million intercessors for forty days of fasting for this cause. Sixty-nine of the one hundred twenty major warlocks killed themselves among each other. Of the others, some came to Jesus and the rest left. The throne of Satan was physically burned. Thousands received Christ in their hearts, and now the city is considered a Christian city.

In 1996 we established the first 24-hour Prayer Tower in Mexico City, linked to the other thirty cities, and to eight countries in Latin America. As the first great testimony of the Tower, the Lord gave us the order to preach in three weeks to the most idolatrous state in Mexico, called "Puebla," in order to stop a volcano from exploding as a judgment of God to that city.

As an incredible miracle, the Lord opened for us the TV and all the radio stations, the most important newspapers (in all of these it was forbidden by the law to speak about God or the gospel). The message of salvation was widely preached. We mobilized, by the hand of God, more than one thousand evangelists, and the government surrendered to help us. In this three-week Organization Evangelism, more than three million people in six cities received the gospel of Jesus Christ.

Glory to God! Mexico is coming to Christ because the Army of God in this nation is taking its place. Hallelujah!

**Torcuato and Ana Luca de Tena**

### HOUSE OF PRAYER FOR ALL NATIONS—PAPUA NEW GUINEA

In September 1990, God spoke to my heart in Singapore while on a trip to Korea, to attend *Asia Pacific Missions Congress* "VISION ENFOLDED." He said, *"I am going to do a quick work and will cut it short."* During that time I began to sense something in my spirit that later on I was introduced to as the vision of the Prayer Networks.

Returning from Korea with that sense of urgency in my heart, God led us on to start *Christ for the Nations Ministry.* After writing out the ministry's objectives, I realized that two of the objectives seemed to be connected to the word that God had spoken to me in Singapore.

These two objectives were:

**Prayer Center:**

Training and equipping Intercessors and seasoned prayer warriors through prayer retreats and seminars to do the will of God in the end times.

**Bless Israel:**

The ministry (Church) has a privilege and an obligation to stand with the Nation of Israel in the area of praying and giving to Israel. I had also written down to establish a *House of Prayer for All Nations Papual, New Guinea* (Isaiah 62:6-7; Psalm 122:6).

Three years later Rev. Michael Maeliau, the South Pacific Regional Prayer Leader whom I also met on the trip to Korea in

1990, introduced me and the ministry to the Prayer Networks: *South Pacific Prayer Assembly*, *International Fellowship of Intercessors*, *Jerusalem House of Prayer for All Nations* and others. Because it was written in the framework of the ministry's vision we fully participated in these Prayer Networks and will continue as long as the Lord tarries.

## Establishment of the House of Prayer for All Nations— Papua New Guinea

Through much praying and supporting the nation of Israel, we felt led to send a prayer watchman to Israel. Early this year the Lord burdened my heart that it's time we have a 24-hour prayer watch and to establish a *House of Prayer for All Nations—Papua, New Guinea*. The Lord surely provided a beautiful house with natural surroundings situated in Lae, second largest city in Papua New Guinea. The house is now used as the 24-hour prayer watch; Scriptures based on Isaiah 56:7.

## Dedication of the House of Prayer

*The House of Prayer for All Nations—Papua, New Guinea* was dedicated and launched on the 7th of September 1996, witnessed by Pastors and Leaders of various churches in the city. We felt the presence of the Almighty God and the humble spirit of intercession. The first group of five intercessors was led by Lutu Kisu, our 1995 watchman candidate to Israel. They spent ten days of prayer and fasting during *All Nations Convocation Jerusalem* held in September 1996.

### Progress

The progress is gradual but we believe God will bring intercessors. It has also been heavy upon our hearts to reach nineteen provinces and see that we have a Network of nineteen prayer watches set up all over the nation. The Lord miraculously brought pastors and leaders to our recent Leadership Conference held on 29th November-1st December. Hallelujah! The need to set up 24-hour prayer watches in the nineteen provinces was shared along with Blessing Israel by supporting financially and materially. The strategy was laid out and we have reached ten provinces—nine prayer watches are set up plus the *House of Prayer* and we have three in the infant stage. Thank God!

These are the strategies used by the *House of Prayer for All Nations— Papua, New Guinea* and the nine other established prayer watches:

## a) Daily Prayer Focus:

Monday- Pray for the vision of the ministry to continue.
Tuesday- Pray for the Body of Christ.
Wednesday- Pray for the Nation of Israel, the return of the Jewish people.
Thursday- Pray for the governments of the world.
Friday- Pray for world evangelism - salvation of the Gentiles.
Saturday - Pray for families - salvation needs.
Sunday- Pray for anointing-worship leaders, preachers of the Word.

## b) International Prayer Alert: *Aliyah*, the return of the Jewish people.

We are also sensitive to the leading of the Holy Spirit in what He wants us to pray.

### Honor and Privilege

It is our honor and great privilege to know this ministry of *Progressive Vision International, Jerusalem House of Prayer for All Nations* and to get involved with these prayer networks worldwide for the return of the Jewish people to their land and to their God, as well as Gentiles coming to know God.

**Pastor Eric Efore**

# APPENDIX II

## HOW TO START A 24-HOUR WATCH OR WATCH GROUP

1. If you desire to be a part of a Watch, ask the Lord if it is His will for you to join one that already exists in your area. If none exist, talk to your pastor and pray that God will raise up someone to start the Watch, whether that would be you or someone else.

2. In the meantime, be a faithful Watchman yourself by beginning to practice the *Twenty Aspects of Being a Watchman* (reread and study Chapters 5 & 6). Then keep a daily Watch of at least a one hour, if possible—or two to three hours, if so directed.

3. If the Lord shows you to start a Watch, reread Chapters 7-9 and Appendix—A, Biblical, Historical and Contemporary Watches. Ask God to show you which model of Watch to start and how to start it. Contact us for more information on our Watches or on how to contact leaders of any other Watches mentioned (see order form in *The Watchmen—Supplement*)

4. If the Lord shows you to join an existing Watch, be a faithful Watchman and give a copy of this book to the leader to encourage and help him. Faithfully pray for him.

5. If, after prayer, you believe the Lord may want to start a 24-hour Watch (or a watch group that could eventually lead to a 24-hour watch), and He shows you someone you believe is qualified, give that person a copy of *The Watchmen* and encourage him to read it. Continue praying for him. Follow up with him by asking if the Lord showed him anything through reading *The Watchmen*.

6. If God calls this person to begin a Watch, join the Watch and be a faithful Watchman. If not, keep watching and praying yourself and ask God to show you His way to start the Watch.

7. If you have already started a Watch or are planning to start one, please contact us. God is developing a fellowship among 24-hour Watch leaders and Watchmen. Already approximately 100 nations have 24-hour Watches and we are believing for 200 nations by the end of the century.

8. You are all welcome and encouraged to come as an individual or to lead a team of seven to fifty people, to join us for one week to ten days and participate in Jerusalem Watchmen's week at Jerusalem House of Prayer for All Nations. Numerous watches have been born in different nations as a result of this. Pray about planning a trip in the next year.

# APPENDIX III

## Scripture References

### Chapter 1

Ps 46:10
Ps 90:4
Ps 104
Ps 127:1
Ps 136
Ecc 3:1
Isa 19:23-25
Isa 21:8
Isa 30:15
Isa 32:17
Isa 62:6
Hab 2:3
Mt 24:43
Mt 26:40-41
Mk 6:48
Mk 14:38
Lk 21:36
Heb 13:17
Jas 1:17

### Chapter 2

Ge 1:1,3-4,27, 29, 31
Ge 16:11,13
Ge 28:15-17,21
Ge 32:24-30
Ex 3:6,16
Dt 2:7
Dt 11:12
2Ch 16:9
Ezr 5:5
Job 13:27
Job 29:2-6
Ps 1:6
Ps 66:7
Ps 91:1
Ps 101:6
Ps 121

Ps 141:3
Pr 6:20,22
Pr 15:3
Pr 16:7
Isa 19
Isa 62:6-7
Jer 1:12
Jer 24:6
Jer 31:10
Mt 16:18
Mt 28:20
Jn 20:22
Ac 10:34-35
Php 4:4
Rev 1:9,14-16
Rev 21:5

### Chapter 3

Isa 31:9
Isa 53:12
Isa 59:16
La 2:19
Eze 22:30
Mal 3
Mt 4:1-11
Mt 6:9
Mt 26:36-38,40-41
Lk 2:25-26,30-32
 37,49
Lk 4
Lk 4:13
Lk 21:36
Lk 22:44
Jn 8:44
Jn 17:1,4
Heb 4:15
Heb 7:1-28
Heb 10:19-20
Heb 12:2-3
Rev 1:14
Rev 12:10-11

### Chapter 4

Ge 1:2
Ps 8:2
Ps 91
Ps 133
Isa 9:6
Isa 58:6
Isa 61:1-3
Isa 63:10
Mic 2:13
Zec 12:10
Zec 13:1-2
Mt 12:31
Mt 13:16
Mt 23:37
Mk 3:29
Lk 3:22
Lk 4:18-19
Lk 10:21
Jn 1:9
Jn 12:7,32
Jn 14:14-19,26
Jn 15:14-15
Jn 16:5-11,13-14
Ac 2
Ac 5:1-11,32
Ac 7:51
Ac 9:31
1Co 2:6-13
2Co 13:14
Gal 5:16,22-25
Eph 3:19
Eph 4:29-32
Eph 5:18
1Th 5:19
1Pe 5:7
1Jn 2:20,27
Rev 1:12-17
Rev 2:7

## Chapter 5

Ps 1:2-3
Ps 100:4
SS 2:8-11
SS 5:10-16
Isa 21:11-12
Isa 64:4
La 2:19
Hab 2:1
Mt 11:30
Mt 16:18
Mt 24:42-44
Mt 26:34-35,37-41, 45-46,70-74
Jn 10:27-28
Jn 15:7-8,16
Php 4:8
Col 4:2
Tit 2:13
Rev 1:14-16
Rev 2,3
Rev 4,5
Rev 4:8

## Chapter 6

Ex 14:13-14
Jdg 7:13-22
Ps 100:1-2
Ps 102:16
Ps 120-134
Isa 21:6-8
Isa 52:7-10
Isa 56:7
Isa 58
Isa 62:6-7
Jer 30:11
Jer 31:6
Eze 3:17-19
Eze 33:6-7
Mal 3:8-10
Mt 18:19-20
Mt 26:40
Mk 13:35
Lk 12:22-40
Jn 15:7-8

Ro 11:25-26
Ro 14:12,17
Eph 6:11-14
1Ti 2:1-2
Heb 12:22-24
Rev 3:2-3
Rev 16:15
Rev 21:13-14

## Chapter 7

Ge 2:15
Ge 3:5,23-24
Ex 14:23-24
Jdg 7:17-19
1Sa 14:16-17
1Ch 6:31
2Ch 5:11-14
2Ch 6:20-21
2Ch 7:16
2Ch 29:25-26
Ne 1:4-11
Ne 4:9
Ne 12
Ne 12:45-47
Ps 127:1
Ps 132:4
Isa 21:6-12
Isa 35:10
Isa 51:11
Isa 52:7-8
Isa 62:6-7
Jer 6:17,19
La 2:19
Eze 1:26-28
Eze 3:17
Eze 22:30
Da 9:5
Mk 6:47-48
Mk 13:35
Ac 1:9-10,13-15
Ac 2:1-2,4
Tit 2:13
Rev 4,5
Rev 4:8,11
Rev 5:9,11-14
Rev 18,19

## Chapter 8

Lev 6:13
Ps 84:4
Ps 122:6-7
Ps 134:1
Isa 30:29
Isa 62:6-7
Jer 29:7
Eze 37:7-11
Zec 14:4
Mt 21:9
Mk 11:9

## Chapter 9

Ge 12:3
Ge 17:20
Ex 20:13
Ru 3:1-13
Ne 4
Ne 4:6-8
Ps 9:11,14
Ps 24:7-10
Ps 122:6
Isa 19
Isa 21:6
Isa 60:13
Isa 62:6,7
Jer 29:7
Eze 37
Joel 1:13-14
Joel 2:9,16
Joel 3:9
Zec 12:10
Zec 13:1-2
Zec 14
Zec 14:2-3
Zec 24:2-3
Mt 6:9,33
Mt 28:19
Mk 10:13-16
Lk 10:38-42
Lk 11:10
Lk 18:8
Lk 24:46-53
Jn 10:1-18,25-30

Jn 11:1-44
Jn 12:1-8
Ac 2
Ac 4:32
Ro 12:12
Eph 5:25-27
Eph 6:18
1Th 5:17
1Ti 2:1-2
Heb 13:3
Rev 4:8-11
Rev 5:11-14
Rev 16:15
Rev 19:6-7
Rev 21

## Chapter 10

Ps 2:4-9
Ps 27:4
Ps 91:1,7
Ps 104:34
Pr 23:7
Isa 31:9
Mt 6:12
Mt 16:23
Mt 26:41
Lk 21:36
Lk 23:34
Jn 17:15
Ro 12:2
1Co 10:12
2Co 2:11
2Co 10:3-5
Eph 2:6
Eph 6
Eph 6:10-19
Php 4:7-8
2Ti 2:3-5
Jas 4:4-7
1Pe 5:8-9
1Jn 2:15-17
1Jn 4:4
Rev 12:10-12

## Chapter 11

Ge 12:3

Isa 21:6-10
Isa 43:5-7
Isa 49:22
Isa 56:7-8
Jer 16:14-16
Eze 37
Eze 39:28-29
Am 9:14-15
Mic 2:12-13
Mt 23:39
Eph 6:12
Heb 12:26-29

## Chapter 12

Ps 68:6
Ps 87
Ps 122:6
Ps 133
Isa 9:6-7
Isa 19:23-25
Isa 28:14-17
Isa 31:9
Isa 56:4-8
Isa 59:19-20
Isa 62:6-7,10
Jer 1:10
Jer 29:7
Zec 12:10
Mt 6:9-10
Mt 10:23
Mt 24:14
Mt 26:41
Lk 21:24,29-32
Jn 17:21
Ac 2:42
Ro 8:31-39
Ro 11:11-27
Ro 14:12
Eph 2:11-18
Rev 8:3-5

## Chapter 13

Ge 1:14
Ps 2:1-3
Isa 19:23-25
Isa 53

Zec 13:5
Zec 14:4
Mt 2:1-12
Mt 7:15
Mt 24:11-12,22-24
Lk 21:7-12,16-17
 24-26,29-30,32
Jn 7:6
Jn 16:13
Jn 17:17
Ro 8:35-37,39
Ro 11:25-26
Php 1:21
Heb 10:24-25
Heb 13:17
Jas 4:4-5
Rev 6:9-11
Rev 8:4-5
Rev 12:1-2,10
Rev 16-19

## Chapter 14

Ps 45
Ps 119:11
Isa 60:13
Jer 23:29
Zec 14:4
Mt 5:1-12
Mt 13:13-23
Mt 25:1-13
Jn 15:10
Ro 5:25-27
Ro 10:17
Ro 13:14
Gal 2:20
Eph 6
Col 3:12
2Ti 4:8
Jas 2:17
Rev 1:3,7-8
Rev 2,3
Rev 2:4-5,7,10-11,13,
17,25-26,28
Rev 3:2,5,10-12, 18-
19,21
Rev 4:1,8
Rev 5:1-2,5

Rev 6-11
Rev 6:1-2
Rev 12:11
Rev 14:13
Rev 16:15
Rev 17:16
Rev 18
Rev 19:8-9
Rev 20:4,6
Rev 21:22-27
Rev 22:1-4,6-7,10-12,
14,16,18-21

## Appendix

Ge 2:3
Ge 18:14
2Ch 7:14
Ps 81:10
Ps 122:6
Isa 56:7
Isa 62:6-7
Jer 32:17
Mal 3:16
Mt 7:7-8
Lk 18:8
Jn 9:4
Jn 17
Ro 11
Eph 3:20

# APPENDIX IV

## JERUSALEM HOUSE OF PRAYER FOR ALL NATIONS
### Options for Watchmen Participation

All who join us in any of the following options A, B or C, staying at Jerusalem House of Prayer for All Nations, are expected to spend at least three hours a day in individual and corporate worship and intercession (practicing the twenty aspects of watching specified in this book).

Option A - Jerusalem Watch of the King - Continual 24-hour worship at the twelve gates of Jerusalem.

Option B - Jerusalem Watch of the Lord/Jerusalem Watchmen's Week - Continual 24-hour watching using the 20 aspects as in Chapters 5 and 6 of this book. Prayer for Jerusalem, Israel, the Arab Middle East and all nations.

Option C - Prophetic Prayer Pilgrimage - Includes participation in Jerusalem Watch of the King/Jerusalem Watch of the Lord, as well as onsite prayer in different locations. Celebrate Israel's Year of Jubilee (1998) or join us in subsequent years.

Option D - All Nations Convocation Jerusalem, 1998 - the year of Israel's Jubilee, when we hope to have 200 nations represented. You can join us in 1998 or in the year 2000! (In 1996, 188 nations were represented).

## OPTION A

### JOIN US FROM THE NATIONS ON
## JERUSALEM WATCH OF THE KING

*24-Hour Ongoing Praise and Worship Watch*
*Just Established in the Gates of Jerusalem*

*We're Asking for Worship Leaders, Teams of Worshippers and Individual Worshippers to Join Us for One Week to One Year, as God Will Call You.*

*Very Reasonable Accommodations Available in Jerusalem House of Prayer for All Nations*

### Jerusalem Watch of the King
### Suggested Donations For:

1. Groups of fifteen (15) people or more staying for seven (7) days or more: $29.00 per day per person
   full-board, which includes three (3) meals daily and lodging
   sixteenth person, free housing/transportation (to/from airport and on all prayer tours)
2. Groups of seven (7) people or more staying for seven (7) days or more: $32.00 per day per person
   full-board, which includes three (3) meals daily and lodging

3. Groups of seven (7) people or more staying for less than seven (7) days: $34.00 per day per person
full-board, which includes three (3) meals daily and lodging

4. 4. Individuals staying for seven (7) days or more:
$35.00 per day per person
full-board, which includes three (3) meals daily and lodging

5. Individuals staying less than seven (7) days:
$37.00 per day per person
full-board, which includes three (3) meals daily and lodging

6. 6. Individuals - one month - $700.00

## OPTION B

### PARTICIPATE IN

## JERUSALEM WATCH OF THE LORD— JERUSALEM WATCHMEN'S WEEK
### at
## JERUSALEM HOUSE OF PRAYER FOR ALL NATIONS

1. As a seasoned individual Watchman, primarily to watch and pray for one week, $245 full board, short walking trips (others available at reasonable cost).

2. A group of seven or more Watchmen for one week - $224 per person full board.

3. A group of fifteen or more Watchmen for one week - $203 per person full board.

All extra days at same rate per day as the first week, airport pickup available for five or more Watchmen at rate of $10.00 per person each way. Reasonable rates for special side trips. Individuals or smaller groups can take Airport Shuttle (Sherut Taxi) for same price.

## OPTION C

### GROUPS OF SEVEN OR MORE MAY PARTICIPATE IN

## PROPHETIC PRAYER PILGRIMAGE:
### at
## JERUSALEM HOUSE OF PRAYER FOR ALL NATIONS

**Staying on the Mount of Olives and Praying Where Jesus Prayed
Touring the Holy Land of Israel and Walking Where Jesus Walked**
*Participate in 24-Hour Watchman's Week
Where Jesus Will Soon Return!*

**10 days and 9 nights in Israel $429 without airfare!
Includes food and lodging for 9 nights and 10 days, airport transfers and all tour transportation, but does not include entrance fees or gratuities.
8 days in Jerusalem, Bethlehem, Bethany, Mt. of Olives -**
Old City, Walk on the Walls as Watchmen, Gethsemane, Via Dolorosa, Calvary, Garden Tomb, Western Wall, Temple Mount, David's Tomb, Upper Room, Shrine of the Book - Dead Sea Scrolls - Book of Isaiah, Knesset - Government Building of Israel, Lazarus' Tomb, Home of Mary and Martha, Bethphage (where Jesus got on donkey), Mt. of Olives (where Jesus prayed the Lord's Prayer), Site of Ascension and

Second Coming. Attend a service at a Messianic Congregation - Local Messianic Jewish and Arab Pastors speaking, as well as *Jerusalem House of Prayer* Staff Members sharing about Jerusalem and Israel

**Day 9** - visit the Galilee, Nazareth, Cana, Tiberias and Boat Ride on the Sea of Galilee, Capernaum, Mount of Beatitudes, Place of the Loaves and Fishes

**Day 10** - visit Jericho, Mt. of Temptation, Qumran, and the Dead Sea**
--pray for the walls to fall down in your city and your life—where they fell down in Jericho!
**Masada* - Optional $25 per person additional on day of Dead Sea

We could do something similar to above itinerary with
**8 days and 7 nights**
**(5 days in Jerusalem - 1 day in Galilee - 1 day at Dead Sea)**

As available: 1) From the 1st to the 10th of the month
2) From the 11th to the 20th
3) From the 21st to the 30th
Should bring your group as close as possible within these time periods
If the flight connections do not work out with the 10 days/9 nights,
we can adjust the tour price and number of days accordingly
Minimum number of people: 7
25% Deposit 100 days prior to arrival
Write to us and we will suggest departure dates based on airline service from your city.

## <u>OPTION D</u>

### PREPARE TO JOIN US IN THE THIRD

## ALL NATIONS CONVOCATION JERUSALEM
## 20 september - 3 October, 1998

### In the City of the Great King!

In 1994, <u>140</u> nations attended -
In 1996, there were over <u>180</u> nations!
There was a special move of the Holy Spirit
in worship, intercession, repentance and reconciliation
between individuals and between nations!
In 1998, the *Year of Jubilee*, we hope to have <u>200</u> nations
Plan now to join us and lead a team from your nation or plan to join us or lead a group
for the year 2000 (30 September - 13 October)

14 Nights and 15 days in Jerusalem and Israel including half board, airport transfers,
two half-day tours in Jerusalem and three-day All Nations Prayer Tour: <u>$1198.</u>
If you bring nine paying Watchmen from your nation, the tenth one is FREE or
for eighteen paying, the nineteenth and twentieth are FREE (land arrangements).
**Pray about helping to sponsor a Third World delegate.**
**We hope to have at least one from every nation.**
**$1198 (land arrangements) or $2198 (land and airfare).**

# APPENDIX V

## Other Materials Available to
## Help Watchmen and Watches
### (Pray about being a distributor in your nation)

1.  Copy of Individual Watch Log
2.  Copy of Sign-up sheet for 24-hour Watch
3.  Copy of our Community Watch and Corporate Prayer Schedule of *Jerusalem House of Prayer for All Nations* in Jerusalem
4.  Copy of Tenth Anniversary Newsletter of *Jerusalem House of Prayer for All Nations*
5.  Information about coming to Jerusalem to participate in *Jerusalem Watch of the King* on twelve gates of Jerusalem (primarily worship) or *Jerusalem Watch of the Lord* (all 20 aspects of watching)
6.  Addresses of Watche Models included in *The Watchmen.*
7.  International Monthly Prophetic Prayer Alert for each day to pray for Jerusalem, Israel and the nations--available upon request and donation (mailed, faxed or e-mailed)
8.  Audio and video on "Praying for the Peace of Jerusalem - Removing the Stones"

Audio:   $4 each One tape
        $3.50 each Ten or more
Video:   $12 each One tape
        $8 each Ten or more

9.  Copy of audio and video of "Being a House of Prayer for All Nations and Jerusalem"

Prices same as audio/video in item #8 above

10. Large poster (similar to cover of book) to frame and put in your Watch room or Church

                      $10 each One large poster
                      $6 each Ten or more
                      $4 each Forty or more
Smaller posters   $2 each One small poster
                      $1.50 each Twenty-five or more
                      $1.00 each Seventy or more

11. More copies of book, *The Watchmen**

                      $15 each One copy
                      $12 each Ten or more
                      $10 each Twenty-five or more
                      $7.50 each Fifty or more

$6.50 each One hundred or more

12. Copies of book, *Let My People Go\**, Year of Jubilee Edition on *Aliyah*, the return of the Jewish people to Israel

$7 each One copy
$5 each Ten or more
$4 each Twenty or more
$3.50 each Fifty or more

*If ordering *The Watchmen* or *Let My People Go* from within the United States, please order from MorningStar Publications. Call 1-800-542-0278.

13. Music worship tape called *Watchmen on the Walls* by Lana Portnoy

$10 each One tape
$6 each Ten or more
$5 each Twenty or more

14. Video: *Aliyah from the Americas to Jerusalem*

$12 each One tape
$8 each Ten or more

15. Video: ***188 Nations** present for All Nations Convocation Jerusalem 1996!*

Prices same as video in item #14 above

**Prices shown are for purchase in Jerusalem. If items are to be mailed, please include an additional 25% for postage. All prices listed in this book will be honored until at least December 31, 1999. You may pay by check, money order, credit card or bank transfer.**

See tear-out order sheet on following page.
To order any of the above, please send donation or designated amount to:

*Jerusalem House of Prayer for All Nations*
**P. O. Box 31393 . 91313 Jerusalem, Israel**
**Tel 972 2 627 4126 . Fax 972 2 626 4239**
**e-mail: jhopfan@compuserve.com**

# Jerusalem House of Prayer for All Nations

## Order Form (Prices on previous two pages)

☐ 1.    I am interested in starting a 24-hour Watch for Jerusalem, Israel and my city, nation and all nations. Ps 122:6; Jer 29:7; Isa 56; Isa 62

☐ 2.    Please send a sample of: _____Individual Watch Log, _____Watchman Sign-Up Sheet, _____Community Watch and Corporate Prayer Schedule of *Jerusalem House of Prayer*.

☐ 3.    I am interested in starting a weekly watch group (based on one of the Biblical watch times (see chapter 6, *The Watchmen*) for Jerusalem, Israel, and my city, nation and other nations, as led by the Holy Spirit.

☐ 4.    I would like a copy of the Tenth Anniversary Newsletter of *Jerusalem House of Prayer*.

☐ 5.    I would like to receive Jerusalem House of Prayer for All Nations newsletter for 1 year.

☐ 6.    I am interested in participating in *Jerusalem Watch of the King (Worship Watch)* in Jerusalem (list dates) beginning_____ until _____.

☐ 7.    I am interested in bringing a watchman team of _____Watchmen to participate in *Jerusalem Watch of the Lord/Jerusalem Watchman's Week* beginning_____ until from the nation of _____.

☐ 8.    I am interested in bringing a *Prophetic Prayer Pilgrimage* to Israel of _____Pilgrims, beginning_____ until_____ from the nation of _____.

☐ 9.    Please send me the addresses of the 24-hour Watch models included in *The Watchmen*.

☐ 10.   Please send me the monthly International Prayer Alert. Enclosed is a donation of $_____. Indicate if to be sent via _____Mail, _____Fax, or _____E-mail.

☐ 11.   Please send me _____tapes of *"Praying for the Peace of Jerusalem-Removing the Stones."* audio, video. Enclosed is $ cost plus shipping (see previous page).

☐ 12.   Please send me tapes of *"Being a House of Prayer for All Nations and Jerusalem."* _____audio, _____video. Enclosed is $_____ cost plus shipping (25%).

☐ 13.   Please send me _____large posters, _____small posters similar to cover of *The Watchmen*. Enclosed is $_____ cost plus shipping (25%).

☐ 14.   Please send me _____copies of *The Watchmen* by Tom Hess; enclosed is $_____cost plus shipping (25%).

☐ 15.   Please send me _____copies of *Let My People God* by Tom Hess; enclosed is $_____ cost plus shipping (25%).

☐ 16.   Please send me _____music worship tapes called *Watchmen on the Walls* by Lana Portnoy. Enclosed is $_____ cost plus shipping (25%).

☐ 17.   Please send me _____video tapes of *"Aliyah from the Americas to Jerusalem."* Enclosed is $_____ cost plus shipping (25%).

☐ 18.   Please send me _____video tapes of *"All Nations Convocation Jerusalem 1996."* Enclosed is $_____ cost plus shipping (25%).

☐ 19.   I am interested in attending *All Nations Convocation Jerusalem 1998 (ANCJ98)* from the nation of _____. We hope to have 200 nations represented.

☐ 20.   I plan to lead a delegation of 10 or more to *ANCJ98* from my nation. Please send me a free video tape of *ANCJ96*.

☐ 21.   I would like to apply for your staff in Israel (send resume, photo and Pastor's recommendation letter when applying and ask for staff application). Check time and list staff position interested in: _____6 months, _____1 year, _____2 years. Staff position interested in: _____.

☐ 22.   I would like to be a distributor of your material in my nation.

**Please Print:**

Name: _____

_____
Address                                        City/State                                ZipCode

_____
Telephone                                      Fax                                        E-mail

**Method of Payment:**

☐   Check/Money Order Enclosed:  Amount  $_____

☐   Wire Transfer:  Amount $_____   Please enclose copy.

    Credit Card Amount  $_____

    Card # _____/_____/_____/_____   Exp. Date _____/_____

    Card: ____VISA,  ____Mastercard,  ____American Express

        ____Diners Club,  ____Isracard,  ____Eurocard

**Donations to:** *Jerusalem House of Prayer for All Nations/Progressive Vision International*
**Checks:** Make payable to **Jerusalem House of Prayer for All Nations.**
Mail to: P.O. Box 31393, 91313 Jerusalem, Israel
Tel 972 2 627 4126 Fax 972 2 626 4239
E-mail: jhopfan@compuserve.com

**Wire Transfers to:** *Progressive Vision International* General Account #17-103-241,
Riggs National Bank of Washington DC / Branch #31, Routing #054-00-00-30,
650 Pennsylvania Ave. SE Washington DC 20005 USA, Tel: (202) 885 6000
(Designate if for Specific Need/Please send us a copy of your wire transfer)

**Wire transfers to:** *All Nations Convocations Jerusalem* Account #375011,
Bank Hapoalim, Branch 12-784, HaHaganah 21, Jerusalem, Israel

**Wire transfers to:** *Attn: Tom Hess, Swiss Bank Corporation:*
Thunstrasse 4, CH-3110 Munsingen, Switzerland;
CHF#98-204,609.1; USD#98-204,609.2; DM#98-204,609.3; FR fr #98-204,609.4; PC-30-188-0